Geomedia

Geomedia

Networked Cities and the Future of Public Space

SCOTT McQUIRE

polity

First published in 2016 by Polity Press

Polity Press
65 Bridge Street
Cambridge CB2 1UR, UK

Polity Press
350 Main Street
Malden, MA 02148, USA

ISBN-13: 978-0-7456-6075-2
ISBN-13: 978-0-7456-6076-9(pb)

A catalogue record for this book is available from the British Library.

Library of Congress Cataloging-in-Publication Data

Names: McQuire, Scott, author.
Title: Geomedia, networked cities and the politics of urban space / Scott McQuire.
Description: Cambridge, UK ; Malden, MA : Polity, 2016. | Includes bibliographical references and index.
Identifiers: LCCN 2016011369 (print) | LCCN 2016030536 (ebook) | ISBN 9780745660752 (hardback) | ISBN 9780745660769 (paperback) | ISBN 9781509510641 (Mobi) | ISBN 9781509510658 (Epub)
Subjects: LCSH: Public spaces. | Digital communications. | Mass media and culture. | Information technology--Social aspects. | Urbanization. | BISAC: SOCIAL SCIENCE / Media Studies.
Classification: LCC HT185 .M39 2016 (print) | LCC HT185 (ebook) | DDC 307.76--dc23
LC record available at https://lccn.loc.gov/2016011369

Typeset in 11 on 13 pt Monotype Bembo by
Servis Filmsetting Ltd, Stockport, Cheshire
Printed and bound in Great Britain by CPI Group (UK) Ltd, Croydon.

For further information on Polity, visit our website: politybooks.com

Contents

Acknowledgements

Writing a book involves a long journey that, while often solitary, finds company with many people along the way. As this work developed, it has benefited from being shared with many scholars around the world. In particular, I would like to thank my colleagues at the University of Melbourne in the Media and Communication Program and the Research Unit in Public Cultures. I would also like to acknowledge my PhD students and the many Masters students who have taken my Media Convergence and Digital Culture subject over the last few years. Working with you all has helped to shape my thinking here. I am also grateful to Paolo Favero at the University of Antwerp for the opportunity to visit just as I was completing this writing; to the Strelka Institute and the City of Moscow for the opportunity to present some of this work at the Moscow Urban Forum in 2014; to Allan Cameron and Luke Goodes for inviting me to the 'Media Ubiquity: Spaces, Places and Networks' conference at the University of Auckland in 2014; to Karen Becker for inviting me to 'Beyond the Frame: The Future of the Visual in an Age of Digital Diversity' conference in Stockholm in 2014; to Patrik Svensson for the opportunity to visit HUMlab-X at Umea University in 2014; to Heloisa Pait for enabling me to present several talks in São Paolo and Bauru in 2013; to Vicki Smith and her colleagues at Aotearoa Digital Arts for their hospitality at the 'Mesh Cities' symposium in Dunedin in 2013; to Seija Ridell and her colleagues Jani Vuolteenaho, Outi Hakola and Sami Kolamo for inviting me to 'The Spectacular/ Ordinary/Contested Media City' conference in Helsinki in 2013; to Justin O'Connor and Wang Jie for the opportunity to visit Shanghai Jiao Tong University in 2011 and 2012; to Victoria Lynn for the chance to speak at Adelaide Festival Artists' Week in 2010; and finally to John Hutnyk at Goldsmiths, where I first gave a public presentation on Google Street View and returned several times along the way.

At an institutional level I would like to acknowledge the financial support of the Australian Research Council through the projects 'Large Screens and the Transnational Public Sphere' and 'Right to the City: Participatory Public Space', as well as support from the Melbourne Networked Societies Institute. The Faculty of Arts at the University of Melbourne funded a period of study leave in 2015 that facilitated the completion of this work.

I owe a personal debt to many colleagues who have collaborated on parts of this research: to Audrey Yue, Ross Gibson, Sean Cubitt, Cecelia Cmielewski, Meredith Martin, Amelia Barikin, Xing Gu and Matt Jones who all contributed to the 'Large Screens and the Transnational Public Sphere' project, and to Danny Butt, Dale Leorke and Danielle Wyatt for the 'Participatory Public Space' project. Last but certainly not least to my dear friend Nikos Papastergiadis who has been a collaborator on all these and many other projects. Salute!

To all my extended family, and especially to my partner Sarah and our sons Lachie and Alistair: thanks for living with this process and making life so much fun!

I would like to dedicate this book to my sister Lisa whose creativity and enthusiasm for designing wonderful spaces has always inspired me.

Introduction

From media to geomedia

In less than two centuries cities have shifted from being exceptional locales to become the globally dominant setting for social life. As late as 1900, Great Britain was the only nation with a predominantly urban population. By 2007, the majority of the world's population could be defined as city dwellers, with the number forecast to continue to rise rapidly (United Nations 2014: 7). The apparent continuity of this threshold masks numerous transformations. Not only is there a vastly expanded scale of urbanism, but city life has become subject to new dynamics, including far greater cultural diversity, new patterns of regional and transnational mobility, and growing pressure to develop more sustainable modes of urban living. If the contemporary city is a social experiment whose ends remain uncertain, it is one being lived without a safety net.

This book focuses on what I will argue is one of the key features distinguishing twenty-first-century urban experience from earlier modes of urban inhabitation, namely the extension of networked digital media throughout urban space. New media technologies from smart phones utilizing place-sensitive data to LED screens embedded in central city locations contribute to a new spatialization of media as an integral part of the contemporary city. This is what I seek to grasp in terms of the transformation of media into geomedia. Through this lens I want to explore the future of urban public space.

Geomedia is a concept that crystallizes at the intersection of four related trajectories: convergence, ubiquity, location-awareness and real-time feedback. Let me unfold each briefly, beginning with ubiquity. Throughout most of the twentieth century, access to media was conditioned by a paradigm which can, at least in retrospect, be described in terms of scarcity and fixity. In other words, people had to travel to particular sites in order to watch, listen or be connected. Telephone calls linked handsets hardwired into particular places. To see a film, you travelled to a specialized viewing chamber – the cinema. Television was primarily viewed in the living room of the family home. When personal computers began to spread from the early 1980s, they followed a similar pattern, and were situated on desktops in home and office. While these different media platforms were deeply implicated in the profound transformations in spatio-temporal experience that defines modernity (McQuire 1998), up to the 1990s 'media' nevertheless remained confined to a relatively restricted set of sites within the city. Despite a few exceptions (such as newspapers, billboards and transistor radios), we could say that media were part of public culture, but generally not situated *in* public space.

This has changed decisively in the present. Mobile and embedded media devices, coupled to extended digital networks, recreate the city as a media space in which content and connection are seemingly available 'anywhere, anytime'.[1] If this condition has been long-desired, and remains to some extent a dream (there are still numerous black spots and blank spaces in which networks function poorly or not at all), ubiquity has made media an increasingly important part of urban routines. While fixed media platforms certainly haven't disappeared in the present, they now function as nodes situated in relation to more extensive media flows. 'Watching television' can still refer to the sort of familial, living-room experience inherited from the dreamtime of the 1950s, but can equally refer to viewing content streamed to a mobile phone on a bus or to a Wi-Fi-connected laptop in a park, or watched on a large video screen permanently located in a central city public space.

The key point I want to draw out in this context is that ubiquity is not just about the capacity to do the same thing – such as watch television – in a new place, but involves a profound transformation of social practice. A common response to the perceived incursions of television on social and cultural life in the 1950s was 'don't watch it'. But abstinence was always a flawed strategy in so far as it failed to recognize that 'television' was implicated in the recalibration of larger sociopolitical logics, ranging from the public sphere and political life to the hyper-coordination of industrial production in accord with mass marketing beamed direct into consumers' homes. Such deep and wide-ranging impacts are difficult to simply *switch off*.

In similar vein, the ubiquity of digital media is currently transforming the social space of the city in complex ways that extend well beyond the choices available to individual users. If communication has always been situational, and new media technologies generally provide the means for altering the spatio-temporal parameters of 'situation', the ubiquity of digital media now extends this transformative capacity across broad swathes of social life. As a result, contemporary processes of social interaction are being shaped less decisively by traditional modes of urban boundary formation, such as the hard infrastructure of the built environment. Instead, the process of social encounter has become more susceptible to new patterns of relational exchange characterized by distributed, iterative communication practices that often enjoy global extension.

The second broad trajectory driving the transition to geomedia is the enhanced role of location in framing both the functionality of media devices and the 'content' they access and generate. Like ubiquity, this is a relatively recent development. While Geographic Information Systems (GIS) date from the late 1960s, it wasn't until the Clinton directive authorizing wider availability of GPS data for civilian use in May 2000 that a wave of experimentation with new devices, services, applications and practices was triggered.[2] Artist-led experiments with 'locative media' were soon overtaken by an explosion of commercial services following the release of the iPhone in 2007.

Contemporary location-aware devices such as smart phones and tablets combine a number of different systems, including geocoded data, GIS software and GPS tracking capabilities. This assemblage enables devices to pose position-sensitive queries to relational databases, which then relay the information considered most relevant to the position described. 'Placing' information in this way has generated a wide range of new social practices and commercial logics that are now routinely enacted in urban space. When the everyday movements of millions of individuals through the city can leave discernible digital traces, location-awareness assumes a new prominence in urban experience. As McCullough notes: 'With the spread of positioning systems, which in effect make anyone who carries such a system into a live cursor, the city plan itself becomes a living surface' (2004: 88). When Google first integrated location into web search in 2010, location-aware services had not only become the most dynamic and rapidly growing sector of digital media, but were recognized as a key to wider business strategies.[3] In conjunction with ubiquity, location-aware media supports the extension of an urban logic in which the freewheeling mobility of individual users and the calculative analytics of mass tracking have become closely related trajectories.

The third key trajectory underpinning the emergence of geomedia is the 'real-time' orientation of contemporary digital networks. It is important to distinguish this from the older capacity for electronic media to relay simultaneous events to a dispersed audience: this has existed for a century with broadcasting, and was elevated into a specific social form through the 'media event' (Dayan and Katz 1992) carried by live television. What is different in the present is the way the distributed architecture of digital networks opens the potential for 'real-time' feedback from many-to-many, supporting novel experiences of social simultaneity. As I will describe in chapter 1, geomedia alters the valence of the broadcast media event by creating the potential for new forms of recursive communication and coordination between diverse actors even as events unfold.

As Virilio (1997) has argued, the threshold of 'real-time' media is not merely a technical event, but is implicated in a profound reconfiguration of the social relations of time and space.[4] A key strand in my thinking of geomedia is the way that contemporary developments are contributing to the progressive undermining of the primacy of the representational paradigm that has historically underpinned media studies as a discipline. According to this paradigm, which can be traced to Platonic roots, the event always comes first and mediation necessarily involves re-presentation through some form of symbolization or signification.[5] In this Platonic logic or *rhythm*, the event is always primary and mediation is inevitably secondary and belated. The explanatory power of this model has arguably been waning ever since live broadcasting via radio and later television became powerful forms of orchestrating synchronous social experiences on a national scale. However, the uncertain relations between live media and event have assumed a new potency in the present, as 'real-time' feedback multiplies and spreads into the interstices of everyday life.

The fourth strand underpinning the condition of geomedia is convergence. Convergence is often defined according to a narrow technical logic, describing the merging of previously separate systems of broadcasting, computation and telecommunications in the context of digital technology. However, the logic of convergence also extends to a broader process of remaking, impacting on business, institutional and regulatory settings as much as social, political and cultural practices. In so far as convergence names this complex process of transforming 'old' media while also elaborating the emergent 'new', it informs my choice of 'geomedia' to name the heterogeneous family of technologies – devices, platforms, screens, operating systems, programs and networks – that constitute the contemporary mediascape. If convergence breaks down the differences separating older mediums such as photography or broadcast television from the computing and telecommunications sectors, this is not just because the older media have become increasingly computational and networked, but because the so-called ICTs have become increasingly mediatized. In this context, many of the historic differences embedded in terms such as 'camera', 'phone', 'computer' or 'television' no longer operate. Using 'geomedia' to name this condition is a strategic choice, in so far as it helps to foreground the increasingly complex relations of 'media' to 'immediacy' in contemporary practices of social encounter.

In summary, geomedia should not be understood as simply referring to the emergence of specific types of new device (as is the case with many studies of 'mobile media') or in relation to the effect of single functions (for instance, the focus on geolocation in studies of 'locative media'). Rather, my aim is to conceptualize the different *condition* that media enters in the twenty-first century. This condition, situated at the confluence of the trajectories I have described in terms of ubiquity, positionality, real-time and convergence, is characterized by a profound contradiction.

On the one hand, media now span the globe with greater facility, spread and speed than ever before. Everyday interactions often enjoy global reach at little cost and effort. Along this axis, digital media are extremely powerful *space-time machines*, enabling the extensions of human perception, social organization and cultural protocols that were first analysed by those such as Harold Innis and Marshall McLuhan in the 1950s and 1960s. This capacity to span distance and contract time has often fed fantasies of overthrowing matter, such as those associated with cyberspace in the 1990s (see for instance Dyson et al. 1994). But this was always a one-sided analysis, and its bias has become more obvious in the present. Digital media have become increasingly personalized and embedded, and are widely used to activate local situations and connect to particular places. In other words, as much as digital media enable *emancipation* from place, they have also become a key modality of contemporary *placemaking*. It is this paradoxical conjunction of connection and disconnection – of emplacement and displacement, of the articulation or *jointing* of the local and the global, of media and immediacy – that I am wanting to grasp with the concept of geomedia. Geomedia constitutes a new context for the *production* of public space, impacting on how we conceive and exercise our incipient 'right to the city', how we negotiate social encounters, and how we experience relations of proximity and distance, presence and absence.

The ambivalence of the digital

The transformation of media into geomedia cuts across a variety of debates concerning media, cities and social life. Alteration of the 'place' that media technologies occupy in the city means that experience of both media and urban space becomes subject to new dynamics. Diverse and often contradictory tendencies are being played out simultaneously, underlining the fact that current transformations are both profound and uncertain in their ends.

In fact, what is most striking about the present is the volatility and polarization that characterizes analysis of the digital future. On the one hand, the sorts of decentralized communication platforms and practices of peer-based exchange and networked collaboration that have developed around the Internet have found diverse manifestations in the contemporary city. The distributed capacity of digital networks means that multiple inputs can be more easily solicited and incorporated, giving practical import to the ideal of a 'participatory public space' in which urban ambiance might be defined and redefined by a city's inhabitants. But accompanying this *generativity* of new peer-based practices are vastly expanded capacities to collect, archive, aggregate and analyse a new range of data. Location-filtered Internet searches and geo-tagged social media posts, mobile phone signals, sensor networks and smart cards for urban transit systems now complement older staples such as CCTV and credit cards in producing an urban communication infrastructure capable of constructing increasingly rapid and precise feedback loops between mobile subjects and their particular urban routines. In a context in which so many actions leave a digital trace, and transaction costs have fallen to historic lows, the sort of anonymity that helped to foster the dynamic public culture of the modern city is at risk of disappearing. As the capacity to store, process and retrieve previously inconceivable volumes of data becomes increasingly cheap and rapid, the entire logic of data use in urban governance is changing. Policies based on retrospection are switching towards prediction.

Urban space suffused with data is the precondition for what Saskia Sassen (2011a, 2011b) has evoked as the potential for an 'open source urbanism' – an urbanism defined by more horizontal, multiple and responsive feedback loops between inhabitants and 'the city'. However, Sassen (2011a) warns that the 'smart-city' agenda is shadowed by the ever-present danger that it may tip over into the technocratic fantasy of totally managed space. Here the genuine innovation of open source urbanism is usurped by what Gilles Deleuze (1992) famously termed 'control society', in which the older spatial strategies of segregation and physical containment that underpinned Foucault's disciplinary regimes are displaced by ubiquitous processes of digital modulation. The demand to negotiate the tension between the potential for new modes of citizen involvement and self-organization and the tendency for such projects to be marginalized by, or to themselves produce, new forms of technocratic control, situates the marked ambivalence of the digital present. I would hasten to add that this is not something that can be resolved by an act of will, as if we could simply 'choose' a single desired pathway over all others. The ambivalence of the digital is not simply the fact that a rhetoric of freedom often masks a new logic of control (Chun 2006), but stems more from the extent to which what Stephen Graham aptly calls 'countergeographies' often depend on the very same digital tools as do contemporary strategies of control:

> The new public domains through which countergeographies can be sustained must forge collaborations and connections across distance and difference. They must materialize new publics, and create new countergeographic spaces, using the very same control technologies that militaries and security states are using to forge ubiquitous borders. (2010: 350)

This ambivalence situates the complexity of the challenge regarding what sort of city – media city, smart city, sentient city – we want to inhabit in the future. How can we invent new protocols, practices and platforms that embrace the benefits of data-based infrastructure operation, while also leaving room to develop the distributed communicative capacity that might facilitate a new era of urban democratization? If answering such a question is today centred around debates over the role of large-scale media platforms and 'smart-city' solutions, it is also tied to our capacity to collectively imagine and enact new articulations between media and public space.

Public space and the 'common'

In the early stages of writing this book during 2011, public spaces across the world, from Tahrir Square in Cairo to Tompkins Square in New York, were being occupied by diverse groups of citizens. These events, often grouped under headings such as 'Arab Spring' and 'Occupy Wall Street', should not be hastily united into a single front, ignoring their vastly different stakes and varied political conjunctures. But they do signal two things central to my inquiry. First, that the appropriation of public space remains a vital mode of political action in the present. Second, that contemporary forms of 'occupation' differ significantly from earlier modalities of taking over the city. How should we understand this new condition?

As Bernard Stiegler notes, the *koine* or common is 'the condition of all public space' (2011: 151). But such commonality has never been a simple relation. David Harvey argues that public space cannot be equated with a 'commons' in any unproblematic way, but has always been a highly contested zone (2012: 72–3). Public space is dependent on state power, and is implicated in the uneven process of capitalist urbanization, but also emerges from class-based practices of inhabitation. Harvey adds:

> To the degree that cities have sites of vigorous class conflicts and struggles, so urban administrations have often been forced to supply public goods (such as affordable public housing, health care, education, paved

streets, sanitation, and water) to an urbanized working class. While these public spaces and public goods contribute mightily to the qualities of the commons, it takes political action on the part of citizens and the people to appropriate them or to make them so. (2012: 72–3)

Harvey underlines the extent to which many of the qualities we associate with public space are not handed down from on high, nor achieved once and for all, but are subject to ongoing struggle. Reversing the order of Stiegler's proposition, we might argue that the fate of public space is today a fundamental index of how we treat the common. In fact, Lefebvre made a somewhat similar observation nearly half a century ago: 'Let us be contented with the notion that the *democratic* character of a regime is identifiable by its attitude towards the city, urban "liberties" and urban reality, and therefore towards *segregation*' (1996: 141).

Struggles around urban space and urban 'liberties' have gained markedly greater prominence over the last two decades. As Pask notes:

> key word searches of 'public space' in newspaper archives show an exponential leap in the number of articles since the mid-1990s. The specifics are often different, but the themes remarkably similar: citizens' groups, grassroots collectives, sometimes even local governments themselves, leading a charge to create public space where it does not yet exist, to reclaim it from where it was lost, and to rejuvenate it from states undesirable or incomplete. (In Hou 2010: 227)

This new prominence undoubtedly reflects the profound challenges to public space that emerged under conditions of neo-liberal urban development, as previous forms of 'the common' have become subject to market disciplines and privatization. Pask adds: '"public space" has now become a driver of social movements and activism in its own right – and a particularly strategic one at that' (in Hou 2010: 231). This perspective is shared by a number of the most thoughtful analysts of the present, including Zygmunt Bauman who argued that 'public places are the very spots where the future of urban life [. . .] is being at this moment decided'

(2005: 77) and Saskia Sassen who contends 'that the question of public space is central to giving the powerless rhetorical and operational openings' (2011c: 579).

But the strategic importance of public space in contemporary questions of power and urban life is not simply the recapitulation of an older problematic of public space. Rather, this renewed emphasis on public space is also the result of historical changes in what constitutes the 'common'. In *Commonwealth* (2009), Hardt and Negri argued that production is no longer rooted in the old common of 'nature' (natural common) but increasingly depends on the 'artificial common' of languages, images, knowledges, affects, habits, codes and practices. As a result, it is not 'nature', but the city that now grounds what they call biopolitical productive activity:

> With the passage to the hegemony of biopolitical production, the space of economic production and the space of the city tend to overlap. There is no longer a factory wall that divides the one from the other, and 'externalities' are no longer external to the site of production that valorizes them. Workers produce throughout the metropolis, in its every crack and crevice. In fact, production of the common is becoming nothing but the life of the city itself. (Hardt and Negri 2009: 251)

This does not mean that the old 'nature' ceases to exist or is somehow rendered unimportant. Rather, what Hardt and Negri call the biopolitical threshold points to historic shifts in the relation between knowledge and economy that have been variously grasped under descriptors such as postindustrial society, information society, knowledge society, informational capitalism and communicative capitalism. As informational goods assume precedence over other forms of production, control over media platforms, network protocols and intellectual property (copyright, trademarks and licensing) becomes fundamental to economic operations. At the same time, and as part of the same process, the 'artificial common' of languages, images, affects, habits and communication practices becomes subject to new forms of intensive cultivation and harvesting. As I will argue below (chapter 2), the routine activities of social life that support the 'artificial common' are precisely what is targeted by the commercial logic of geomedia that is now unfolding across urban public space. But as I will explore in chapters 3 and 4, geomedia also opens new potentials to remake the urban as a social space.

What models are adequate to conceptualizing networked public space as digital platforms become increasingly important to how we navigate the city and interact with others? What are the lines of force and agency that operate in this context? These contradictory tendencies, in which public space is both critical to the elaboration of the common, but also a key site for its inscription into new market dynamics and strategies of surplus appropriation, form the striated field of this inquiry.

The structure of this book

My analysis of geomedia is advanced through three chapters that might loosely be termed case studies. 'Googling the City' (chapter 2) uses Google Street View as a lens to explore the implications of proprietary urban data platforms. Beginning with a description of Street View as a distinctive form of urban imaging, the chapter traces its growing importance to Google's overall business strategy. I argue that the new centrality of imaging to mapping, and of mapping to the digital economy, is predicated on the expanded affordances of both digital images and digital archives. By connecting Street View to the broader logic of the smart city, I further argue that the new *operationality* of the digital archive is a key feature in how the city is being reconfigured in contemporary social practices and political imagination. 'Participatory Public Space' (chapter 3) suggests how we might begin to reverse engineer this emerging mass surveillance apparatus. Beginning with a call for critical analysis of current rhetoric around 'participation', it focuses on contemporary digital art in public space in order to explore the emergence of new models of public encounter in the context of sociotechnical networks. By tracing the longer history of 'situation' in art practice, and linking this to the 'social turn' in contemporary art, I seek to understand the potential for public media art to contribute to new situated practices of urban appropriation.

Chapter 4, 'Urban Screens and Urban Media Events', continues this emphasis on investigating social encounter in contemporary public space. Drawing on fieldwork into the use of large video screens situated in public space, I build a model of what I call the 'urban media event'. I argue that the situated practices of collective communication that are emerging around 'second-generation' urban screens demand a rethinking of the relation between public sphere and public space. I further argue that these practices have the potential for developing new models of citizen-engagement as well as providing avenues for distinctive experiences of transnational communication.

While these three exemplars were deliberately chosen to explore different trajectories and emphases, it is important to recognize at the outset that they are not entirely separate but interconnected and overlapping scenarios. What they share is framed and contextualized by the opening and closing chapters. The first chapter maps the key changes spanning public space and media that have converged to produce contemporary networked public space. I begin by reformulating Henri Lefebvre's (1996) problematic of 'the right to the city' by asking how we might address the right to the *networked* city. I proceed by situating geomedia in relation to the historic role of public space as a key arena for encounters between strangers in the modern city. I then consider the tensions that became manifest in the seeming inability of institutionalized urban planning to address the importance of spontaneity and casual street life in the modern city. I argue that these tensions are increasingly evident in the dominant agenda of the contemporary 'smart city'. From the media side, I explore the complex interplay between public events, urban space and media that was initiated around broadcast television in the mid-twentieth century. I use this as the basis for investigating the emergence of new modalities of urban occupation and social encounter over the last two decades. I conclude by arguing that the new affordances of the condition that I describe as geomedia have profound implications for how we theorize the relation between 'media' and 'immediacy'. This is the theme I return to in chapter 5, where I focus on the implications of geomedia for the operation of power and how we think the relation of the human to the technological.

It may be evident from this outline that the problematic of geomedia is difficult to fit within existing disciplinary orientations. Clearly, there are a wide range of debates in different disciplines – from media and cultural studies to urban sociology, urban geography, architecture and urban planning, and human-computer interaction (HCI) to name a few – that have been concerned with the impact of digital media on cities broadly, and on public space more specifically. But disciplines have their own histories, and this includes the historical dominance of particular frameworks, approaches and conceptual formations. Writing from a disciplinary perspective rightly demands understanding new phenomena in terms of its implications for this or that discipline. My approach here is a bit different. Rather than policing demarcation disputes or adjudicating claims to disciplinary priority, I have been more interested in exploring the way in which the nexus between geomedia and public space is generative of new phenomena, and therefore demanding of new conceptual alignments.

The last few years have seen the emergence of interdisciplinary clusters addressing topics such as urban communication, urban informatics and media architecture.[6] There has also been renewed interest in bridging the divide that has long separated debates over 'public space' from those over the 'public sphere' (Low and Smith 2006) and more effort to take human-computer interaction research outside the lab and into the city.[7] Architecture has given greater attention to ephemeral interventions and temporary inhabitations, as well as displaying a welcome (if overdue) enthusiasm for exploring the *social* effects of networked digital media. A number of media scholars, including Gordon and de Souza e Silva (2011), Frith (2012), Farman (2012) and Wilken (2014), have sought to explore the implications of mobile media for urban space. 'Design' in a broad sense is now being elevated by some as a potential meta-discipline (McCullough 2013). While I certainly can't claim to be 'across' all these debates, or to exhaust their different resources, I have certainly learnt from my engagement with them. In the process, I have endeavoured to follow what Morley (2009) aptly termed a less 'mediacentric' mode of studying media. I have also sought to resist the temptation of attempting to resolve the growing contradictions of the relation between 'media' and 'immediacy' by simply appealing to some new third term as horizon or ground. As Stiegler (2001) argues, the attempt to leap 'beyond' deeply entrenched oppositions usually ends up reinscribing them. Generating new conceptual frameworks requires a different logic, following what Stiegler calls *composition*, in which experimental relations are established among the old terms.[8] This is what I hope to have begun here.

When McLuhan famously posited 'new media' as the new 'nature' he was referring to the capacities of media to restructure both individual sensory experience and the scales and rhythms of communication as social practice.[9] Today his precocious understanding of media ecology must be revisited. Media literally surround us in urban life, and this state of immersion reconfigures relations between site, boundary and agency across all scales, from the psycho-acoustic space of the body and the nominally private space of the home to the abstract territory of the nation-state and the incipient apprehension of the world as global network. In this context, it is increasingly important to ask: can we still oppose 'media' to the 'immediacy' of face-to-face experience, as we have done for centuries? Is the present defined by the loss of existential nearness, as Heidegger (1971: 165) famously lamented in his broadside at broadcast television? Or are we now becoming more attuned to the contradictions that were embedded in old formulations? Perhaps what is lost in the present is not the possibility of 'nearness' but the terms of an older ontology? Any answer to this question is immensely complicated by the extent to which, as Kittler (2009) notes, philosophy has always remained blind to the question of media, to the fact of mediation as its own condition of existence.[10] This need to rethink the relation of mediation to immediacy outside the metaphysics of presence constitutes a vital horizon of this work.

Finally, I would note that, while the focus of the book is the interplay between geomedia and urban public space, what occurs in this arena will likely have wider ramifications. Faced with profound challenges that have now assumed planetary proportions, the need for inventing new solidarities between heterogeneous actors who are both locally embedded and transnationally extended has never seemed so urgent. A key thread of my argument in this book is that networked public space is today a vital laboratory for incubating and practising the sociotechnical skills – which is to say, the new forms of communication, collaboration and cooperative action – needed for this complex task.

1

Transforming Media and Public Space

The right to the networked city

In 1968, Henri Lefebvre posed the question of urban space in terms of 'the right to the city'. Contrary to the top-down ethos that dominated modern urban planning, Lefebvre argued that the capacity for a city's inhabitants to actively *appropriate* the time and space of their surroundings was a critical dimension to any modern conception of democracy. Lefebvre's right to the city is not a formal rights agenda, but relates to the capacity of city dwellers to live as *inhabitants* rather than to merely occupy the city as *habitat*. 'Appropriation' stands as a general term for various forms of citizen-led action that would enable the reinvention of the politics of everyday life that Lefebvre did so much to put on the urban agenda.

In 'the right to the city', Lefebvre announces what was already becoming a familiar theme in the 1960s – the death of the city. However, this was not merely a lament. Rather, he is concerned with the impact of industrialization on the form of the city, and the consequent need for the reinvention of the *urban* – something

which he distinguishes from *the city*. Lefebvre argues that industrialization had created a double dynamic of implosion-explosion, in
which the evisceration of the city centre proceeds in tandem with
the extrusion of urban boundaries. 'From this situation is born a
critical contradiction: a tendency towards the destruction of the
city, as well as a tendency towards the intensification of the urban
and the urban problematic' (Lefebvre 1996: 129). If the city takes
different historical forms, the urban is something that he defines in
a manner akin to an older generation of urban sociologists – such
as Georg Simmel and Louis Wirth – as a 'way of life'. The urban
is primarily a condition of social complexity and encounter with
difference that fosters a new dynamism of social life: 'As a place of
encounters, focus on communication and information, the *urban*
becomes what it always was: permanent desire, disequilibrium, seat
of the dissolution of normalities and constraints, the moment of
play and of the unpredictable' (Lefebvre 1996: 129).

Lefebvre's writings influenced a generation of urban researchers
in France and elsewhere and also achieved some traction in urban
policy, particularly in Europe. More recently, the theme of the
'right to the city' has been revisited and taken up anew by writers
including Don Mitchell (2003) and David Harvey (2008, 2012),
who argues that 'the right to the city' is 'one of our most precious
and yet most neglected rights' (2008: 23). I want to use Lefebvre's
concept as a provocation for thinking about the right to the city in
the context of pervasive digital networks. If the right to the city is
fundamentally concerned with social encounter, communication
and practices of appropriation, how should we think the right to
the *networked* city?

What I want to establish across the different parts of this chapter
are key trajectories in the transformation of both media and public
space that have combined to produce the current conjuncture. If I
initially sketch these as somewhat separate, in order to elaborate the
emergence of distinct histories and bodies of thought, this is not to
ignore the fact that the present is defined by their increasing intersection. It is worth recalling at the outset that concern over the role
and future of public space in the industrial capitalist city has been
coextensive with its emergence. This became particularly acute in

the late twentieth century, as the demise of many older industrial urban spaces led to explicit strategies for urban 'regeneration'. Renewed concern with, and desire to reinvent, the urban over the last two decades has coincided with the profound transformation of media technologies associated with computerization and digital convergence. Media, which was once associated primarily with the demise of public space and the commercialization of the public sphere (a logic grasped by Habermas (1989) as 'refeudalization'), is today one of the keys to the city's possible reinvention. Geomedia, which I characterized above in terms of the convergence of media sectors, the ubiquity of digital devices and platforms, the everyday use of place-specific data and location-aware services, and the routinization of distributed, real-time feedback, has become a major force shaping the contours of public space. By altering the rhythms and spatiality of social encounters, geomedia has become critical to the *politics* of contemporary public space.

How should we understand this politics? Nearly a century ago, Robert Park memorably characterized city-making as 'man's most consistent, and on the whole, his most successful attempt to remake the world he lives in more after his heart's desire' (1967: 3). But the search for a constructed utopia was not a one-way street: in remaking the city as lifeworld, Park added, 'man' finds that he 'has remade himself'. David Harvey strips this sentiment of its gender bias, while sharpening its political implications, arguing that 'what kind of a city we want cannot be divorced from the question of what kind of people we want to be' (2012: 1). My broad argument in this book is that, in the twenty-first century, how we imagine and implement the digitization of the city and the networking of public space will prove pivotal to what kind of future city we inhabit. In many respects, how we deal with this threshold will offer a template for what 'kind of people' we will become. This is not to assert that there will be a single outcome across different cities and societies, but rather that the threshold of digitization manifests a tipping point. It poses a set of questions with deep implications for the future of urban inhabitation.

As cities become increasingly media-dense spaces, the older modes of boundary-formation that previously defined the geometries and rhythms shaping everyday life have become subject to significant reworking. The function of urban public space as the locus for distinctive practices of social encounter and communication is being extensively recalibrated by new logics. Contrary to many pronouncements, 'place' has not disappeared, but particular sites and practices are now routinely 'opened out' spatially and temporally, reframed by new potentials for recording, archiving, analysing and retrieving various streams of information. Enhanced capacity to 'connect' to others supports a new prominence of transversal and transnational exchanges in social life, but also generates anxieties arising from the incursion of Others into previously circumscribed places and local practices. Geomedia is one name for the condition in which these new scales and speeds are inserted into the weft and warp of everyday life.

Will geomedia be used to submit social life to increasingly intense processes of scrutiny and micro-evaluation, aiding and abetting the commodification of the common, the intimate and the personal which have become the most valuable forms of marketing knowledge? Or will the nexus between geomedia and public space become a critical forum for the incubation and elaboration of social practices that might enable a reinvention of the urban? Posing the issue as a choice between two apparently separate and easily separable trajectories is misleading. As I argued above, the ambivalence of the current digital conjuncture is marked by the high degree of entanglement of contradictory trajectories. This has confused some of the terms belonging to an older language of political critique.

When Lefebvre extolled the urban in terms of encounter with difference, spontaneity and play, he was appealing to an idea of the urban everyday as a reserve or reservoir of resistance to 'authority':

> this urban life tends to turn against themselves the messages, orders and constraints coming from above. It attempts to appropriate time and space by foiling dominations, by diverting them from their goal. It also intervenes more or less at the level of the city and the way of inhabiting. In this way the urban is more or less the *oeuvre* of its citizens instead of imposing itself upon them as a system, as an already closed book. (1996: 117)

Today the urban everyday is precisely the terrain that many applications of geomedia progressively target. In the 1960s, Lefebvre could claim that: 'The use (use value) of places, monuments, differences, escape the demands of exchange, of exchange value' (1996: 129). The prospects for such 'escape' seem far more complex in the present. As Jonathan Crary argues, the contemporary 'everyday' is an increasingly uncertain ground for the elaboration of counter-practices:

> Even though, at various points in history, the everyday has been the terrain from which forms of opposition and resistance may have come, it is also in the nature of the everyday to adapt and reshape itself, often submissively, in response to what erupts or intrudes in it. [. . .] [N]ow there are numerous pressures for individuals to reimagine and refigure themselves as being of the same consistency and values as the dematerialized commodities and social connections in which they are immersed so extensively. Reification has proceeded to the point where the individual has to invent a self-understanding that optimizes or facilitates their participation in digital milieus or speeds. (2013: 69–70, 99–100)

From this point of view, one can immediately note the growing ambivalence surrounding Lefebvre's appeal to 'play', in a context in which modes of play are now directly implicated in generating economic value.[1] This is not to dismiss the potential for playful engagement to support the invention of new social relations, but to note that concepts such as play, appropriation and participation demand critical scrutiny and careful deployment in the present.

The key driver of this new degree of colonization of 'lifeworld' by 'system' is the tightening circuit fostered by the extension of digital technologies that has enabled the integration of previously separated systems and sectors. Bernard Stiegler describes this as a logic of *hyper-industrialization*:

> With the advent of very advanced control technologies emerging from digitalization, and converging in a *computational* system of globally integrated production and consumption, new cultural, editing and programming industries then appeared. What is new is that they

are technologically linked by universal digital equivalence (the binary system) to telecommunications systems and to computers, and, through this, directly articulated with logistical and production systems (barcodes and credit cards enabling the tracing of products and consumers), all of which constitutes the hyper-industrial epoch strictly speaking, dominated by the categorization of hyper-segmented 'targets' ('surgically' precise marketing organizing consumption) and by functioning in real time (production), through lean production [*flux tendus*] and *just in time* (logistics). (2011: 5)

Hyper-industrialization is characterized by the growing integration of production, consumption, finance, logistics and marketing. This convergent logic finds its peak expression in contemporary digital 'platforms' – such as Apple's iTunes, Amazon and various offerings by Alibaba, where software enabling 'one-touch' purchasing is linked to both credit facilities and logistics systems (warehousing, distribution) – but also to cultural practices and social relations. User-created content such as product reviews, comments and ratings systems function to lubricate processes of exchange under the rubric of 'sharing', joining social practices and market logics in a tight loop – this is what *your* 'friends' did/liked/read/listened to/watched/bought *today*. Seen in this light, the dominant forms of digital culture are less the carrier of new freedoms – whether conceived in terms of the consumer utopia of Anderson's (2006) 'long tail' or in terms of the new possibilities for 'participation' enabled by convergent media platforms identified by Jenkins (2006) – than a powerful and historically unprecedented force of *synchronization*.

For Stiegler, the driver of this synchronizing force is the historical failure of contemporary capitalism to generate the conditions for its own replacement, despite the massive growth in its productive capacity. In fact, this political failure is closely connected to the chronic instability engendered by increasingly rapid technical development, manifest in the explicit shift to accelerated production cycles based on 'permanent innovation' – and its corollary, perpetual obsolescence. Stiegler argues that 'hyper-industrial' capitalism has initiated a decomposition of capitalism's older political-symbolic terrain, which was dominated by the nation-state and the myth of a unified national culture. However, the failure to develop other values and beliefs that might replace national governance and the homogeneous culture in which the national imaginary was long grounded has led to the wholesale submission of social life to the logic of consumption. Stiegler argues that instead of rethinking the limits of national belonging and addressing the inequalities of the global system of production, we have entered a period of 'decadence', in which belief in a viable future is blocked. Awareness of the need for systemic change in the face of global challenges such as resource inequality and climate change is complemented by paralysis of meaningful action.

In this context, the immense communicative resources of the digital are being squandered, channelled into instrumental forms of data-gathering and user-profiling deployed primarily for marketing and security purposes. When 'consumption' has become the consumption of individualities, 'culture' becomes directly integrated into the consumption system. 'Culture' becomes a means of generating the data (the *datum* of intimacy) used to profile consumers, to target messages and communications. Part of the problem is that this orientation, which becomes ever more frantic, tends to obscure other possible relations – to communication, to technics, to other people, to being in the world.

Overreliance on commodity consumption as the measure of 'the good life' – and of individual worth – leads to a short-circuit of the desire and belief necessary for social progress. It not only blocks our relation to our own singularity, but prevents that singularity becoming the basis for a relation to the collective. Stiegler argues:

> Every human being is constituted by his or her *intimate and original* relation to *singularity*, and first of all by the knowledge that he or she has of *their* singularity, of the necessity of their being-unique, and this is why herdish behaviours, almost like the image we have of human cloning, provoke a tremendous malaise among those who endure them, a dangerous dissatisfaction with oneself and a profound loss of belief in the future, the paradox being that this malaise and this feeling of loss in fact reinforce the herdish tendency itself, through a retroactive loop

constituting a political tendency. It is this circle that must be broken: this *and decadence and the obligations it creates for us as political task*. (2011: 28)

In the decadence of the present, Stiegler argues, hope and fear come to oppose one another. In the fading of a vision of the future, hope often gives way to resentment (*ressentiment*) and fear to panic, leading to archaic symptoms and the kind of 'herdish' hyper-synchronization manifest in phenomena from global marketing fads to virulent nationalisms, jihadisms and increasingly anxious border policing.

How, then, might this cycle be broken? I have discussed Stiegler's analysis in some detail in this context because, even as he acknowledges the implication of the digital in the current impasse, he also recognizes its critical importance to any way out. In this vein, he argues that contemporary 'tele-technologies' not only threaten democracy but 'are also the only possible way to invent new forms of social bond and civil peace' (2010: 177). This assertion is linked to Stiegler's (1998) adaptation of Gilbert Simondon's thesis that all human societies exist in relation to a 'technical system' which is traversed by evolutionary tendencies. Such tendencies may induce changes, not only in the technical system, but across the other systems constituting society. As such, Stiegler contends that, in so far as 'digitalization is a mutation of the global technical system', it inaugurates a process of 'adjustment' that '*constitutes a suspension and a re-elaboration of the socio-ethnic programmes which form the unity of the social body*' (2011: 10).

From this perspective, Stiegler argues that the digital is also the source of a potential 'jumpstart' that might enable the inauguration of a new epoch. Such a 'jumpstart' will not arise from opposing 'culture' to 'industry' as its complete outside (as with nineteenth-century romanticism), nor yet from submitting 'life' to the imperatives of technological development (as is the case with hyper-industrialization).

Rather, and to the complete contrary, it is a matter of the invention of a new order, and the constitution of *a new mode of industrial development* as well as of cultural *practices* (and practices *irreducible to mere usages*), at the very moment that culture, or rather the *control* of culture, has become the heart of development, but has done so at the cost of a becoming-herdish which is also a generalized becoming-wild [*devenir-inculte*], and which can only lead to a political mis-belief and dis-credit. (Stiegler 2011: 15)

The argument that I advance in this book is that the nexus of the urban and the digital constitutes a critical site for this potential invention of a new order, one that links cultural practices to the 'industrial' logic of digital technologies in a new way. But this is a complex and problematic terrain to develop. What Sassen (2011c) terms the 'urbanization of technology' recognizes that technological imperatives can be, and are, continually modified and shaped by particular instantiations and cultures of use. At the same time, it is evident that techno-logics are also remaking cultures of use according to new scales and speeds of interaction.

My particular interest in this book is the way in which processes of 'becoming public' in networked cities are drawing together different modalities, scales and practices of communication, techno-logics and social agency, bridging the immediate and the mediated in ways that change both. If *publicness* necessarily entails the possibility of constructing some kind of 'commons' as the space of communication and social encounter, today this common space must be thought in the context of the growing heterogeneity and new mobilities of urban populations. How might new forms of assembling and acting with others in public contribute to the reinvention of cultural practices, values and beliefs so as to enable us to move beyond the current impasse? How can we affirm what we share without repeating the damaging political legacy of older, essentialist models of social bonding based on idealizations of a unified culture, language, religion, race or nation? How can we invent and consolidate a sense of belonging that finds its strength and common dimension in differences? In what circumstances might digital public space offer a basis for developing cosmopolitan forms of civility, not as the province of a well-travelled elite but as *social skills* enacted in everyday existence? Or is the vision of the looming 'smart city' directing us elsewhere? These are the questions I take up in what follows.

Living with strangers

In Hannah Arendt's (1958) important analysis of the transformation of notions of public and private in modernity, classical public space is fruitfully conceptualized as the 'space of appearance' for political action. However, we miss the full scope of Arendt's argument if we assume that public space is something that already exists, ready and waiting as the stage to house such activity. Paralleling Lefebvre's (1991a) critique of theories which conceptualize space as an 'envelope' waiting to be filled, Arendt argues that the 'publicness' of public space is precisely what has to be established through processes of public assembly and public speech. It is these fundamentally *political* actions of gathering and communicating that *constitute* publicness in and through their enactment. As Judith Butler (2011) has emphasized, this approach has two major implications for thinking about 'publicness'. First, it suggests that 'publicness' needs to be prised away from the privilege that classical liberalism granted to individual agency. Second, it gives far more weight to the constitutive dimension of embodied assembly.

> In the first instance, no one mobilizes a claim to move and assemble freely without moving and assembling together with others. In the second instance, the square and the street are not only the material supports for action, but they themselves are a part of any theory of public and corporeal action that we might presuppose. (Butler 2011)

Public space can be productively defined by the tensions generated by this double role: it is both support for the kind of common action with others that constitutes the 'appearance of the political' in Arendt's terms, but also part of what is at stake in any such action. In other words, the 'publicness' of public space is never simply given but is precisely what is produced through the *political* actions of public assembly and collective speech. Today, this relation has become more complicated, since the exigencies of 'speaking' and 'acting' with others in public need to take into account the multiple ways that public speaking and acting are reframed by digital networks operating according to new scales, intensities and temporalities.

Defining public space as a fundamentally political space of speech and assembly underlines a second paradox. If public space is indissoluble from what is shared – from the 'commons' – it is also and at the same time a space of difference and dissensus. In fact, public space could be said to be most authentically *public* in so far as it is able to assemble and stage such dissensus (Mouffe 2007). It is this contested and agonistic space that all claims to constitute a 'public' capable of speaking must traverse.

This agonistic role assumes a particular weight in the context of the modern city, where public space became the primary contact zone for new types of social encounters – spontaneous and ephemeral interactions between strangers. What might be called the *structural* conditions for the formation of a distinctive modern urban sensibility emerge in the mid-nineteenth century in the context of the marked acceleration in the transition to urban-industrial capitalism. In this period, many cities experienced extremely rapid growth in scale and social complexity, as displaced rural workers were drawn into urban employ in workshops and factories. The pioneering urban sociology of those such as Tönnies and Durkheim established the formal analytic coupling that came to dominate the sociological understanding of this new milieu in terms of the distinction between *Gemeinschaft* and *Gesellschaft*. This was most frequently framed in terms of the displacement of traditional ties based on kinship and personal knowledge by the more anonymous forms of social interaction and more impersonal forms of modern governance, including the market system and formal contracts. Max Weber's renowned 1921 essay on the city opens by defining the city in precisely these terms: 'Sociologically speaking, this would mean: the city is a settlement of closely spaced dwellings which form a colony so extensive that the reciprocal personal acquaintance of the inhabitants, elsewhere characteristic of the neighbourhood, is lacking' (Weber 1968: 1212).

However, it was Georg Simmel who emphasized the formative role of the stranger in the *cultural* experience of the modern city. For Simmel, 'big-city' life produced a new type of urban subject: a stranger who neither 'moved on' in the traditional manner of the itinerant travelling from town to town, nor was 'made familiar' according to the process of assimilation characteristic of smaller, more tight-knit communities. Rather, the stranger inhabited the modern city precisely by remaining an unknown quantity. The onset of the city of strangers upset the customary spatial relations of social life. As Simmel put it: 'the distance within this relation indicates that one who is close by is remote, but his strangeness indicates that one who is remote is near' (1971: 143). This uncertain quality of 'dwelling-with' while remaining 'distant-from' constitutes the modern city as the site of an existential tension that has only intensified into the present. How can 'community' be constituted and sustained when older forces of unification, such as shared cultural and religious experience, and especially a single common language, are attenuated, disrupted or absent?

Simmel suggests that living among strangers instils urban life with new possibilities for personal and cultural freedom, but also places it under a general shadow of depersonalization and loss of cultural bearings. His coupling of invention and alienation as the twinned trajectories of urban modernity returns regularly in twentieth-century urban thought. Louis Wirth's influential 1938 essay 'Urbanism as a Way of Life' recognizes that the capacity for urban dwellers to compare different cultural mores is what underpins the new freedom to reinvent tradition, but also heightens the risk of Durkheimian *anomie*. Wirth's description of the modern city as 'a mosaic of social worlds in which the transition from one to the other is abrupt' (1994: 71) was profoundly shaped by the explosion of migration to the 'new world'.[2] If cultural difference is constitutive of the modern city, for Wirth it also constitutes a potential obstacle to attaining the desired norm of social unity.[3]

Simmel's legacy can also be recognized in Richard Sennett's

optimistic appraisal of the *ideal* of modern urban culture.[4] For Sennett, learning to live among strangers is central to the modern *political* task of ameliorating absolutist belief systems. Big-city life is the precondition for the development of modern democracy not only because it subjects individual experience to the series of 'jolts' necessary to establish a more relational framework of belief, but also in so far as it provides the lived basis for the emergence of a public language of cosmopolitan civility. A key lesson from Sennett's (1978) seminal book *The Fall of Public Man* is his demonstration that public sociability is not natural but learned. Sennett traces the emergence of *civility* as the modern replacement for feudal bonds built around obligation and deference, arguing that it is a complex social relation that needs to be actively experimented with, learned, practised and nurtured. Public space is the 'medium' for the emergence of this more cosmopolitan culture, in which the potential for establishing social solidarity is no longer so tightly linked to remaining in one's place of origin. It is a theme Sennett returns to in his book *Together* (2012), where he argues that the sort of complex societies engendered in contemporary cities characterized by high degrees of diversity and mobility require novel forms of social cooperation: 'a demanding and difficult kind of cooperation [that] tries to join people who have separate or conflicting interests, who do not feel good about each other, who are unequal, or who simply do not understand each other' (2012: 6). Following Simmel's insight that the existential quandary of the modern city is how to sustain social relations amongst strangers, Sennett reposes this in the present as the challenge 'to respond to others on their own terms'.

This task has arguably become more demanding as patterns of migration have become more complex and jagged, and new mobilities have redefined rhythms of urban inhabitation (Papastergiadis 1999, 2012; Georgiou 2013). What is often most 'familiar' in the present is the celebrity host on television or the personalized homepage of a social network, while the neighbour living next door remains unknown and seemingly unknowable. Recognizing this is not to advocate that we should address this situation by seeking to return to the seemingly more stable and homogeneous social formations of the past. Such nostalgia is not only misleading but can be dangerous. As Jean-Luc Nancy has argued:

> the thinking of community as essence [. . .] is in effect the closure of the political. Such a thinking constitutes closure because it assigns to community a *common* being, whereas community is a matter of something quite different, namely, of existence inasmuch as it is *in* common, but without letting itself be absorbed into a common substance. Being *in* common has nothing to do with communion, with fusion into a body, into a unique and ultimate identity that would no longer be exposed. Being *in* common means, to the contrary, *no longer having, in any form, in any empirical or ideal place, such a substantial identity, and sharing this* (narcissistic) *'lack of identity'.* This is what philosophy calls 'finitude' [. . .] (1991: xxxviii)

Nancy reminds us that the reason Aristotle gave for humans living in cities was not based on 'need' but on a 'higher' reason: the sharing of a *logos*. If *logos* is notoriously hard to define (reason, language, etc.), Nancy insists it is something 'whose only worth lies in being exposed (among other ways, as when a face lights up), that is, in being shared' (1991: xxxviii). Our challenge in the present is to learn how to share the commonness of 'community' in the context of multiplicity without erasing our differences under a facade of false consensus. Nancy argues that, as much as this task demands a new sense of 'community', it also requires new practices of 'communication':

> How can we be receptive to the *meaning* of our multiple, dispersed, mortally fragmented existences, which nonetheless only make sense by existing in common? In other words, perhaps: how do we communicate? But this question can be asked seriously only if we dismiss all 'theories of communication', which begin by positing the necessity or the desire for a consensus, a continuity and a transfer of messages. It is not a question of establishing rules for communication, it is a question of understanding before all else that in 'communication' what takes place is an *exposition*: finite existence exposed to finite existence, co-appearing before it and with it. (1991: xl)

Communication occurring in public space has a strategic stake in this rethinking of the relation between community and communication. A critical element of Sennett's argument – and one that brings the issue of public space to the fore – is his insistence that responding to others on their own terms is not just a question of ethical attitude. It is not simply a matter of wanting to 'do the right thing' (to paraphrase Spike Lee) but is something that requires *social skill*. For Sennett, like Lefebvre, skill 'emerges from practical activity' (2012: 6). In particular, the experience of encountering others in public is a key avenue for developing the social skills needed for co-existence. This emphasis on the role of embodied practice in developing social skills underscores the need to move beyond the privilege that Habermas (1989) gave to rational debate as constitutive of the political public sphere. This is not to valorize the so-called 'irrational', nor to dismiss the value of purposive-rational discussion in politics, but to recognize that embodied and affective interactions also play critical roles in building public sociability as a commonly held skill – which is to say, a skill held not by particular individuals, but *held in common* as relations between a collective of people who remain different from one another.

Acting in public demands we negotiate an always-unstable balance between autonomy and cooperation, between the need to assert singularity, and the desire to find common ground with others. These different tensions frame the way in which we need to re-pose our initial question: under what settings can the nexus between geomedia and public space offer the potential for fostering the skills of a cosmopolitan civility?

The death and life of public space

The largely affirmative understanding of the modern city as the site for the invention of new forms of cultural dynamism advanced by Simmel, Lefebvre and Sennett has scarcely been uniform. In fact, it has long been shadowed, if not overshadowed, by a perception of the modern city as a chaotic space requiring a new logic of organization. As Benjamin (1999: 839) reminds us, the dominant image of the nineteenth-century city was of a *labyrinth* inhabited by surging and unpredictable crowds. This perception of the modern city as an unruly space at the mercy of the 'mob' was one of the major currents that led to Haussmann's pioneering 'regularization' of Paris beginning in the 1850s. It also informed the subsequent emergence of urban planning as a formal discipline dedicated to imposing a more rational order on the messy realities of city life.

The need to re-order the city in response to the fast-changing conditions of industrial capitalism became a fundamental tenet of the *Congrès internationaux d'architecture moderne* (CIAM) in the 1920s and 1930s under Siegfried Giedion's stewardship.[5] The key document formalizing these settings was CIAM's Athens Charter of 1933. Among other things, the Athens Charter made explicit the priority for planning the city from the functional perspective of circulation rather than social encounter. Like Le Corbusier's acclamation of the street as 'a traffic machine' (1971: 131–2), and Giedion's clarion call for 'abolition of the corridor street' (1967: 822), the stated aim was to produce an urban space optimized for rapid transit. While public space does not disappear in such visions, it is increasingly subjugated to the technocratic ideal of function-ally separated activity zones that came to dominate modern urban planning.[6]

A peak expression of this logic is found in the post-war devel-opment of the shopping centre or large-scale mall: a car-based destination carved out from the rest of the city in which the older functions of the street are largely internalized. While social life continues to exist in the mall (Morris 1988), it does so in a space that has ceded the mixed functions common to older marketplaces from the agora to the high street to a privately controlled space dedicated to consumption. By the close of the twentieth century, shopping-centre development was increasingly central to urbaniza-tion strategies, as cities overflowed older boundaries and large-scale 'corridors' became the primary unit of urban development.

Opposition to the logic of functional zoning had begun to grow even as it was being put into wider practice in the aftermath of the Second World War. As Sadler (1998: 24) points out, the lag between theory and implementation at a policy level meant that, even as CIAM's settings were being subject to trenchant criticism in 1950s architectural circles, they were being built into cities across the globe. While the various critics, including Lefebvre, the Situationists, the Smithsons, Reyner Banham and a range of other Marxist and anarchist urbanists, were scarcely unified in either philosophy or programme, what they did share was a growing concern that technocratic urban planning was eliminating the very features of spontaneity and social encounter that had made the modern city particularly valuable as a social form. From this perspective, the loss of 'the street' is devastating, not because it is the most desirable public space, but because it is the most complex and multifarious in terms of social interaction. Constant's influential conception of 'unitary urbanism', developed around 1960, stressed the role of the street as a communication and contact zone rather than merely a space of circulation:

> Historically, the street was more than a mere traffic artery. Its additional function, which may have been even more important than its role as thoroughfare, was as a collective living space where all the public events – markets, festivals, fairs, political demonstrations – took place, as well as encounters and contacts between smaller numbers of individuals, in short, all those activities that do not belong to the more intimate, private domain. (1998: 134)

When streets become mono-functional – whether through functional zoning, domination by motor vehicles, over-commercialization or because they simply 'disappeared', as in Paris under Haussmann and in the Bronx reshaped 'with a meat ax' (Caro 1974: 849) by Robert Moses in the 1940s – the entire character of a city's public life changes. A significant turning point in the battle over the city street was the publication of Jane Jacobs' *The Death and Life of Great American Cities* (1961), which Kasinitz extols as possibly 'the single most influential book on American urban space of the last half a century' (1994: 93). Jacobs' book is notable for its impassioned defence of the social life of the street. However, when it was first published, Jacobs' praise for the complexity of street life

as a 'higher form' of social order ran in marked contrast to existing policy settings and urban practices. As McCullough observes:
'the density and diversity that we know now as the basis for good
urbanism were the very targets of modernizing "urban renewal"'
(2004: 187). William Lim recalls the hostility towards those seen
as blocking 'progress': 'vocal protests by many urban theorists and
grassroots activists were ignored and even ridiculed' (2012: 28).

Where Jacobs' work differed from most of her contemporaries
was in her extensive use of empirical observation. Instead of laying
down prescriptions as to what urban life *should* be like, she advanced
her argument in favour of mixed spatial use on the basis of what she
saw already existing around her in Greenwich Village. Suggesting
that sidewalks have 'other uses' than circulation, Jacobs argued that
'well-used streets' are those capable of attracting a variety of users
across the day, drawing together an informal coalition of residents,
workers, shoppers, itinerants and strangers. Continual and varied
use is what establishes a virtuous circle, in which the presence of
people attracts more people, not least by promising the pleasure of
watching others go about their business (Whyte 1980). Because the
well-used street is a well-watched street, it becomes a safe street in
which the presence of diverse strangers can be enjoyed rather than
construed as threatening. Well-used streets promote the sort of
serendipitous social encounters that Kasinitz extols as 'the essence
of urbanity' (1994: 94). For Jacobs, casual encounters are central to
social bonding and establishing urban trust:

> Most of it is ostensibly utterly trivial but the sum is not trivial at all.
> The sum of such casual public contact at a local level – most of it
> fortuitous, most of it associated with errands, all of it metered by the
> person concerned and not thrust upon him by anyone – is a feeling for
> the public identity of people, a web of public respect and trust, and a
> resource in time of personal or neighborhood need. The absence of
> this trust is a disaster to a city street. Its cultivation cannot be institu-
> tionalized. (1961: 56)

The 'web of public trust' is what enables a balance to be struck
between desire for privacy and the need for differing degrees of

contact that don't necessarily blossom into personal intimacy. 'This balance is largely made up of small, sensitively managed details practiced and accepted so casually that they are normally taken for granted' (Jacobs 1961: 59). However, in the absence of appropriate spaces and opportunities for casual social encounters, people are forced to either formalize such arrangements (which tends to be self-defeating), or to forego them. Jacobs notes: 'The more common outcome in cities where people are faced with the choice of sharing much or nothing, is nothing. In city areas that lack a natural and casual public life, it is common for residents to isolate themselves from each other to a fantastic degree' (1961: 65).

The work of Jacobs and others focusing attention on the importance of street life situates one of the critical implications of the extension of geomedia into public space. Will the capacity for low-cost distributed communication facilitate casual and serendipitous social encounters with others, extending and deepening them in new ways? Or will the new digital urban infrastructure sterilize such encounters, submerging spontaneity under the kind of predictive analysis enabled by high volumes of data? This is one of the key tensions running through contemporary smart-city planning and rhetoric.

Public space in the smart city

Like Lefebvre, the work of Jacobs eventually found purchase in urban planning circles. In some respects, one might argue that it has never been more widely cited or influential than in the present – which is not to say that it is always followed. This change in urban policy settings was initially driven by the growing recognition of urban crisis. The widely televised destruction of St Louis' Pruit Igoe housing complex in 1972 – provocatively seized by Charles Jencks as the birth of 'postmodern' architecture – signalled a critical threshold in acknowledging the failure of modern urban planning. By 1975, New York – the iconic modern city – was near bankrupt. President Ford's initial refusal to supply a loan facility led to the *New York Daily News*' blunt headline: 'Ford to City: Drop Dead'. The riots and looting that followed the power blackout of 1977 seemed to mark the end of a certain urban dream.

For many theorists writing around that time, there was an overwhelming sense that the modern city had lost its coherence. In his 1984 essay, 'Postmodernism, or, the Cultural Logic of Late Capitalism', Fredric Jameson drew on Kevin Lynch's (1960) concept of urban 'legibility' to argue that the postmodern city was fundamentally disorienting. Paul Virilio (1986a) went further to posit the total collapse of the distinction between city and country, resulting not only in the loss of 'downtown' but also the paradoxical formation of a new 'omnopolis'. When Goethe had described Paris as a universal-city in 1727, he was extolling a unique place that concentrated far-flung splendours from all around the globe. In contrast, Virilio's (1997: 74) omnopolis was characterized by the collapse of distance and the spread of a homogeneous commercial culture in which the same objects, brands and experiences spread all over the world. In a context dominated by resurgent neo-liberalism, a marked pessimism towards the future of public space was evident, particularly in the United States (Davis 1990; Sorkin 1992).

Two decades on, it is striking that, while many of the trajectories driving such analyses – market globalization, urban sprawl, dominance of private cars and mediatized public culture – remain operative, and have in many respects intensified, there has nevertheless been a marked change in urban discourse. This has been partly the result of the upsurge of new and accelerated urbanizations, most notably in China (Keith et al. 2014), but also across other parts of Asia and Africa.[7] The rapid growth of megacities with over 10 million inhabitants, mostly in Asia, led Rem Koolhaas (2004: 452) to assert that the city can no longer pretend to be a 'western' construct.

But reappraisal of the urban future has also been driven by a significant transformation in the urban discourse emanating from the old centres. This new urbanism is marked by a number of contradictory currents. The widespread programmes of urban regeneration sparked by the paradigm case of Manhattan 'loft living' (Zukin

1982), which restored New York's fashionable image, were subsequently expanded into broader 'creative cities' agendas (O'Connor 2006). These were tightly predicated on leveraging the digital 'revolution' to fast-track a desired transition from manufacturing to knowledge economies (Pratt 2008). While these shifts contributed to a partial reversal of earlier planning settings, and have produced success stories defined by more 'vibrant' neighbourhoods (Franklin 2010), they also fed other headings. The redevelopment of older inner-city industrial spaces around the world has become implicated in successive cycles of urban gentrification, resulting in new patterns of urban stratification.[8]

More recently, the rhetoric of the 'creative city' has been trumped by the growing prominence of 'smart-city' agendas. In these visions digital technology is not just the gateway to a new creative economy, but is being handed responsibility for sustaining a new era of urban inhabitation. But what do we mean by 'smart city'? In a technical sense, smart-city operations are generally defined by the use of multiple, large-scale and varied data sets to provide 'insights' into urban mobility, resource use and the like. As Batty and colleagues put it, this involves 'constellations of instruments across many scales that are connected through multiple networks which provide continuous data regarding the movements of people and materials' (Batty et al. 2012: 482). If smart-city rhetoric often taps into older fantasies of urban control, it's emergence as a practical possibility is very contemporary. As the cost of networked sensors, data storage and analytic capacity have become lower by orders of magnitude, it has become feasible to collect data about all kinds of urban systems and behaviours, to process it and to apply it – potentially in real-time – so as to act on those same systems and behaviours.

This new potential raises a host of questions. As Batty and colleagues note: 'Cities however can only be smart if there are intelligence functions that are able to integrate and synthesise this data to some purpose, ways of improving the efficiency, equity, sustainability and quality of life in cities' (2012: 482). Data and data analytics are now being harnessed according to visions in which 'smart cities' become more competitive, functional, secure, liveable and sustainable (Kitchin 2014: 8). This variety of ambitions situates the grey zone found in most contemporary elaborations of the smart city: the slippage between claims to generate and analyse data to empower citizens and improve 'liveability', and schemes for generating and analysing data to refine capabilities for *managing* cities.

While I am not disputing the potential for utilizing data in order to promote efficient resource use, I do think there are significant problems with the smart-city agenda as it is currently elaborated. In particular, it tends to be vendor-driven, often comes with expansive claims about what can be learned from 'data', and, while it deploys a rhetoric of transparency, closer inspection reveals fundamental asymmetries. These settings have serious implications for public space in the future city.

Critics such as Anthony Townsend (2013: 18–19) and Adam Greenfield (2013) emphasize the fact that the contemporary smart-city narrative has unusually strong commercial origins, driven by companies such as IBM, Siemens, Cisco, Samsung and Microsoft. Greenfield comments: 'It's as if the foundational works of twentieth-century urbanist thought had been collectively authored by United States Steel, General Motors, the Otis Elevator Company and Bell Telephone rather than Le Corbusier or Jane Jacobs' (2013: 13–14). As Schaffers et al. point out: 'smart city solutions are currently more vendor push than city government pull based' (2011: 437). These origins help to explain – but not justify – a narrowness in conception of smart-city 'stakeholders', as well as a marked lack of interest in local terrain and local culture that is displayed by 'enterprise-level' smart-city solutions.

A second issue is that the vision of creating a smart city using real-time 'big data' depends on a chain of problematic assumptions regarding the apparent neutrality of data and data analytics, as well as a disturbing fetishism as to what data can actually reveal about urban life (Mattern 2013). When Siemens proclaims that the future city 'will have countless autonomous, intelligently functioning IT systems that will have perfect knowledge of users' habits', adding that 'The goal of such a city is to optimally regulate and control resources by means of autonomous IT systems' (Wohllaib 2008:

68), they elaborate a programme built on positivist assumptions about the capacity for technical systems to model relations and states without bias or distortion. Yet such assumptions have been widely critiqued in both philosophical and practical terms. Even putting aside the well-known problem that any act of observing or measuring inevitably impacts on the situation being studied, designers know that the practical construction of any technical system involves trade-offs over capacities and outcomes (Greenfield 2013: 53). Proposing a singular and uncontested value of 'optimization' fails to address either issue. Siemens' language here buys into the big-data fallacy proposed by Chris Anderson (2008), in which sufficient quantities of data obviate any need for interpretation or 'theory'.[9] The smart-city agenda compounds the problem by treating the city as comprised largely by a series of technical systems that can be best managed by sophisticated algorithmic tools. Such solutions (or what Morozov (2013) aptly calls 'solutionism') are the new and powerful face of urban technocracy.

Third, the smart city is generally conceived as consisting of proprietary platforms. This is particularly the case for what Greenfield (2013: 11) calls the 'canonical' smart cities: blank slate developments such as New Songdo in Korea or Masdar City in the UAE, for which Cisco and IBM have respectively constructed prototype integrated urban systems. But the same logic also affects the much broader drive to retrofit existing urban infrastructure. This process concerns not only the proliferation of networked sensors, RFID readers and digital vision systems (such as number plate recognition systems) that complement older CCTV networks, but also relates to the growing tendency to incorporate citizen devices into the data net. As Greenfield notes, mobile phones and tablets are 'treated both as interface objects and as sources of the most granular data regarding our whereabouts, activities and intentions' (2013: 11).

Reliance on big data has particular implications for research. Thatcher points out that the preponderance of proprietary data sets is matched by proprietary analytic systems in this space. This constrains both the kinds of 'questions' that can be asked, and the answers that will be received, even when one is researching data gathered through citizen-operated devices such as mobile phones: 'rather than fully capturing life as researchers hope, end-user inter-actions within big data are necessarily the result of decisions made by an extremely small group of programmers working for private corporations that have promulgated through the mobile applica-tion ecosystem' (Thatcher 2014: 1766).

Smart-city proposals often deploy a rhetoric of informational transparency and citizen empowerment. However, data access tends to remain highly asymmetrical. Greenfield's (2013: 43–4, 60) analysis of three 'exemplar' smart-city developments revealed little or no planning for systematic provision of open raw data to citi-zens. Instead, citizens were to be given 'alerts' based on processed data. In any case, for access to raw data to be really useful, citizens need to have access to advanced analytic capacity – something that is generally lacking. This kind of asymmetry also extends to problems faced by both 'clients' (often municipal governments) and citizens in understanding the implications of data collection. In fact, what data 'means' depends on how it can be used, and this shifts all the time: what you could do with a photograph fifteen years ago is very different to what you can do with it today. All of these factors impact on our capacity to make critical judgements about decisions and alternatives. As Nissenbaum remarks:

> With the advent of actuarial prediction based on data aggregation, mining, and profiling, however, decisions are made that we do not understand; even those making the decisions may not understand the decisions being made because the highly complex algorithms whose outputs are statistically significant correlations defy the ordinary theo-ries that have guided our actions in the past. (In Nissenbaum and Varnelis 2012: 32)

Finally, and perhaps most disturbingly, there has been a con-spicuous lack of dialogue about alternative visions in this space, as arguments about the 'quality' of urban life have been largely subsumed by a technology-driven agenda. As Schaffers et al. note: 'Technology push is still dominant in the actual research agenda' (2011: 437). While those such as Batty et al. (2012: 492) argue strongly for smart-city data to constitute a 'public good', how this might be manifested when commercial interests are increasingly tethered to provision of platforms and control over data is likely to form one of the key battlegrounds for the future of the city.[10]

Faced with growing streams of digital data, cities around the world have begun to integrate different data sources and networks into single hubs, including some that provide public-facing information on 'city dashboards'.[11] But most displays are directed towards city managers. Arguably the most ambitious is the *Centro De Operações Prefeitura Do Rio* (a partnership between the Rio de Janeiro city government and IBM), which draws together data streams from thirty agencies. In the control room, urban 'management' becomes a matter of optimizing flows of energy, matter and information. Despite the sophistication of the system, one is left wondering what has happened to the capacity to understand the city as a complex of social encounters that are experienced and lived rather than 'optimized' and managed.

Rem Koolhaas (2014) argues that the rise of smart-city rhetoric is symptomatic of a critical failure in urban imagination: 'We stopped thinking about the city at the exact moment of the explosion in urban substance in the developing world. The city triumphed at the very moment that thinking about the city stopped. The "smart" city has stepped into that vacuum.' Koolhaas adds: 'This confluence of rhetoric – the "smart city", the "creative class", and "innovation" – is creating a stronger and stronger argument for consolidation. If you look in a smart-city control room, like the one in Rio de Janeiro by IBM, you start to wonder about the extent of what is actually being controlled.'

As I argued in the previous two sections, unpredictable and unplanned forms of association have been the creative heart of modern urban life. As Hardt and Negri put it: 'In addition to the immersion in the common produced by and productive of social life, another quality defines the metropolis: the unpredictable, aleatory encounter or, rather, the encounter with alterity' (2009: 251–2). A major concern with contemporary smart-city strategies is that part of 'what is actually being controlled' – wittingly or unwittingly – is the capacity for public space to continue to function as the medium for these sort of aleatory encounters. This plays out across two related registers: how we design urban public space, and the new traceability of public encounters in the context of geomedia.

One of the key criticisms of modernist planning and design was not only its tendency for top-down implementation, but its related propensity for being overly prescriptive. As those including Whyte (1980), Watson (2006) and Stevens (2007) have argued, prescriptive design constrains the capacity for inhabitants to *appropriate* their surroundings in Lefebvre's terms. Saskia Sassen (2011b) argues that contemporary smart-city agendas are repeating the same mistake: instead of appreciating the value of 'incompleteness', and thereby designing systems that might enable inhabitants to 'urbanize' technology through varied forms of local practice, the focus remains too strongly on the digital as a technique for centralized command and control:

> I think that the model of 'intelligent cities' as propounded by [. . .] the telepresence efforts of Cisco Systems misses this opportunity to urbanize the technologies they mobilize, and futilely seeks to eliminate incompleteness. The planners of intelligent cities, notably Songdo in South Korea, actually make these technologies invisible, and hence put them in command rather than in dialogue with users. One effect is that intelligent cities represent closed systems, and that is a pity. It will cut their lives short. They will become obsolete sooner.

Koolhaas (2014) concurs, arguing that by dint of prioritizing safety and security as the main selling points of the smart city, urban spontaneity is being traded off in favour of predictability:

> The rhetoric of smart cities would be more persuasive if the environment that the technology companies create was actually a compelling one that offered models for what the city can be. But if you look at Silicon Valley you see that the greatest innovators in the digital field have created a bland suburban environment that is becoming increasingly exclusive, its tech bubbles insulated from the public sphere.

How we might use geomedia to design 'incomplete' or 'unfinished' urban spaces that facilitate rich forms of urban appropriation and social encounter is something I take up further in chapters 3 and 4 below. The issue has become increasingly important for another reason. As we enter what the novelist William Gibson evocatively described as an era of 'affordable privacy', it is apparent that the role of 'the street' as the site of the sort of serendipitous encounters that animated so much modernist thought is being overtaken by new capacities to monitor and regulate social movement.[12] Greater heterogeneity of the urban population and greater mobility are matched by an ever-growing desire to track, control and manage movement in public space. Tracing movement and sorting identity is no longer about seeking to regulate the flows at specific border control points but has become a more general logic deployed throughout urban space. In this context, Greenfield argues that the lack of concern with anything resembling a traditional public sphere in canonical smart-city proposals is particularly troubling

> given certain inherent capabilities of a thoroughly instrumented environment, namely the ability to identify individuals via the analysis of unique biometric signatures; track their movement through the space of the city; monitor and assess their utterances and other behaviour; and predict likely courses of action, including future patterns of movement and association, based on that assessment. (2013: 68)

The 'secure' environment of the smart city can all too easily assume an ominous political tenor. Moreover, tracking and tracing is no longer the sole prerogative of the state, but has become central to contemporary commercial agendas. What happens to urban experience when everyday processes of communication, navigation and social encounter come to be intimately tied up with the new logistics of surveillance and the digital trace? What kind of urban life is incubated when privacy is 'dead' and the mutual anonymity that gave rise to the distinctive public culture of the modern city is increasingly threatened?[13]

The threshold of geomedia holds a particular and significant responsibility in relation to the future of casual and 'unplanned' activity in urban space. On the one hand, digital technologies offer an emergent and still relatively unexplored potential for using distributed feedback to alter urban ambiance so as to produce temporary experimental zones and new collective forms of social interaction. On the other hand, public encounters are increasingly subject to massive data capture, carried out not only by automated systems controlling urban infrastructure but by a fast-growing culture of volunteered information and *self*-reporting. How we might negotiate this new condition is one of the central concerns I explore in the following chapters.

The revolution will not be televised

Having traced the transformation of public space from the formation of the modern city to the dilemmas of the networked present, I now want to focus on transformations emerging more from the media side of my equation. In the preface to his influential *Relations in Public: Microstudies of the Public Order*, Erving Goffman made a brief reference to 'the current unsafety and incivility of our city streets' (1971: ix).[14] The causes underlying Goffman's observation could certainly be debated: as much as 'unsafety and incivility' was a function of urban blight, it was also a measure of the extent to which the streets had become a key arena for challenges to political consensus in the United States and across much of the globe in the 1960s. The new social movements of the time were distinctive in part for the extent to which they used public space as a key contact zone: an arena of protest, but also of public communication that involved the invention of new forms of action and display, ranging from sit-ins to fashion and performance art. These innovative forms of publicity were themselves implicated in the new conditions of public culture established by the rapid growth of broadcast television. It is the vicissitudes of this relation between media and public events that I want to examine further here.

In this section I will trace how the spatial organization that corresponded to the broadcast era supported a particular set of relations between media and social life. The emergence of the private home as a key media centre in the post-war era eventually gave rise to what Dayan and Katz (1992) influentially called the 'media event'. In the next section, I will argue that the terms of this *broadcast* media event have been increasingly put into question by the transition to geomedia. The proliferation of media *on* the street is generating a different type of media event characterized by public viewing and distributed feedback. While the second trajectory does not simply replace the first, it substantially refigures the production of 'public events' in the conditions of networked public space.

Growing perception of the street as an arena of 'unsafety and incivility' in the 1960s heightened the role that television took in orchestrating the public sphere in this period. Watching television allowed viewers to stay 'in touch' while remaining safely at a distance, according to the logic announced by Hutchinson's (1946) 'window to the world' that has remained such a lasting trope for understanding television. However, the relation between television and event has always been complex. For those in the street, a different dynamic was at work. As the anti-war movement grew in the US through the 1960s, trust in television declined markedly: the 'window to the world' was increasingly recognized as selective and partial in what it allowed to be seen (Gitlin 2003). Growing realization that mainstream media were part of the problem bled into broader critiques of capitalism, gender politics and consumer culture. 'The whole world is watching' chanted by protestors outside the 1968 Democratic National Convention in Chicago gave way to Gil Scott-Heron's acerbic assertion in 1970 that 'the revolution will not be televised'.[15] Recognition of the need to make your own media as an integral part of any project to remake society had arrived.

When Scott-Heron's slogan re-appeared on Occupy posters in 2011, the relation between media, public space and 'media events' had again changed significantly. Video activist Shay David (2014) proclaims: 'The revolution will indeed not be televised. It will, however, be streamed.'[16] However, the transformation seems more complex than the neat transcendence of old forms and limitations that his statement suggests. While the logistics of media production and distribution in the digital era alleviate some older restrictions around access and visibility, they also establish new constraints. This is what I want to unfold here.

First we need to recognize that the growth of broadcast television in the second half of the twentieth century was profoundly implicated in the transformation of both the private space of the home, and in the orchestration of a new genre of 'media events'. The rapid growth of television cannot be reduced to a simple cause–effect relation; as Raymond Williams (1974) argued, it was a function of the ways that the new communication platform could be articulated with an evolutionary phase of capitalism. What we now recognize as the broadcast television ecology was pivotal in the retooling of capitalism from a wartime production economy towards one based on lifestyle consumption centred in the private home. Television rapidly became the primary conduit for carrying advertising *into* the home, establishing the communication logistics necessary for the full development of the Fordist production of consumer goods. But its impact far exceeded simply showing a new range of products and models: as Stiegler (2011: 109) notes, television also showcases *model behaviours*. A century after Nietzsche proclaimed the death of God, the meaning of life seemed increasingly to be found in consumption, and desire was aggressively channelled into a 'good life' defined by individual accumulation.

Beyond this function, television became an important driver of post-war politics, establishing the conditions for the transformation of local and regional political affiliations into national-presidential politics (even in formally non-presidential systems), and heightening the link between celebrity and political currency that is still powerful in the present. Along a related register, television was instrumental in the progressive relocation and partial integration of 'local' cultures into expanded national and global circuits of cultural exchange. It is from this perspective that we can begin to situate the institutionalization of broadcast television in relation to paradigmatic social and political shifts associated with late twentieth-century urban society: the move away from tighter-knit, more persistent urban groupings to looser and more diffuse associations characterized by greater mobility, diversity and spatial extension; the professionalization of politics which comes to be increasingly centred around organized forms of media display; and the reworking of subjectivity in which the diminished influence of traditional socializing institutions is counterpointed by the rise of 'the media' as a key resource for what Beck, Giddens and Lash (1994) call 'reflexive' identity formation.

The rise of broadcast television also corresponded to the consolidation of a particular spatial disposition of the city. The great suburban dispersion of the post-war era placed heightened importance on communication infrastructure linking private life with the public sphere. Television fitted this *structural* need – defining itself in the process – as it became the primary mechanism carrying the political public sphere, as well as representations of cultural life and market relations, *into* the home. As the habitus of broadcasting was established, the cellular architecture of network television came to typify the distinctive recasting of the relation between citizens and *polis* as one between a mass of essentially private individuals. In contrast to Arendt's description of the *vita activa* in classical life, it was no longer the public arena but the private home that now stood as the privileged site of 'authentic' experience.

It was in this historical context that television leveraged its novel capacity for the production of spatially extended experiences of social simultaneity to inaugurate a new category of events – what Dayan and Katz (1992) aptly called *media events* – exemplified by the Apollo moon landing in 1969. While Dayan and Katz define the 'media event' in restricted terms, I am more interested in exploring the implications of this new social logic based on the mass consumption of public events by audiences located in the privacy of their own homes.[17] In the context of live broadcasting, 'face-to-face' encounters suddenly found themselves counterpointed by a new regime: relayed happenings that arrived from distant *elsewheres*, and which could be watched simultaneously with others across a multiplicity of sites. The fact that this experience has become so commonplace in the present should not obscure its epochal implications, or its manifest contradictions. To understand the new logic of the public event that emerges during this period, I

want to trace these tensions along two key trajectories: the politics
of representation, and the temporality of re-presentation.

Media visibility in the broadcast era was inevitably shaped by
limitations on the number of channels available in any particular
territory.[18] Scarcity of outlets was fundamental to the architecture
of broadcast media, and inevitably focused critical analysis around
questions of 'gatekeeping' and 'representation'. The key issue for a
politics of media representation in the broadcast era tended to be
the (lack of) diversity making up a presumed 'national conversation' on the one hand, and strategies for gaining access to scarce
resources such as the most visible channels, roles and time-slots
('prime time') on the other. This frame is most evident in ongoing
debates over the on-screen visibility of various minorities, ranging
across both 'fiction' and 'non-fiction' programming. Who is interviewed or portrayed? Who appears on camera? Whose voice is
heard and whose opinion is positioned as authoritative? Scarcity
also situates the high threshold that had to be crossed for something
to become visible as a 'media event' in this period.[19]

While the constraints imposed by scarcity of outlets are widely
acknowledged, the temporal effects of live broadcasting remain
more shadowy. Nevertheless, a key dimension of broadcast logic
was the extent to which 'events' were increasingly orchestrated
for the media. If this is already becoming evident in the political
sphere at the moment of Kennedy's ascension (exemplified by his
famous 1960 debates with Nixon in which radio and television
audiences displayed markedly different responses to the respec-
tive candidates), it plays out over ensuing decades in terms of the
growing imperative to shape and control media coverage of formal
politics by borrowing professional techniques from the advertising,
marketing and film industries. By the 1980s, designing the public
appearances of politicians for photo-ops, or scripting for sound-
bites, had become second nature. By the 1990s 'best practice' was
defined overwhelmingly in terms of accelerated responsiveness
to media cycles, exemplified by the mantra adopted for the 1992
Clinton election campaign: 'speed kills'.

Of course, such a logic scarcely remains confined to formal
politics. Growing reliance on 'soft power' as the complement to

military firepower meant that securing favourable media coverage became increasingly important to waging military campaigns,
particularly after Vietnam. Media blackouts give way to saturation
information, as traditional forms of censorship came to be complemented by strategies of information provision and the 'embedding'
of journalists as favoured mechanisms for shaping war coverage.
Speed is also critical in this domain. Virilio (1989) reminds us that
during the German *blitzkrieg* of 1939 a special unit was deployed
to shoot film at the front line and get it onto cinema screens in
Berlin and other German cities the following night. By the 1990–1
Gulf War, the extent to which the strategic use of media as a technique for military operations had converged with techniques for
the governance of the civilian population had become even more
evident. This was manifest not only in the rolling 24/7 coverage
of the conflict pioneered by CNN, but also by the fact that the
same 'missile-cam' images were shared by military analysts and
the public watching 'live' on their television sets at home (Wark
1994).

   This growing integration of media publicity with (destructive)
event was not destined to remain a state prerogative for long.
Reflecting on the 1993 attacks on the World Trade Center towers
in Manhattan, Virilio noted: 'With the New York bomb, we thus
find ourselves faced with the latest escalation in the kind of military-political interaction that is based simultaneously on a limited
number of actors and *guaranteed media coverage*' (2000: 19, emphasis
added). If the 1993 attack foreshadowed the extent to which planning an event and calculating its sociopolitical effects had become
inseparable from planning its media dissemination, the same logic
was fatally evident in the 2001 attacks that finally levelled the
Trade Centre towers. The seventeen-minute delay between the
first and second planes enabled television cameras to be in place so
the second collision could occur 'live' on screen.[20] The fact that
the event was designed to take time (the fires that melted the concrete core and resulted in the collapse of the towers took almost an
hour) ensured maximum visibility.

   What does this tell us about the relation between 'media' and
'event' at the close of the broadcast era? First, we need to underline

the way in which the logic of the *campaign* – instructively, a term deployed equally across contemporary military, political and marketing operations – has infiltrated public events of all genres and scales. Second, while 'rapid response' communication used to be restricted to powerful actors such as the military and police, it has been progressively seized by others, including those variously dubbed 'terrorists' and 'activists'. In this respect, we might note that *rapid response* is now being progressively integrated into 'private life'. Older habits, such as staging key family rituals including weddings and birthdays for the camera, are now being elevated into a more generalized performativity, and self-representation has assumed the attributes of a *permanent campaign* of *self-construction* waged on social media platforms.

Third, it has become increasingly evident that the screen's role in 'mediating' between the viewer at home and events in the world outside cannot be too hastily reduced to the sort of binary oppositions between 'reality' and 'representation', or between 'active' participants and 'passive' spectators, that have so often been called on to regulate this space. To caution against this reduction is not to deny the manifest limits of all televisual witnessing: what television displays of any event is inevitably the product of multiple filters that assume technological, economic, ideological, institutional, sociocultural and other dimensions. Nevertheless, if we want to account for the historically distinctive *force* unleashed by television's novel capacity to redistribute live events, we need to recognize that the televisual constructs a complex psychosocial relation to public events. Most of the time, the presumed separation between 'event' and 'media coverage' is held in place by an amalgam of habits and routines including professional codes of production and social practices of viewing. However, there have long been signal occasions when this habitual frame is ruptured. In moments such as the 9/11 attacks, the seemingly safe mediation of the screen gives way to an uncanny *immediation* in which unpredictable affect radiates outwards. Instead of a mechanism that enables distancing by imposing a detached and largely *touristic* relation to the scene of the other, television becomes the vehicle for the uncanny transmission of traumatic experience.[21]

Shadowing the well-known economic effects of the 9/11 attacks, Matusitz (2013) notes that surveys taken in the immediate aftermath found that 21 per cent of Americans across the nation had difficulty sleeping because of nightmares about the event and concerns about subsequent attacks.[22] Other indicators of massive and widely distributed psychosocial affect included a notable rise in the use of mental health services and antidepressant prescriptions, as well as rises in the perceived importance of survival, safety and security values, and a concomitant decline in self-esteem and self-actualization values. Perhaps the most striking measure was a 2005 poll in which nearly half (46 per cent) of adult respondents in the US cited the 9/11 terrorist attacks as the single most significant event in their lifetime (Matusitz 2013: 88–9). (In comparison only 2 per cent cited the collapse of communism, 3 per cent the Vietnam War, and 6 per cent the Iraq War.) While such results are shaped by many factors, including the fact that the 9/11 attacks occurred on 'home' territory, I would argue that part of their perceived magnitude and intensity stemmed from their extraordinary visibility as a 'media event' watched 'live' in the home.

Occupying networked public space

9/11 remains a distinctive 'media event' in another sense: it coincides with the closure – which is not yet the *end* – of the broadcast era. Even as the destruction of the World Trade Center towers was witnessed on television by millions, the spatio-temporal settlement of broadcast media was coming under increasing pressure. What happens when the orchestration of the 'media event' is opened up – even partially – to new actors?

In *The Wealth of Networks*, Yochai Benkler (2006) posits a broad distinction between the 'industrial information economy' (IIE) and the 'networked information economy' (NIE). 'Old' media including cinema, music recording, publishing and television are characterized as belonging to the IIE, typified by the need for relatively large-scale capital investment to support the process of fixing and distributing information. Benkler argues that the fact that 'making initial utterances', such as producing a song or a film, has a relatively high cost compared to the additional cost of making copies favoured the modern development of cultural industries that privileged the production of relatively few, high production-value artefacts that could be widely distributed. If 'technological reproducibility' (Benjamin 2003) creates the conditions for 'mass' audiences, Benkler also emphasizes the historical settlement in which this model fosters tendencies towards both commercialization and concentration in the production and exchange of information.[23]

In contrast, what Benkler terms the NIE emerges at the junction of two different technological developments: the transformation of the personal computer from a tool for calculation and data analysis into a ubiquitous media and communication device, and the availability of relatively cheap, global connectivity through the Internet. Where domestic television was only a 'receiver', the computer came to combine the means for accessing and generating content in the same device. This fusing of production and consumption also underpins the design of key Internet platforms, most famously Tim Berners-Lee's (1997) protocols for the World Wide Web. Once the personal computer met the new distributive architecture of the Internet, the business model of the IIE was rendered increasingly vulnerable. A major tipping point was reached when a critical mass of people gained access to the combination of hardware and software enabling easy reproduction of (relatively) lossless digital copies *and* low cost distribution of these files. This produced the 'perfect storm' of Napster in 1999–2000, and launched a raft of fights over copyright, intellectual property settings and responses to 'piracy' that are still ongoing.

However, the implications of the NIE extend well beyond its impact on the older media industries. Benkler argues that the 'peer-based commons production' enabled by networked computing is the portent of a deeper social and economic shift:

> What characterizes the networked information economy is that decentralized individual action – specifically, new and important cooperative

and coordinate action carried out through radically distributed, non-market mechanisms that do not depend on proprietary strategies – plays a much greater role than it did, or could have, in the industrial information economy. (2006: 3)

Michel Bauwens (2005) extends this vision further, contending that peer-to-peer (P2P) networks hold the potential to foster post-capitalist modes of cooperative economic activity and political organization. Arguing that P2P projects are characterized by what he calls 'equipotentiality' – merit-based participation in which skills are communally validated through the process of collaboration – Bauwens underlines the extent to which contemporary capitalism has become dependent on P2P infrastructure, particularly in computing and communication. If this currently produces what he calls 'netarchical capitalism', like Stiegler he argues that it also creates the conditions for the emergence of alternatives:

This still nascent P2P movement (which includes the Free Software and Open Source movement, the open access movement, the free culture movement and others), which echoes the means of organization and aims of the alter-globalization movement, is fast becoming the equivalent of the socialist movement in the industrial age. It stands as a permanent alternative to the status quo, and the expression of the growth of a new social force: the knowledge workers.

However, as Bauwens notes, the extent to which the sort of collaborative models pioneered in the context of the distributed online production of software can be effectively translated into other contexts remains to be seen. This is the point at which the problematic of public space elaborated by those such as Lefebvre, Sennett and Butler conjoins contemporary debates over digital media. One of my key arguments in this book is that the networking of urban public space has become a critical laboratory in which capacities to develop social skills in relation to embodied others are being experimented with.

The occupation of public space, as the space of appearance of the political, has always carried a symbolic dimension. However, today one might suggest it is *primarily* symbolic. As Virilio (1986b) argued, taking control of the space of a city is no longer sufficient for taking or holding military-political control. This strategic change is caught up in wider historical transitions, as the city has morphed from a relatively autonomous political unit demarcated by fortification and possession of an independent army (Weber 1958) to become part of the more extensive political, economic and territorial framework of the nation-state. Nevertheless, the strategic value of urban warfare does not disappear entirely, and in some respects assumes a new prominence in the post-Cold War context.[24]

How, then, should we understand the *political* effects of occupying public space in the context of post-broadcast media? Assembling a mass of bodies at a specific site remains an important tactic for garnering media attention, as much for official rituals and ceremonies as for unofficial actions and political protests. Contemporary occupations of public space still frequently conform to the older protocols for gaining broadcast media visibility, by providing the 'raw material' – the familiar drama of crowds, speeches and possible confrontation – that fits the highly formalized demands of TV news bulletins. The frisson of desire and emotion palpable in many public protests remains a key news currency, and is arguably the reason that mainstream media cover protest actions despite indifference or even hostility towards the aims of protestors.[25]

However, two factors have changed decisively in the present: first, the logistics of organizing public assembly, and, second, the extent to which those assembled can now produce and disseminate their own accounts of their actions. Eric Kluitenberg notes the way social movements such as Reclaim the Streets began to use the new affordances of distributed digital media to create distinctive modes of public mobilization in the late 1990s:

> Reclaim The Streets was reliant on coordination in space in real-time, or as close as they could possibly get to it. Too slow and the action would fail. The networks of RTS had to be simultaneously open and relatively insular – open to allow enough participants to have a real party in the streets, and insular so that its location and time would not

be disclosed ahead of time outside of the participant network. SMS text messaging allowed for exactly that function. In its early inception, before it was recognised as a cash-cow for telecommunications companies, SMS permitted free messaging to a list of addresses of any length. [. . .] The fact that unlimited numbers of subscribers could be notified on the fly of the start of an event produced a rare tactical opportunity that RTS activists seized eagerly. The protocol thus produced a new social formation, retroactively identified as the flash mob. (2011: 42–3)

A decade later, social media platforms were leveraged for similar tactical ends across the Middle East. Following the self-immolation of Tunisian street vendor Mohammed Bouazizi in December 2010, a Facebook group and Twitter posts to #sidibouzid were instrumental in publicizing country-wide protests in January. In the months that followed, social media was used to organize 'days of rage' right across the region at relatively short notice (Joseph 2012).[26] To recognize this is not to subscribe to the facile branding of 'Arab Spring' protests as Facebook or Twitter revolutions, as if the complexities of long-standing and diverse political struggles can be truncated to a single deterministic instance of technology-led liberation (see Khondker 2011; Hirschkind 2011). Rather, it is to acknowledge that the new capacity to coordinate mass public action cheaply and quickly alters one of the long-standing constraints on public assembly. The *Arab Social Media Report* (Dubai School of Government 2011: 5) notes that Facebook posts calling for public protest resulted in street actions in all but one instance. Where the capacity for rapid mobilization was once the prerogative of highly centralized institutions such as the military, digital networks have made this capacity increasingly available to other social actors.

The capacity to publicize and mobilize enables a range of further effects. The very act of occupying public space is frequently transformative for those involved, altering the horizons of personal and collective imagination, and engendering or enhancing political solidarities. Taking collective action in public can lessen feelings of isolation, while the shared articulation of political demands often lends them a new credibility, not least in the eyes of those making the demands. An important dimension of this is the new capacity for self-reporting that enables distribution of public protest – and its distinctive forms of public expression – along new routes. In the 2011 protests, events were not simply reported 'on' by media professionals but were witnessed from within by numerous participants who distributed their accounts via websites, blogs, social media and online video. The intended audience was often other protestors, but also 'the world'. Kluitenberg notes:

> The predominant image of the protests is no longer that of the distanced media professional, or even of the artist, who is after all still a professional of sorts. It is not even clearly the perspective of the 'activist', as most of the protesters do not regard themselves as activists. They are much rather ordinary citizens longing for some form of meaningful social and political change, and new modes of expression and self-determination to recapture their sovereignty as political subjects. (2011: 47)

Practices of self-reporting not only reduce reliance on professional media coverage to define an event, but also enable the process of 'reporting' to adopt a new temporality. No longer confined to forming a belated record, media now contribute to the dynamic elaboration of the event even as it unfolds. This generates new relations between action undertaken by those on the street and those watching elsewhere. Rayya El Zein notes:

> Assessing the framework of how the Revolution was watched becomes more grounded when we consider that both protesters and Mubarak seem to have been keenly aware of the potent politics of being seen. The regime's constant and brutal crackdowns on journalists and their equipment reflect an anxiety about the infectious power of specifically seeing resistance. And Tahrir protesters were constantly aware of the potential and the danger of being seen or remaining hidden. At night, panicked voices described what they feared others couldn't or wouldn't see. And in daylight, an outward, visual embodiment of resistance, a performance of defiance, was made apparent in cultural activity. (In Ortiz and El Zein 2011: 4)

While it is difficult to assess the full range of psychosocial impacts generated by the dense feedback networks that characterized these protests, it is evident that the growth of self-organized media played an important role in building political momentum by raising awareness, providing affirmation and normalizing dissent. In an article written in New York shortly after the abdication of Egypt's President Mubarak, El Zein described how public performance became integral to Tahrir's political effect:

> Protesters held signs declaring identity and resistance that display an exponential capacity to riff, elaborate on, and embellish the basic articulation of political demands. They gathered in the millions, sustaining each other with song, comedy, murals, and memorials. In these creative gestures, Egyptian protesters invited others to watch them and implicitly, to join them. Creative output actualized the political revolution. (In Ortiz and El Zein 2011: 4)

A decade earlier Brian Holmes (2007) had underlined the new convergence between art and activism in the protest cycle that began in the late 1990s, as different protagonists sought to develop forms of activism that were both more meaningful for participants and more effective in gaining media attention. Such creative political actions serve not only to build solidarity among those involved, but can influence other media coverage. In Egypt in 2011, graffiti, hand-made signs, posters and performances circulated via the Internet onto the world's television screens.

In conceptualizing the emergent condition that she terms the 'global street', Saskia Sassen draws attention to the way that the different logics of networks and cities become intertwined in particular situations and moments, according to 'the capacity of collective action in the city to *inscribe* a technology'. Arguing that networks are never simply technical but 'deliver their utility through complex ecologies that include (a) non-technological variables (the social, the subjective, the political, material topographies), and (b) the particular cultures of use of different actors', Sassen adds:

> Thus a Facebook group of friends doing financial investment aims
> at getting something through using the technical capability under-
> lying Facebook that is quite different from the Cairo protestors
> organizing the next demonstration after Friday's mosque services.
> This difference is there even when the same technical capabilities are
> used by both, notably rapid communication to mobilize around one
> aim – going for an investment or going to Tahrir Square. (2011c:
> 578)

Focusing on the capacity for collective action in a city to *inscribe*
a technology moves us towards a better understanding of how
networked public space is constituted at the nexus of place, media
and the cultural practices of embodied social actors. This highlights
the distance we have moved from the 'media event' described
by Dayan and Katz (1992), where 'event' and viewer-witnesses
occupied largely separate spheres. In contrast to the 'broadcast
media event', with its heavy reliance on professional orchestration, the different affordances of geomedia *in* and *as* part of urban
space enable public events to be shaped by multiple, intensive and
iterative streams of 'feedback' even as they unfold. While this has
received most attention in relation to public protest, the implications of what I will later call the 'urban media event' are much
broader. I will explore this further in the context of large screens
situated in public space in chapter 4.

The composition of geomedia

When the term 'cyberspace' was first popularized following the
publication of William Gibson's novel *Neuromancer* in 1984, it
fed into an already established tendency to treat the Internet as a
parallel world that existed largely separate from the rest of social
life. Today, most critical scholarship has shifted profoundly. It
is instructive to compare two books that Bill Mitchell published
barely a decade apart. In *City of Bits*, Mitchell forecast the wholesale displacement of 'bricks' by 'bytes', announcing a new city that

would be formed by 'the growing domination of software over materialized form':

> This will be a city unrooted to any definite spot on the surface of the earth, shaped by connectivity and bandwidth constraints rather than by accessibility and land values, largely asynchronous in its operation, and inhabited by disembodied and fragmented subjects who exist as collections of aliases and agents. Its places will be constructed virtually by software instead of physically from stones and timbers, and they will be connected by logical linkages rather than by doors, passageways, and streets. (1995: 24)

By way of contrast, in *Placing Words*, Mitchell argues against precisely the oppositional logic that he evoked in his earlier account. Instead of 'domination' we have interlacing: 'Physical spaces and the information space of the WWW no longer occupy distinct domains – meatspace and cyberspace in the provocative trope of the cyberpunk nineties – but are increasingly closely woven together by millions of electronic devices distributed throughout buildings and cities' (2005: 16, 18).

Does this mean the old interpretation of 'cyberspace' was always wrong? Or has a new understanding been driven by changed circumstances? Both propositions ring true to some extent. If simply opposing the 'virtual' to the 'physical' was always of dubious value, the migration of computerized digital media from desktop and living room to pocket and streetscape has thrown this limit into stark relief. A wide range of descriptors have emerged to name this new spatiality, including Shaun Moores' (2003) 'doubling of space', the 'hybrid space' favoured by Kluitenberg (2006, 2011), de Souza e Silva (2006) and Frith (2012), and what Benford and Giannachi (2011) call 'mixed reality'. However, collective enthusiasm to disown what is now regarded as a misguided idealism can easily become an alibi for avoiding more difficult questions about the models we use to think the relation between the urban and the digital. Take, for example, Lev Manovich's (2006) influential concept of *augmented space*. Derived from the computer science terminology of Augmented Reality, Manovich defines augmented space as 'physical space overlaid with dynamically changing information' (2006: 220). While this formulation has the attraction of not being tied to any particular device, platform or content, it nevertheless perpetuates the idea that the city consists of an underlying physical stratum that is *subsequently* affected by the introduction of 'dynamic information' – by media. McCullough deploys a similar frame when he opposes the 'augmented city' to the city as 'unmediated experience': 'Yet, however much augmented the city is also unmediated experience: fixed forms persist under all these augmentations and data flows, and for that you might be thankful. Without persistent environments, the sense of confusion and flux might only worsen' (2013: 8).

While there is a common sense appeal to such formulations, in which buildings and data flows remain separate 'layers' (akin to a Photoshop image), my concern is with the way they replay an older understanding in which 'media' are simply add-ons to an already-existing social reality. In contrast, I am arguing that the contemporary reworking of social experience is far more profound. The threshold of geomedia involves the recalibration of what we call the physical, the material, the embodied and the face-to-face, as much as it impacts on the virtual, the immaterial, the disembodied and the remote. In a context in which various practices and modalities of communication-at-a-distance have become routinized, the 'face-to-face' assumes new valences, if only by dint of the fact that it is now one form of social encounter among others. Once communicating 'face-to-face' becomes *optional*, it becomes subject to *decision* in new ways. The insertion of this kind of decision across a wide range of practices and protocols marks the extent to which social life is being fundamentally reworked in the contemporary era. Kittler's reflection is pertinent: 'As Heidegger wrote in his essay on Parmenides, the ancient Greek philosopher who stimulated his thought on the typewriter, whether or not we personally ever use the typewriter is not important. What is important is that all of us are thrown into the age of typewriting, whether we like it or not' (in Armitage 2006: 29).

Today we are all 'thrown' into an age of digital urbanism, whether we use particular devices or services or not. Geomedia cannot simply be 'turned off', but are implicated in the wholesale restructuring of social practices including the public terrain of embodied encounters. Leaving your phone behind for the day, or losing network access, does not mean that the city somehow reverts to an underlying pre-digital state as a default. Rather, those so affected commonly experience a (relative) lack, often marked by frustration and anxiety. As Jason Farman notes:

> The very practice of embodied space is becoming entirely reliant on the seamless interaction between our devices and our landscapes. The representation of space is not outside of the lived experience of that space. It is entirely incorporated into the production of embodied space. We have thus moved beyond the theorization of our mobile devices as a type of prosthetic to our bodies – an extension of ourselves out into the material world – but instead have to conceive of our devices as absolutely integral to the very foundations of embodied space in the digital age. (2012: 46)

This is the shifting context that I have sought to situate in this chapter, focusing on the transformed conditions of urban encounter and public events. These themes will be developed in relation to specific examples more extensively over the next three chapters.

Despite the importance of digital networks in orchestrating this new condition, it is premature to declare that the 'old media' are simply dead. Broadcast logics continue to exist and adapt even as they are increasingly pulled into the operational paradigm of digital networks. While it is arguable that attaining *public voice* is no longer so difficult in the present, this does not so much solve the problem of political visibility as relocate it. While there is a new level of porosity in the media system, the capacity to become visible remains unevenly distributed. Broadcast television remains extremely powerful, and, while viewers (and advertising revenues) leach away from 'free to air' broadcast services, this is neither as rapid nor as monolithic as many have asserted. Many facets of media gatekeeping structures persist: it is worth remembering that events in Tunisia went largely unreported in the West until the president fled. Mainstream media silence forced activists to adopt novel strategies, such as their appeal to celebrity Stephen Fry in order to leverage his million plus Twitter 'followers'.

Moreover, it is clear that the new multiplicity of media outlets cannot be automatically equated with diversity of opinion. Current digital media ecologies depend heavily on recirculating 'old media' content, which carries implications for the diversity of sources, frames and issue agendas. Even more significantly, the capacity to produce and distribute content does not guarantee attention. While new forms of low-cost public communication such as blogs and vlogs have the potential to find large audiences, very few do: for every viral sensation, the vast majority of posts find only the indifference of 'zero comments' (Lovink 2008). In an overcrowded mediascape, a key issue today is arguably less one of gaining public voice than of being *heard* when everyone is speaking at the same time. If overabundance of information has made *attention* the new pivot of scarcity, this arguably accentuates the importance of professional marketing and the public relations apparatus in constituting public visibility in the present.[27] Above all, this situation underlines the extent to which the older politics of representation inherited from the broadcast era is today embedded within a new *politics of search*. The older 'gatekeeping' functions of editorial teams in filtering information and knowledge are today supplemented, and even supplanted, by the black-boxed algorithms of proprietary search engines.[28]

While entry barriers to media production and distribution have become significantly lower in the digital milieu, this trajectory exists alongside increased global concentration at the level of the platform. New potential for peer-to-peer practices of funding, production and distribution of media content is matched by the contemporaneous rise of a small number of *global* media companies with unprecedented scale and reach. The heavy dependence of digital communication on privately owned platforms such as Facebook, WeChat and Twitter makes the public culture they sustain highly susceptible to new forms of political intervention. In this vein, we might recall the shutdown of the Internet in Egypt for five days in January 2011, or the PRISM programme of mass surveillance that was revealed by Edward Snowden in 2013.

Even the primary article of faith that has long defined the Internet in terms of 'many-to-many' communication seems far less solid than it once was. Pressure from content owners has resulted in restrictions on hardware capabilities, as well as the mandating of new legal and technical constraints on the use of digital content (Gillespie 2007; Lessig 2004). As Google's development of YouTube exemplifies, monetizing user-generated niche content does not exclude delivering a range of professional premium content. In addition to deploying pay-per-view and subscription 'channel' strategies, Google has invested heavily in studio space in order to enable its 'YouTube stars' to develop proprietary content. As one commentator quipped (Stenovec 2014): 'The Internet video world is starting to look a lot like . . . traditional TV.'

These different headings suggest that Benkler's distinction between the IIE and the NIE should not be overstretched to form too neat an opposition. Like many others, Benkler tends to fall back on the claim that certain tendencies are an inevitable consequence of the 'nature' of digital technology. In this vein, he argues: 'Because of the redundancy of clusters and links, and because many clusters are based on mutual interest, not on capital investment, it is more difficult to buy attention on the internet than it is in mass media outlets, and harder still to use money to squelch an opposing point of view' (2006: 13). Even before the success of China's 'Great Firewall', it should have been clear that many attributes of the so-called 'nature' of digital networks were, in fact, related to the historical moment of their deployment. While broadcasting emerged at the height of an era of state-led nation formation, the Internet was mainstreamed in an era of resurgent neo-liberalism. Where state control of the broadcasting spectrum once seemed 'natural', private ownership and light-touch market-led regulation of digital infrastructure and services now assumes that status, despite the large amounts of public investment underpinning the historical development of the Internet backbone.

What does this signal for the future of geomedia and its impact on urban public space? The point of my discussion here is not to disparage metaphors such as 'augmented space', and especially not to insist on a new master term of analysis. Rather, it is to recognize the real difficulties of thinking the *relationality* of urban space in a present defined by increasingly complex interactions between media and immediacy. My approach in this book is defined not so much by the ambition for a radical jump beyond the oppositional logic that has defined these terms, but by an attempt to reconsider their deployment. Instead of seeking a new term or relation that might somehow transcend the historical binary between media and immediacy, my aim is to explore the tensions and contradictions that characterize the contemporary instantiations of digital media in public space.

Noting that the connections between the digital and the non-digital are inevitably 'mixed, contradictory and lumpy', Saskia Sassen suggests that 'the overall outcome might be described as a destabilizing of older formal hierarchies and an emergence of not fully formalized new ones' (2006: 328). Sassen's framework, with its focus on 'frontier zones' of contact, stresses the need for situated analyses of the ways in which the different orders overlap and interact. In perceiving the thickness and complexity of inter-actions, and the differentiated consequences and varied outcomes of different situated practices, we may begin to think the relation between immediacy and mediation differently, gradually loosen-ing the chokehold that the metaphysics of 'presence' has long held over this domain.

Public spaces capable of productively combining the histori-cal affordances of the urban with the connective and distributed attributes of digital networks have become 'frontier zones' for investigating new modalities of public communication involving experimental coalitions of actors. In what follows, I will explore how different modes of *becoming public* are enhanced or blocked by particular combinations of media working in conjunction with architecture and interface design, institutional protocols, and more or less formalized cultural practices. What settings might facilitate the reinvention of the urban – defined by social practices of sim-ultaneity, communication and appropriation – in the context of public encounters that frequently assume both local and global coordinates?

2

Googling the City

The city as database

In 2011 German-born artist and photojournalist Michael Wolf received an honourable mention in the World Press Photo Award for his 'A Series of Unfortunate Events'. The images, which show things like street accidents or unusual urban sights, aren't all that striking. What is most noteworthy is that they were culled entirely from the Google Street View database. As Wolf (2011) describes his process: 'I'm not taking a screenshot. I move the camera forward and backward in order to make an exact crop, and that's what makes it my picture. It doesn't belong to Google, because I'm interpreting Google; I'm appropriating Google.' I'm not really concerned with Wolf's justification of his practice, which stands in a long line of modernist tactics of image appropriation. A century ago, mass printed imagery inspired the photomontage of Dadaist artists such as Hannah Höch and John Heartfield. More recently, there have been numerous projects in which artists and curators have used digital images as raw material for producing new work. Wolf treats Street View as another 'territory of images' – to use

Alan Sekula's evocative phrase for a photographic archive – that can be mined. What I'm more interested in asking here is: just what kind of *territory* is Street View, and how might it change our conception of the photographic archive?

Almost all media coverage and most academic analysis of Street View has concerned its impact on privacy. While these debates have raised important and still unresolved issues, I am keen to expand the parameters of discussion. The dominant tendency is to focus on whether Street View images capture recognizable individuals, fitting the legal conception of privacy in the Western tradition which emphasizes individual control over certain categories of information. My concern is how data-driven projects such as Street View underpin the transformation of the *social* space of contemporary cities. From this perspective, Street View indexes two significant trajectories: the transformation of the photographic image in the digital milieu, and the consequences of the digital archive in the context of the developing smart city. Street View provides an emergent and not-yet-consolidated model of how previously untapped dimensions of urban life are being converted into images, at a moment in which images are themselves being converted into key forms of urban data. What are the stakes at play in this shift from an older logic of urban representation to one of large-scale data aggregation involving practices spanning digital capture, GIS metadata, automated image analysis and networked dissemination? If Street View indexes a still emergent apprehension of the city *as* data, it demonstrates the way in which digital databases change the logic of the archive, and also the relation of 'data' to 'world'.

Fascination with the city as 'database' has been around at least as long as the electronic computer, and its statistical underpinnings can arguably be traced to the period in which nineteenth-century sociology began to deploy statistical analysis to address the new scale and complexity of urban life (Hacking 1990: 46–64). However, even if we accept that the origins of the 'information revolution' were established prior to the twentieth century, we also need to acknowledge the more recent threshold of what Hellerstein (2008) has called the 'industrial revolution of data'. Declining cost of data processing and growing capacity for capture, storage and analytics combine to push the database city from incipient logic to operational reality, in which data is literally warehoused in temperature-controlled server farms situated in strategic (tax-effective and network-efficient) locations around the world. If the nineteenth-century urban database sought to map distributions and concentrations across a relatively static space – an ambition that could best be described in terms of using *statistics as history* – the ambitions of the twenty-first-century smart city have tilted decisively towards real-time information flows and *predictive* capabilities. It is in this context that the archive becomes what I term an *operational archive*, in which inert and finished sets of data (such as photographs) become increasingly open to ongoing supplementation and modification, but also to distributed forms of use which themselves generate value. The aim of this chapter is to explore how this new logic of operationality as manifest in Street View is impacting on urban public space.

Rolling out Street View

Google launched Street View on 29 May 2007 as a complement to the aerial and satellite imagery available through its popular Google Maps application. Google Maps had launched in 2005, following the purchase of Where-2 Technologies, a Sydney-based start-up run by Danish-born brothers Lars and Jens Rasmussen. Google Maps replicated a number of existing web-based map services (such as MapQuest), which it soon outstripped. It quickly established Google's leadership in online mapping, a position it continues to hold today.

Unlike Google Maps, Street View didn't replicate an existing service but offered something new. The service comprised a database of digital images captured at street level by cameras mounted on moving vehicles. Each image could be zoomed, tilted and panned 360 degrees, and the database was navigable by clicking an overlay of directional arrows visible on the user's screen. The intended effect, according to Google's press release, was to enable users to experience a virtual promenade: 'By clicking on the "Street View" button in Google Maps, users can navigate street level, panoramic imagery. With Street View users can virtually walk the streets of a city, check out a restaurant before arriving, and even zoom in on bus stops and street signs to make travel plans.'[1] Street View initially offered images of the central areas of five cities in the United States: the San Francisco Bay Area, New York, Las Vegas, Denver and Miami. However, even from day one, it had global ambitions: in Lars Rasmussen's words, the aim was 'to be a world map' (quoted in Moses 2008). Street View soon spread across other cities in the US and then to other countries, beginning with parts of Europe, Australia and Japan in 2008.[2]

At the time of writing Google has photographed more than 3,000 cities and locations on seven continents. Clearly this still does not cover the whole world: there are dark zones, particularly in Africa, that haven't been photographed and may never be. Despite the gaps, which reflect Google's estimate of 'return on investment', Street View's scale remains noteworthy. When Street View opened in Australia, I remember being both fascinated and puzzled. I could understand the business logic behind Google Maps, but how did it make sense to photograph every street in a city, and claim that you were going to do this all around the world? Unlike the thousands of webcams already streaming from myriad urban locations, Street View images were neither 'live', nor refreshed regularly.[3] Unlike the hundreds of thousands of photographs of city locations publicly available on photo-sharing websites, Street View images didn't try to claim any particular aesthetic value. Image resolution was deliberately low.[4] While the 'promenade' enabled by Street View images had some utility, this seemed nowhere near as great as Google Maps, which quickly became the web's most popular mash-up. In comparison, Street View seemed like some kind of strange art project.

Street View as image archive

Street View's distinctiveness rests squarely on two attributes: its systematic adoption of street-level perspective, and the unprecedented scale of its imaging ambition. In fact, the two are closely connected. Compared to photography from above, street-level perspective has always seemed to offer far less capacity to *master* urban space. In the nineteenth century, seeing the city from on high became a key technique for representing urban space, as photographers exploited hills, towers and eventually balloons to gain a vantage point on cities that were fast overflowing their previous bounds. In comparison, street-level images offer more fine-grained detail, but prove far more difficult to integrate into unified conceptions of urban territory. The specificity of photographs, coupled to the camera's unruly multiplication of possible perspectives, seemed to undermine all such ambitions. One might say that the camera generated too many images, and yet not enough. Systematically capturing street-level images at the scale of an entire city so as to organize them according to its map was always a possible means for solving this problem, but was logistically and financially forbidding. Even in the image-saturated cultures of modernity, where the city had become the primary theatre of operations for so many photographers, such an undertaking was never seriously contemplated. How many images would be needed? How could they be captured, let alone stored, correlated and retrieved? Who would ever see them?

These questions of scale and perspective beg comparison between Street View and earlier urban image archives. One salient point of reference is Charles Marville's pioneering project in which he photographed Paris at the time of Haussmann's 'reconstruction' of the city between 1856 and 1871. Marville was unusual for his time, first in his adoption of a street-level point of view in photography, and, second, in his systematic approach to photographing the city. His project stands on the cusp of a new use of images. It marks the beginning of the transition from the scarcity of hand-made images to the *seriality* of technological images, and points towards the modern apprehension of the city as database. This trajectory suggests a second point of reference: Dziga Vertov's 1929 'city-symphony' film *Man with a Movie Camera*, which Lev Manovich provocatively describes as 'perhaps the most important example of database imagination in modern media art' (2000: 239). As I have argued elsewhere, the projects of Marville and Vertov are exemplary in so far as they each constitute key thresholds in which a new media platform (photography and cinema respectively) was directly implicated in the emergence of a new understanding of urban space (McQuire 2008). My argument here is that Street View indexes a similar kind of threshold or rupture in relation to the digital. To understand the terms of its operation, I begin by considering the changing logistics of photographic capture, before investigating how what Dourish and Mazmanian (2011) term the *materiality* of the database separates Street View from earlier archives.

Marville's project to photograph the streets of Paris undoubtedly appeared excessive to many of his contemporaries. Even two or three decades after the invention of the camera, the nineteenth-century visual economy remained dominated by 'handmade' images typified by painting and drawing. In this context, producing hundreds of images to 'map' changes across a single urban territory was unprecedented.[5] But while Marville produced an archive of unprecedented scale and system, it soon paled in comparison to those that followed. Eadweard Muybridge shot an astonishing 100,000 photographs for his eleven-volume work *Animal Locomotion* first published in 1887. Even this kind of enterprise, once the sole province of the professional photographer, no longer seems exceptional. Digital cameras, the inclusion of cameras in 'phones', and the availability of cheap online storage has inflated image production right across the board. While precise figures regarding their size are volatile, the trajectory established by the massive image databases held on platforms such as Flickr, Facebook and Instagram is clear. Collections that were once numbered in hundreds and thousands now have to be reckoned in billions (and soon trillions).[6] Street View belongs to this recalibration of photography for the era of 'big data': in giving us more images of the city, it changes the social relations of the urban image – which is to say its social and political effects, and its insertion into chains of economic value.

It is instructive to recall that Marville's archive of Paris was still formally organized around a typology of generic urban scenes drawn from older visual practices such as drawing and lithography. But what was most striking was not this superficial adherence to older genres but his incessant multiplication of 'examples'. Rather than one streetlight, Marville photographed almost one hundred. Instead of a few streets, Marville photographed hundreds, usually several times each. In the corpus that he built over fifteen years, each image came to function less as an autonomous picture than as a member of a set. For this reason, as much as each image offers the concrete point of reference that we associate with photographic documentation (it depicts *this* street seen from *this* direction at *this* precise moment in time), the overall effect of Marville's work points elsewhere. Instead of the aesthetic discourse that histori-cally belonged to the 'picture' understood as a discrete image, his work points to the *relational* meaning established by the (potentially infinite) series. Here the meaning of each image is conditioned as much by its place in the wider set as by what it shows. This shift is precisely what Benjamin (2003) later distilled into the contrast between the 'ritual function' of the 'cult image' and the 'exhibition value' of 'technologically reproducible' images, particularly when he hints that the photograph might be understood as a *statistical* form.[7] In retrospect, we might argue that Marville's work offers a precocious and incomplete expression of this emergent condition, in which the photograph shifts from 'picture' to 'data'. This is the condition that is today being rendered *operational* by the creation of digital image archives of unprecedented scale.

If photographing every street in every city around the world still seemed financially and logistically forbidding when Street View was first mooted, it was precisely the sort of 'crazy' idea that appealed to Google's data-driven founders. As Levy comments: 'Google – as its very name implies – is geared to handling the historic expansion of data that the digital revolution has triggered. Competitors, especially those who were successful in a previous age, were slow to wrap their minds around this phenomenon, while Google considered it as common as air' (2011: 43–4). Marc Levoy recalls that a forerunner of Street View, the Stanford City Block Project, was initiated in March 2001 when Google co-founder Larry Page 'gave us a videotape he had captured while driving around the Bay Area, and challenged us to invent a way to summarize the video with a few images'.[8] Today, the ambition of Street View not only seems less outlandish but increasingly obvious. This transition is still worth remarking. As data acquisition, storage, processing and retrieval have become exponentially faster and cheaper, the horizons of social imagination shift. What was once unimaginable – a database of images showing every street in the world – becomes almost prosaic. For Google, Street View is only one of a suite of projects that seek to leverage their enormous competitive advantage in 'big data'. But it is one that is increasingly vital to their core business.

In the nineteenth century, the invention of photography initiated a vast expansion of imagery which completely reconfigured the social relations of the image. Scarcity gave way to abundance, and new practices of production, distribution and display transformed the social conditions of representation and witnessing. Marville's project sits on the cusp of the industrialization of image production that began in the 1880s on the back of new cameras, film stocks and printing techniques. What Street View confirms is the extent to which photography has itself been rebooted in the twenty-first century. Older problems of fixing, printing and preserving images have been displaced by concerns over capture and compression formats, data storage, and search and display protocols.

In the process, large-scale image archives such as Street View have raised the bar in terms of fulfilling that most tantalizing modern fantasy: the production of a comprehensive picture of 'big city life' in all its variety. What the Street View image gives up in terms of the deliberate compositional choices available to a human photographer, it replaces with its distinctive combination of automatic capture and saturation coverage. The selectivity of the photographer's eye gives way to a deliberate non-selectivity, as the need for 'sampling' gives way to the possibility of 'whole of population' measurement.[9] In this regard, Street View follows the logic of what Virilio (1994) aptly dubs the 'vision machine': an imaging apparatus that obviates the need for any human agent. With Street View, the Google car equipped with its special camera apparatus has literally become a *vision machine*, concerned less with the transport of people or objects than the production of images as data.

The desire to produce a *total image* of the city has proved a remarkably persistent trope in modernity. Faced with the growing complexity and scale of urban life, images shot from a church tower or hill were no longer sufficient. The task of visualizing the city as some kind of 'whole' increasingly devolved to specialized techniques of representation, particularly the topographic map on the one hand, and aerial (and satellite) photography on the other. Both seek to master the increasing size and complexity of the city through distance and abstraction. Street View's distinctive ambition in this regard is to reunite the 'view from below' with the abstract, relational structure of the map. When the map becomes the interface for a vast archive of urban imagery, a new sense of urban totality begins to emerge; one based on the multiplicity, relationality and searchability of the digital archive. The description of Bing Streetside (Microsoft's Street View competitor) by one of its developers situates the paradox of this new threshold: 'Moving beyond aerial photography, as we start to image all the way down to the street level, that's when the map really becomes sort of 1:1 with real life.'[10] The hallucinatory merging of map and territory that was once imagined by Borges (1975) has returned as apparent social fact.

Faced with the recurrence of this hallucination, it seems important to ask: what kind of a 'text' does Street View produce? Where Marville's choice of slow exposure times tended to erase pedestrian life in favour of solid urban structure, Street View reverses this emphasis, generating images that emphasize transitory appearances and – arguably – a far more *liquid* city. This is evident in the image transitions between what Google engineers call 'tiles': the separate sets of 'shots' from a single position that are stitched into panoramic views. While at first transitions tended to be jerky, they have since become more fluid, as the software has been reprogrammed to stretch and blur objects from frame to frame. One might say that Street View is no longer comprised of 'jump cuts' but 'morphs'. Such a comparison suggests that, despite the fact that it is composed entirely of still images, the experience of using Street View shares as much with cinema as it does with an older heritage of photography. Clicking through the Street View database generates sequences of images, comparable to producing a kind of *film* in which the user is the *director* organizing the selection and duration of different 'shots'. However, this analogy offers less the resolution of the problem I'm exploring than an indication of the complexity of the terrain.

'Reference' has always been at the heart of the evidentiary appeal of photography: how does an image correspond to the world it depicts? While this relation has never been the direct, mechanistic connection fantasized by positivist theories of 'objectivity', the equivocation of reference inevitably became a more explicit concern with the advent of cinema. With moving images, the *time of viewing* is structurally embedded in the image for the first time in history. This novel affordance generates enormous potential for creating new kinds of texts. What the viewer sees can be organized in advance, chosen by a director who *directs sight* according to the logic of montage. As film matures as a *textual* system, the meaning of different images comes to be centred less around seemingly direct photographic correspondences between individual shots captured in particular times and places, and instead depends more on the *relations* established between multiple shots as parts of organized sequences. This uncanny marriage between the gravitational pull of photographic reference and its perpetual unmooring by the plasticity of montage is precisely what constitutes the paradox of cinema: the constant swings between claims about the luminous reality of its images and counter-claims about its unprecedented capacity to *counterfeit* the world (McQuire 1998).

In one sense, Vertov's *Man with a Movie Camera* is a triumphant celebration of precisely this paradox. Vertov seizes the camera's capacity to reconstitute time and space as plastic dimensions and mobilizes this in the service of a self-reflexive narrative. Image fragments shot in several cities over months are recomposed into what he termed an 'organized memo', with the dual aim of showing a day in the life of the city *and* the process of constructing a film (Vertov 1984: 18–19). For the Constructivist Vertov, the ambition is to create a realistic film opposed to all 'fictional' scenarios. To this end, he exploits all techniques in the cinematic arsenal – rapid montage, fast-motion, freeze frame, multiple exposure, moving camera and so on – in order to assemble a series of dynamic (and often didactic) contrasts between the old and the new, setting politically decadent and progressive forms of social life against one another.

Can we compare watching Vertov's film with exploring Street View as if it were a film? The reason I feel authorized to pose such a question is partly because Vertov's film explicitly invites us to consider how its 'data' is organized into a textual system. This is most evident in the sequence in which the film editor (Vertov's wife, Kuznetzova) is shown handling film strips, animating and freezing them on a flatbed editing suite, snipping them with scissors and even gluing together the film we are apparently watching. Of course, this self-reflexivity – which is arguably what inspired Manovich's claim concerning the film's 'database' quality – remains fictive. A founding limit of celluloid cinema was precisely the fact that shot selection *had* to be made prior to screening. While unexpected events might seem to unfold on-screen in the moment, the sequence of the film and the duration of its shots was inevitably set in advance of the viewer.

In contrast, Street View is defined by the simultaneous availability of all 'shots'. Since the order in which images are seen will be a function of different users selecting particular points of entry and exit, or choosing links, there is a sense in which a final order can never be fixed and always remains to be decided. As Manovich notes, from this perspective, database and narrative are antagonists: 'As a cultural form, the database represents the world as a list of items, and it refuses to order this list. In contrast, a narrative creates a cause and effect trajectory of seemingly unordered items (events). Therefore, database and narrative are natural enemies' (2000: 225).

If meaning and reference in cinema is ultimately a function of a *narrative* system, what, then, is Street View's textuality? Two observations are worth bearing in mind. First, the opposition Manovich poses between narrative and database is becoming less certain, as film-makers and artists utilize the possibilities of *digital* databases to generate new types of open-ended artwork. A salient example here is Perry Bard's web project *Man with a Movie Camera: Global Remake*, initiated in 2005. Bard's project unpicks the fixed 'cause and effect' logic that Manovich attributes to 'narrative'. By enabling people to contribute image sequences interpreting Vertov's original film, and using specially developed software to archive, sequence and stream the different contributions as a 'participatory film', her project instead brings out the database potential of *Man with a Movie Camera*.[11]

Second, it is important to recognize the limits to 'user choice' that any database affords. While Street View certainly offers users a level of freedom in navigating its archive, we need to acknowledge that its images have already been subject to an extensive process of ordering. Given that even the highly efficient, automated image capture pioneered by Google takes time, even contiguous Street View images can never correspond to a single, synchronous time. In other words, what we see on Street View is always already a *montage*; a stitching together of multiple times and perspectives in the interests of creating an integrated image space. This is something that 'cinema' has practised for a century. What is unique to Street View is that, instead of being assembled according to the 'narrative' frames that Vertov and other film-makers might have deployed, the images are arranged according to the dictates of the GPS data gathered in the process of image-capture. In a sense, we might argue that this data constitutes a kind of meta-narrative; one that enables the vast 'list of items' in the Street View database to *cohere* according to a circular relation, in which a heterogeneity of images is integrated, not by genre or aesthetics, but because they belong to a city and are organized according to its map.

Undoubtedly, most uses of this database remain largely functional, and largely consist of someone looking at a place they know, such as their own house, or looking at a place they're planning to visit. Only when we suspend this functional relation do we begin to glimpse the historical significance of ordering the world's cities according to such a system. Street View combines endless repetition with endless variation, assembling more images than anyone – any *human* – could ever hope to see.

Street life in the era of big data

From its inception, Street View's potential to alter certain dynamics of public space was evident. In the United States, Street View's depiction of identifiable individuals performing potentially embarrassing actions in public locations immediately raised privacy concerns. Examples of possible privacy infringements in the initial rollout included individuals leaving a medical centre which tested for STDs, others entering a brothel or passed out drunk, and one seemingly entering a property illegally by scaling a fence (Helft 2007). Google also received criticism for a 'take-down' policy that put the onus on members of the public to complain.[12] Concerns about privacy meant that the release of Street View in jurisdictions outside the US had to be postponed. In contrast to the US, where activities on the street are generally held to constitute a public domain open to representation, privacy laws in Canada and the EU generally prohibit the publication of images that reveal personal details without permission.[13] In response to criticism in the US, Google initially argued: 'Street View only features imagery taken on public property. This imagery is no different from what any person can readily capture or see walking down the street' (quoted in Helft 2007). However, in June 2008 Google introduced software to automatically blur human faces, applying a similar fix to car licence plates a month later.[14] The fact that blurring was also applied retrospectively to images already gathered within the US indicated the uncertain terrain Street View was seeking to occupy, and the depth of feeling it inspired. However, blurring techniques did not satisfy all privacy concerns.

In April 2009, residents in Broughton UK took direct action to block the Street View car from photographing their village (see Ahmed 2009). In May 2009, Street View was halted in Greece pending further explanation of privacy concerns.[15] At the same time, Google was forced to reshoot many areas in Japan, setting its car-mounted cameras about 40cm lower, after receiving numerous privacy-related complaints.[16] But it was in 2010 that Google found itself embroiled in the most serious privacy complaints relating to Street View. This concerned the capture of large amounts of unsecured Wi-Fi data gathered in the course of collecting Street View imagery.[17] While Google denied that the collection of this data was intentional, the episode sparked widespread criticism and legal uncertainty, as different jurisdictions took markedly different responses.[18] Concern intensified in 2010 when Google changed its account, revealing they had not only captured details of Wi-Fi networks, but so-called 'payload data' including entire URLs, emails and passwords.[19] While jurisdictions including France, Germany, Italy and some states in the US issued legal sanctions, others such as the UK did not.[20] The issue has continued to bubble away, following revelations in mid-2012 that not all the captured data was destroyed, as Google had previously claimed.

The privacy concerns arising from this saga are significant and ongoing. Continued uncertainty as to appropriate regulatory response underlines the extent to which Street View, as a novel media platform with global extension, cuts across existing legal settings and cultural terrain. However, serious as such infractions are, it is important to recognize that they are merely the visible tip of a fast-growing data iceberg. Even with the enormous scale of its urban imaging, it is clear that most people are not going to be personally caught in Street View's nets. Focusing too tightly on this possibility risks missing the bigger picture, which concerns how data-driven projects such as Street View are transforming the *social* space of the city. From this perspective, while we might acknowledge that the images captured on Street View can certainly be intrusive, it is evident that the more significant intrusion takes place after the fact, so to speak. It is not so much what the images themselves show but what the maps database entices users to reveal – their habits, preferences, routes and routines – that is critical to the data-hungry economy. The fact that much of this process takes place in the background, in the 'black box' of what Thrift (2004) terms the technological unconscious, means it often escapes attention.

Building on this line of thought, I am arguing that the most significant shift pioneered by Street View is not its generation of photographs of identifiable individuals, but how it enables the wholesale conversion of urban space into data. This capacity has become increasingly important to Google's overall business strategy. Arguably, this importance was far less clear when Street View began in 2007, perhaps even to Google itself.[21] However, it had certainly become evident by 2012, when a very public mapping 'war' erupted with competitors such as Apple.[22] The growing importance of Street View was signalled as early as 2008 by Google's decision to take control of its core data in this domain.[23] In his influential paean on 'Web 2.0', Tim O'Reilly (2005) observed that 'data is the next Intel Inside'. O'Reilly explicitly highlighted the failure of online mapping pioneer MapQuest to protect its core data as the key factor that enabled later entrants such as Google to oust it from a once dominant position:

> The now hotly contested web mapping arena demonstrates how a failure to understand the importance of owning an application's core data will eventually undercut its competitive position. MapQuest pioneered the web mapping category in 1995, yet when Yahoo! and then Microsoft, and most recently Google, decided to enter the market, they were easily able to offer a competing application simply by licensing the same data.

Google had initially established Google Maps by licensing data from third parties including MapQuest and TeleAtlas. Its ability to rapidly dominate a market it came to as a late entrant demonstrates that success is not entirely defined by access to data, but also by capacity to organize, process and deliver it. Nevertheless, control over core data is critical, both in differentiating a service, and in offering a level of protection against potential competition. Street

View today performs both these roles for Google Maps, making it integral to Google's ambitions in online mapping.

In an essay published in the *Atlantic Monthly*, Alexis Madrigal (2012a) offered one of few detailed descriptions of Google's process of building up a master map – what it calls 'Ground Truth' – from a variety of sources.[24] Beginning with a base layer of 'authoritative data' such as the US Government Census Bureau's TIGER database of reference maps, Ground Truth 'operators' combine this data with other sources such as the US Geological Survey, as well as Google's own aerial and satellite imagery. The overall ambition is to build a map corresponding more precisely to the physical terrain it represents. Street View contributes to this endeavour in several critical ways. Since 2007 Google vehicles have travelled over 11 million km along the streets of many of the world's cities (Miller 2014). These journeys generate at least three levels of data that Google can use: driver experience (confirming whether a street shown on a map actually exists, is traversable, etc.); GPS metadata to correlate with the millions of images; and the images themselves. Improved visual recognition capabilities mean that Street View images have themselves become increasingly important as data sources to be mined for increasing amounts of information. In particular, the capacity to extract words on street signs, road surfaces and kerbs, and enter them into Google's index of the physical world, is critical to the operation of Google's Atlas tool, the internal platform built by Google to integrate different streams of 'Ground Truth' data. While this kind of data extraction (part algorithmic, part manual) vastly improved the accuracy of driving directions, providing directions is only the tip of its potential uses. As Google Maps VP Brian McClendon states:

> We can actually organize the world's physical written information if we can OCR [optical character recognition] it and place it. We use that to create our maps right now by extracting street names and addresses, but there is a lot more there. [. . .] We already have what we call 'view codes' for 6 million businesses and 20 million addresses, where we know exactly what we're looking at. [. . .] We're able to use logo matching and find out where are the Kentucky Fried Chicken

signs . . . We're able to identify and make a semantic understanding of all the pixels we've acquired. That's fundamental to what we do. (Quoted in Madrigal 2012a)

The quantities of data involved are large, even for Google. Madrigal (2012a) reported in 2012 that the Maps team were publishing more image data every two weeks than Google possessed in total in 2006, and that this was largely a function of Street View imagery.[25]

More significant than this expansion in the quantity of data is the way the Street View project registers a fundamental shift in the relation imagined between the 'online' and 'offline' worlds. Where Google began life as a company famously dedicated to addressing the problem of organizing data on the Internet, its sights have increasingly shifted towards organization of the physical world *as data*. As Manik Gupta (senior product manager for Google Maps) puts it:

> If you look at the offline world, the real world in which we live, that information is not entirely online. Increasingly as we go about our lives, we are trying to bridge that gap between what we see in the real world and [the online world], and Maps really plays that part. (Quoted in Madrigal 2012a; interpolation in original)

Physical things can become digital data in many ways, from describing them in text, scanning them or attaching RFID tags or sensors to them. But visual capture is arguably one of the most efficient and cost-effective ways for converting the fine-grain detail of the city into data. Google's investment in Street View has pioneered cost-effective, large-scale capture of place data combining images and geolocation. In the process, it has become critical to the continued success of Google Maps. The decision by Apple to pursue their own mapping service in 2012 indicates the strategic importance of this sector in the digital economy.[26] Mapping is particularly critical to mobile device use: being the native mapping application for a billion-plus Android phones globally facilitates Google's dominance in related areas such as location-based mobile search and advertising. Moreover, as Thatcher (2014) notes, Google Maps has become one of the basic platforms on which a host of other data-related urban software operations are now built. Even as Apple left Google Maps, new services such as Uber grew in its place.[27] Mapping platforms are also becoming increasingly important to basic operations in the transport, shipping and retail sectors. Madrigal (2012a) argues: 'Google's geographic data may become its most valuable asset. Not solely because of this data alone, but because location data makes everything else Google does and knows more valuable.' The problem facing any rival wanting to dislodge its lead in this field is the long head start that Google has had in acquiring its own data and integrating it into its mapping and other applications. Madrigal (2012a) concluded: 'I came away convinced that the geographic data Google has assembled is not likely to be matched by any other company.'[28]

Street View as urban world-picture

Street View's development indexes key aspects of the emergent ecology of data-driven urbanism, and underlines the implication of geomedia in contemporary smart-city strategies. In concluding this discussion, I want to work through a number of related issues. The first concerns the transformation of the social relations of the photographic image. Compared to earlier traditions of urban imaging, such as the projects of Marville and Vertov discussed above, Street View imagery is produced less for what it enables a user to 'see' than for its efficient capture of enormous quantities of data. This shift is facilitated in so far as automatic capture of the 'vision machine' has been extended to automated viewing, in which the human eye is complemented by increasingly sophisticated modes of machine analysis. If this limits the value of comparisons with earlier traditions of urban imaging, it also underscores the need to rethink the relation between photographic image and viewer in a context in which each and every act of viewing gains the capacity to generate more data. As Crary notes:

Most of the historically accumulated understandings of the term 'observer' are destabilized under such conditions: that is, when individual acts of vision are unendingly solicited for conversion into information that will both enhance technologies of control and be a form of surplus value in a marketplace based on accumulation of data on user behaviour. (2013: 47–8)

As cities become increasingly data-rich terrains – whether generated by automated transactions such as movement through an urban transit system or volunteered by users posting geotagged images to a social media site – the issue of who controls the data, and how it will be used, is becoming increasingly urgent. While there have been calls for a better aligning of data with the public good (for instance, Batty et al. 2012), they are yet to gain significant traction. The rapid emergence of Street View in advance of any systematic consideration of its privacy implications, let alone of its broader effects on urban public culture, is symptomatic of what has become a radically experimental environment. Google's practice of releasing new services rapidly and dealing with any flak later is symptomatic of a digital urbanism in which seemingly autonomous technological progress is disciplined only by the cut and thrust of the market.

This highlights the changing role of the state in managing the urban public domain. In his book *The Postmodern Condition*, Jean-François Lyotard (1984) hypothesized that information wars would one day be fought between nation-states. If such 'cyber-wars' have become increasingly common, an equally important front is the extension of data battles into the terrain of the urban everyday. Such an extension carries a number of implications. It is instructive to recall that both Marville and Vertov undertook their projects as employees of the state. In contrast, the Street View project was launched not by a state but by a private company with distinctive global ambitions: to organize and manage the world's information. This is not to argue that such a project would somehow be automatically better had it been initiated by a state, or that any state has always acted to further the 'public good', even assuming that such a value could be defined in unitary and non-antagonistic terms.

Rather, it is to acknowledge that the emergence of powerful global digital platforms that cut across national jurisdictions and urban territories changes the way in which citizens – and governments – can influence basic urban processes such as finding the way from one place to another. Any future articulation of the concept of 'public good' now has to speak to these new conditions.

I want to argue that, in producing the Street View database, Google has effectively *appropriated* something – the public appearances of urban space – that previously belonged to no one, and it has converted this common resource into private value. However, conceptualizing such an act of appropriation is difficult. Seizing hold of urban public appearances by building a database of digital images is clearly not the same as earlier seizures, such as the enclosure of the public commons that forced rural workers into urban factories at the dawn of industrial capitalism. Digital images belong to the class of commodities which Benkler (2006) terms 'non-rival' goods. Google can rightly argue that constructing their Street View database does not prevent others (such as Apple) from making their own databases of images of city streets. Moreover, the fact that the possibility of producing such a database is historically new means Google can also argue that it is simply the 'first-entrant' to this field.[29] Finally, the fact that use of the database is 'free' for all non-commercial purposes means that many people tend not to think of Google Street View or Google Maps as private platforms, but accept their regular framing as a type of public service.

In all these respects, Google Maps exemplifies what I mean by an *operational archive*. Unlike a traditional archive, the operational archive is constantly 'under development' even as it is being used. Wolfgang Ernst characterizes this threshold in terms of a shift 'from archival space to archival time', from the archive as 'vault' to 'permanent data transfer' (2004). Second, parts of the archive are made 'freely' available to users. This widespread, distributed usage forms the basis of the archive's commercial value to the platform operator. Operational archives are not only *sources* of information but are themselves tools for *gathering* information about their users. In this sense, we might say that Google Maps functions primarily as a *lure*, since value to Google is derived primarily from the data they can accrue through encouraging user transactions. Third, operational archives are modifiable (at least to some extent) by users. Google Maps supports a number of forms of user-modification and user-contribution, including the capacity to customize maps, to 'Report a problem' or to submit edits using its MapMaker tool.[30] Parts of the archive are also made freely available to third-party developers through various application programming interfaces (APIs). This is a key to the way in which Google Maps has become one of the Internet's 'base platforms' on which a wide range of other applications are built. In his study of a number of software start-ups involved in developing locative mobile apps, Thatcher notes that 'every application relied on mapping information provided by either Google or Open Street Map' (2014: 1772).[31]

If the inclusion of these 'bottom-up' strategies for map modification and user-generated production resembles the open data philosophy of Open Street Map in some respects, the similarity is superficial.[32] The bottom line with Google Maps is that all *processed* data, including user-contributed elements, becomes the proprietary content of Google. Google justify their closed eco-system largely on the basis that it enables improved accuracy and efficiency, including quicker response times to correct errors.[33] McClendon (quoted in Rushe 2012) argues: 'We are making a version of the world, as accurate as we can make it.' In common with other 'smart-city' platforms, Google is now seeking to integrate more and more data streams, such as transit and traffic information, into its maps. The end goal is a real-time vision of the city in motion.

The efficiency and effectiveness of the 'Ground Truth' system is not my main concern here; it is, rather, with the consequences of a private company – or a few companies – building proprietary databases that contain a 'deep map' of the cities of the world, at the historical moment in which digital maps become a key to organizing and integrating multiple other data streams and services shaping urban life. The development of such 'deep maps' places these companies in an enormously powerful position. If this becomes the dominant and unchallenged orientation enabled by the threshold of geomedia, it creates the structural conditions for a wholesale appropriation of the urban – thought of as social encounter, communication and simultaneity – as a technique of value extraction. When fundamental aspects of urban life, such as finding your way around a city or keeping in contact with 'friends', are routinely mediated by profit-oriented digital platforms, the logic of commodification gains a much tighter purchase on more and more aspects of social life. When even micro-scale social actions, from looking at a map to catching a bus or meeting a friend, become susceptible to automatic recording, and every transaction, journey, call and click becomes a sign that can be aggregated and evaluated, it is clear we have crossed a new frontier in the way capitalism seeks to extract surplus value from urban life. It is in this respect that Street View and Google Maps exemplify what Hardt and Negri (2009) call the 'biopolitical' front, what Lash (2010) calls 'intensive culture', and what Stiegler (2011) terms hyper-industrialization, in which all elements of 'life' are at risk of becoming subject to new forms of value extraction through data acquisition.

In an influential article published nearly two decades ago, US law professor Jerry Kang contrasted the level of surveillance enabled by the Internet to what was considered 'normal' in public space:

> imagine the following two visits to a mall, one in real space, the other in cyberspace. In real space, you drive to a mall, walk up and down its corridors, peer into numerous shops, and stroll through corridors of inviting stores. Along the way, you buy an ice cream cone with cash. You walk into a bookstore and flip through a few magazines. Finally, you stop at a clothing store and buy a friend a silk scarf with a credit card. In this narrative, numerous persons interact with you and collect information along the way. For instance, while walking through the mall, fellow visitors visually collect information about you, if for no other reason than to avoid bumping into you. But such information is general – e.g., it does not pin-point the geographical location and time of the sighting – is not in a format that can be processed by a computer, is not indexed to your name or another unique identifier, and is impermanent, residing in short-term human memory. You remain a barely noticed stranger. One important exception exists: the scarf purchase generates data that are detailed, computer-processable, indexed

by name, and potentially permanent. By contrast, in cyberspace, the exception becomes the norm: Every interaction is like the credit card purchase. (1998: 1198)

Kang's point was that most people going about their business in the city wouldn't accept the kind of tracking and tracing practices that were being instantiated in the early days of the commercial Internet. However, instead of modifying Internet data collection, the threshold of geomedia has enabled the progressive extension of such practices into public space. As Nissenbaum and Varnelis note:

Instead of sustaining the freedoms of physical space online, the conditions of Kang's cyberspace seem increasingly to be replicated in (or mapped onto) physical space – social networks, and Internet of Things, pervasive computing, RFID, GPS-enabled devices, location tracking systems and technologies (such as that used by Footpath), and identification through crowd-sourcing (a so-called 'human flesh' search engine). As venture capitalist Harry Weller put it in a recent interview, 'now instead of us surfing the Internet, the Internet is surfing us'. (2012: 16)

Is this an inevitable outcome? While the pace of change in this sector has been extremely rapid, confounding both legal and cultural responses, the trajectory towards pervasive data-gathering has by no means gone unchallenged. As the rollout of Street View demonstrated, turning urban life into data has often been controversial. Despite the mystification around 'big data', it is evident that many people don't like the increasingly intensive colonization of social life by commercial data harvesting – at least when they become aware of it. It is instructive to compare the trajectory of locative social networks such as Foursquare – launched in 2009, and for a brief moment in 2010 one of the web's hottest properties. Foursquare, which combined elements of urban gaming with social location, depended on a 'check-in' model in which users self-reported their location. However, its rapid growth stalled and the company eventually pivoted to split between a recommendation service and a location-sharing service.[34] A similar fate awaited

Facebook Places, which was introduced in 2010 before being axed the following year.[35] Google Latitude was 'retired' in mid-2013. While 'check-in' and location-sharing remain available (for instance in Google+), it seems that once a certain novelty wore off, many people found the idea tedious and intrusive.

Foursquare in particular was dogged by bad publicity around privacy and security issues. For instance, in February 2010, a site known as Please Rob Me was launched. It scraped data from public Twitter messages that had been pushed through Foursquare to list people who were away from their homes (McCarthy 2010; Wilken 2012). Equally concerning were a number of 'stalker' applications such as Girls Around Me, an 'app' produced by Moscow-based developer i-Free. Girls Around Me mashed together Foursquare location data with Google Maps and data from Facebook profiles to display a map showing all the girls in your area who had checked in to Foursquare. By scraping Facebook profiles, Girls Around Me could show pictures and other data such as age and personal interests. Journalist John Brownlee (2012) observed:

> all that *Girls Around Me* is really doing is using public APIs from Google Maps, Facebook and Foursquare and mashing them all up together, so you could see who had checked-in at locations in your area, and learn more about them. Moreover, the girls (and men!) shown in *Girls Around Me* all had the power to opt out of this information being visible to strangers, but whether out of ignorance, apathy or laziness, they had all neglected to do so. This was all public information.

While Brownlee concluded 'I still don't believe that there's anything wrong with what this app is doing', the ensuing furore soon led Foursquare to modify its API.[36] Girls Around Me exemplifies the class of apps engaged in what Thatcher (2014) describes as sniffing for 'data fumes': aggregating and repurposing information that is already being collected by other 'base services' such as Google Maps. While Girls Around Me seemed a step too far to Foursquare, the fact that it was simply aggregating data routinely captured by popular devices and applications received far less attention. A key point in this scenario is the extent to which what Brownlee describes as 'public information' keeps shifting. This might be a function of alterations to the terms of service, such as Facebook's regular shifts in its default settings as it tries to 'monetize' its user-base, but it might equally be a function of new capacities to analyse data. The growing strategic importance of Street View's photographic archive, like the massive archive of user-created photographs on Facebook, exemplify this latter trajectory.

What kind of urban future does this trajectory of geomedia portend? In this chapter, I have argued that services such as Google Street View are symptomatic of an emergent post-national urban imaginary – one in which an increasing role is assumed by the global corporation rather than the state; in which the individual street and individual movements have crossed the threshold of recording; and in which urban data accrues in the operational archives of global digital platforms. If Street View offers a powerful image of a connected world, it is configured with specific traits: the city has become searchable and the process of searching contributes further flows of data to the proprietary platform operator. Here the urban is not the realm of social encounter, simultaneity and difference as Lefebvre figured it, but has become what Heidegger (1977) called a 'standing reserve': not of 'nature' but of data.

As much as apps such as Foursquare offer increased connectivity, they also reveal a concern to *control* urban experience. Like the practice of tele-cocooning (Habuchi 2005), in which mobile devices are used to carve out private zones in public space, location-based services offer a means of *filtering* social encounters with others (Frith 2012). While these tendencies shouldn't be overstated, it is worth recalling Sennett's (2012) argument concerning the importance of public encounters with diverse others as critical to learning the social skills capable of sustaining contemporary urban life. In our search for convenience and control, we need to be attentive to the risks involved in outsourcing the management of social encounter to software. At the simplest level, we might observe that the adoption of personalized digital navigation systems reduces the need for one the most common interactions with strangers: the need to ask directions. Rather than practising skills, such as the capacity for strangers to give and receive advice from each other, by delegating these everyday transactions to 'smart devices' we risk finding that the very abilities needed for co-existence have atrophied when we need them most.

This is an all too common scenario in the contemporary uptake of the digital, where individual convenience looms large and longer-term trajectories, such as the potential for loss of urban amenity and conviviality, receive scant consideration. This imbalance is exacerbated by the fact that commercial digital platforms regularly adopt inflexible models for managing data, so that user choice is commonly reduced to either 'opting out' entirely, or trading off expansive rights over personal data for access to the service. More nuanced settings enabling what Nissenbaum (2011) terms 'contextual privacy' are rare. This aggressive framework might fit contemporary ambitions to convert urban serendipity into pervasive marketing opportunity, effectively extending the logic of the 'Gruen transfer' from the controlled environment of the shopping centre into the city at large. But if we want to make richer and more varied use of the new communicative and place-making capacities of geomedia, we will need to demand other headings.

It is to these other headings that I now turn. While there is an ongoing necessity to focus on the issues such as control over data and proprietary platforms that I have raised here, there is also a clear need to move beyond what might be described as *reactive* responses. Instead, we need to work towards imagining and exploring different agendas for urban communication infrastructure. It is towards thinking about possible new models that I turn my attention in the next two chapters.

3

Participatory Public Space

Rethinking participation in public space

Street View offers a powerful vision of how networked public space might be reconfigured by commercial platforms. But this is not the only possible orientation of geomedia. What I am interested in exploring in this chapter are some recent uses of digital media by artists also working 'in the street'. I want to use contemporary digital art in public space as the lens for focusing on the potential for geomedia to construct more 'open' urban situations capable of supporting experimental forms of being-with-others in public: in short, what I call the question of 'participatory public space'.

There are a number of elements to address in sketching an answer to this question. First, we need to recognize that 'participation' has become a buzzword. Underpinned by the historically low transaction costs of networked digital communication, participation has become an early twenty-first-century *zeitgeist*: a value everyone seems to subscribe to without necessarily sharing a common sense of what might be involved. This absence of accord is not surprising: in fact, the condition for a term to achieve global currency is arguably its capacity to mean different things to different people. However, recognizing its chameleon-like qualities doesn't mean that we should render 'participation' entirely vacant, nor simply surrender it to the highest bidder. Rather, this suggests that we need to deepen our analysis to better understand what participation might involve in different settings and particular contexts.

Focusing on the participatory ambitions of art in public space art is helpful in both broadening and concretizing analysis. Contemporary art has been one of the key zones in which research into the capacity for digital media to facilitate new types of relations to site, to others, to interfaces and to networked places has been actively pursued. Simon Penny underlines the leadership of artists in experimenting with interactive and location-based technologies, but also in thinking about digital interfaces beyond the dominant HCI frame of 'usability':

> in our current era of ubiquitous computation, the universe of live data which was once called 'the virtual' is increasingly anchored into physical and social context via a diversity of digital commodities. The technologies, techno-social structures and modalities of interaction which permit this (re)union were workshopped and prototyped in 'media arts' research and elsewhere over the past quarter century. (2011: 100)

Penny also stresses the way in which the experiential and embodied approach common to art practice has opened crucial orientations that tended to remain closed to other disciplines: 'Because of the sensitivity of artists to persuasive sensorial immediacy and embodied engagement, interactive art practice pioneered research into dimensions of interaction which remained opaque to institutional and commercial labs for many years' (2011: 78). These orientations towards exploring embodied engagement with experimental interfaces and technical systems are crucial in rethinking the composition of public space as digital milieu.

Second, we need to recognize that contemporary ambitions for 'participation' in relation to digital media are not entirely new, and often reproduce certain tensions and contradictions inherited from older settings. There is a memorable scene in François Truffaut's 1966 film adaptation of Ray Bradbury's 1953 novel *Fahrenheit 451* in which Montag (one of the firemen whose 'duty' is to burn books) watches as his wife Linda takes part in the nightly 'tele-play' that includes a part written 'just for her'. In fact, the role involves Linda responding on cue and according to script with single-word answers, in concert with an audience of equally sedated peers. The scene is eerily reminiscent of the occasion when the Nazis made precocious use of live radio to construct a new type of mass ritual, when over one million people gathered under loudspeakers in public spaces in different cities to recite the personal oath to the Führer in unison with his deputy Rudolph Hess.[1] The key difference in *Fahrenheit 451* is that, instead of assembling in public space, each 'participant' in the tele-play remains physically isolated in the nominally private space of their own home. If Truffaut's target was partly this *separation* that Guy Debord saw as one of the primary consequences of spectacular society, it was also what Umberto Eco (1984) described as 'neo-television', in which the one-way communication structure of broadcasting was masked by a rhetoric of *direct address* to each individual viewer.

It is tempting to believe that everything has changed today due to the 'many-to-many' communication architecture of the Internet. However, despite numerous claims about the 'inevitable' democratization of both culture and politics, the situation is clearly more complex. As I argued in chapter 1, the Internet is not always 'many-to-many', nor is two-way exchange necessarily about dialogue.[2] As 'audience participation' has become an explicit commercial strategy of contemporary media platforms, it is increasingly difficult to make direct correlations between the capacity to produce media content and deeper changes cutting across creativity, education and democracy.[3] The growth of 'audience' productivity does not negate the new degree of integration of production and consumption that Stiegler (2011) describes as hyper-industrialization, but is in fact one of its preconditions.

Third, we need to recognize that participation has long been understood as a core attribute of public space. However, as my discussion in chapter 1 sought to emphasize, participation is neither given nor unitary. Public space is always a striated, contested zone with both visible and invisible barriers. For this reason, participation in public space has always had to be thought on a variety of levels, from formal laws regulating access and behaviour, to decisions made in the realm of architecture and urban planning, to the ways in which individual and collective capacities are shaped by socio-economic distinctions and cultural protocols. All these factors combine to influence a person's or group's sense of belonging or not belonging in a public space, and affect their ability to enter, occupy and act in particular spaces, or, conversely, to avoid them, or to withdraw from action.

Designers have long known that the capacity for members of the public to make (even incremental) adjustments to an environment makes it more attractive and congenial. In his influential study of the social dynamics of public spaces, sociologist William Whyte emphasized a range of factors that contributed to 'well-used' public spaces, including seating, provision of food, the role of 'mayors' (official or unofficial mediators of the space) and the availability of attractions (such as buskers). Beyond these specific elements, the key attribute of an attractive public space was the level of design 'openness' allowing some degree of user-configuration of the space. From this perspective, Whyte argued that fixed individual seating was often 'a design conceit' (1980: 35). The ability for a visitor to move a seat, even a few centimetres, enables a ritual of 'appropriation' that not enough urban public spaces afford.

Small differences can make a difference. Geomedia now offers numerous possibilities for altering and adjusting urban ambiance, ranging from the macro scale of smart-city strategies deploying big data to 'optimize' urban settings down to smaller-scale interventions into specific sites and social encounters. It is the small, incremental modifications that Sassen (2011b) emphasizes as the route towards a different kind of smart city: an 'open source urbanism' based on responsiveness to multiple streams of feedback.

We can think of the multiple ways in which the city talks back as a type of open-source urbanism: the city as partly made through a myriad of interventions and little changes from the ground up. Each of these multiple small interventions may not look like much, but together they give added meaning to the notion of the incompleteness of cities and that this incompleteness gives cities their long lives, thereby outlasting other more powerful entities.

History suggests that the aspirations of architects and urban designers to create what Fanck and Stevens (2007) call 'loose space' have proved difficult to realize in modern practice. This includes numerous attempts since the 1960s to include 'the public' in planning processes.[4] My interest here is in what contemporary art practice might contribute to rethinking 'participation' in public space in the context of geomedia. In other words, rather than focusing on avenues for 'speaking back' to the city in Sassen's sense of establishing better feedback loops to authority, I am interested in the potential for using digital media to elaborate new experiences of 'becoming public' that emerge at the junction of digital networks, embodied actors and urban places.

Recalling the importance that those such as Lefebvre and Sennett placed on the experience of being-with-others in public space as the mechanism for developing public civility, I argue that 'art' has today become a key zone for incubating new types of urban encounter in which social relations are to the fore. Such an argument depends on a transformed understanding of art, recognizing not only the increasing connection between activism and certain practices of art (Holmes 2007), but also the historical convergence between art practice and everyday life. Contemporary art projects are no longer content to simply 'represent' the social, but frequently seek to *enact* sociality through forms of dialogue, reciprocity, collaboration and hospitality. As Nikos Papastergiadis argues:

> From modest gestures that interrupt everyday communal practices, to ambitious projects that seek to revitalize the public sphere, art has become a medium for reconstituting the social. Art is now a mode through which cosmopolitan ideals have materialized both in visual forms and through collective social actions. [. . .] This shift in the collaborative demands that we consider not only how art can represent

the conditions of the world but also the way it can enable an alternative way of imagining our participation in the world. (2012: 14)

This transformation in contemporary art practice has grown out
of a longer history of art that explores both the contours of urban
'situation' and the configuration of social relations. In what follows
I will trace the emergence of these orientations in the work of the
Situationist International towards the end of the 1950s, and their
reconceptualization by writer-curator Nicholas Bourriaud in the
late 1990s. I will also draw on Umberto Eco's concept of the 'open
work', first advanced in the 1960s, to think through some of the
specific attributes of networked digital art. The aim of these discussions is to contextualize my analysis of specific examples of digital
art in public space, drawing particularly on the work of Rafael
Lozano-Hemmer and Blast Theory. If my broader concern here is
to understand the potential for geomedia to contribute to a more
'participatory public space', my engagement with specific artworks
and projects is what contributes to the task of elaborating what this
phrase might mean.

Urban participation and the 'construction of situations'

In defining the right to the city in 1967, Lefebvre argued that
'participation' was integral to its practice. 'The right to the city
manifests itself as a superior form of rights: right to freedom, to
individualization in socialization, to habitat and to inhabit. The
right to the *oeuvre*, to participation and *appropriation* (clearly distinct from the right to property), are implied in the right to the
city' (1996: 173–4). However, he also reminds us that there is a
long history of fetishizing 'participation': 'In practice the ideology
of participation enables us to have the acquiescence of interested and concerned people at a small price' (1996: 144–5). This
tension between principles and practice remains common to many
contemporary discussions of urban participation (Brownhill and

Carpenter 2007; Finn 2014). For Lefebvre, genuine participation implies a new practice of inhabitation based on capacities for self-organization and self-management. The recovery of urban life demands 'capacities of integration and participation' which 'cannot be stimulated either by authoritarian means or by administrative prescription, or by the intervention of specialists' (1996: 146).

Crucially, *inhabitation* demands a departure from the instrumental rationality that dominated the functionalist conception of the city. Instead Lefebvre evokes the collective production of urban life as *oeuvre* or work of art. But Lefebvre's understanding of 'art' differs fundamentally from its bourgeois conception: 'To put art at the service of the urban does not mean to prettify urban space with works of art. [. . .] Rather this means that time-spaces become works of art and that former art reconsiders itself as source and model of appropriation of space and time' (1996: 173). To conceive the urban as artwork is to change how we think about art, including who might be considered an artist. Lefebvre envisages a future in which 'everyone' makes art: 'Leaving aside representation, ornamentation and decoration, art can become *praxis* and *poeisis* on a social scale: the art of living in the city as a work of art.' From this expanded perspective, 'the future of art is not artistic but urban' (1996: 173).

This expanded sense of art was shared by the Situationist International (SI), and was central to their distinctive urban critique.[5] In what amounted to the group's founding manifesto, the 1957 'Report on the Construction of Situations', Guy Debord argued: 'Something that changes our way of seeing the streets is more important than something that changes our way of seeing paintings' (in Knabb 2006: 42). To this end, 'art' in a restricted sense would give way to the 'construction of situations'. Debord's well-known definition of the constructed situation emphasizes several features, including ephemerality, emotional intensity and the constant feedback between environment and behaviour:

> Our central idea is the construction of situations, that is to say, the concrete construction of momentary ambiences of life and their transformation into a superior passional quality. We must develop a

systematic intervention based on the complex factors of two components in perpetual interaction: the material environment of life and the behaviors which that environment gives rise to and which radically transform it. (In Knabb 2006: 38)

This emphasis on the relation between material environment and emotional behaviour not only distinguished the constructed situation from more recognized political practices, but underlines its continuing potential as an approach for understanding contemporary everyday life lived in an urban networked terrain.

The SI were adamant in aiming for the total transformation of society. What was distinctive in their approach was their insistence that transformation could not be achieved simply by seizing control of the state (if such a thing is ever simple), but demanded a concomitant process of emotional and psychological transformation. The transformation of individual and collective subjects necessitated the transformation of the *relation* between individual and collective.[6] A second distinctive factor was their emphasis on alienation, understood not simply as an effect of working conditions, but as emblematic of the broader reduction in which wage labour and administered leisure formed two halves of a single, stultified existence. It was from this perspective that *boredom* was seized as a key political issue. In response to the *banality* of the everyday as imposed routine, the SI placed the search for a full and passional life alongside – and even in place of – more traditional revolutionary goals. As Debord expressed it: 'The most general goal must be to expand the nonmediocre part of life, to reduce the empty moments of life as much as possible' (in Knabb 2006: 39).

The city was what was at stake, but was also the lever to achieve this ambition: the construction of new ambiances 'will be both the products and the instruments of new forms of behavior' (Debord in Knabb 2006: 36). To this end, the SI sought new 'data' that would be gained by experience of the city. This demanded new experimental techniques such as the *dérive*, which was conceived as a means for gaining insight into the existing urban environment, but also as a way of actively producing new ambiances.[7]

The aim of constructing situations was ultimately to engender new participatory practices. If, for Debord, the spectacle was defined above all by passivity, the construction of situations would point to a new practice of taking action, or *living*:

> The construction of situations begins beyond the ruins of the modern spectacle. It is easy to see how much the very principle of the spectacle – nonintervention – is linked to the alienation of the old world. Conversely, the most pertinent revolutionary experiments in culture have sought to break the spectators' psychological identification with the hero so as to draw them into activity by provoking their capacities to revolutionize their own lives. *The situation is thus designed to be lived by its constructors.* The role played by a passive or merely bit-part playing 'public' must constantly diminish, while that played by those who cannot be called actors, but rather, in a new sense of the term, 'livers,' must steadily increase. (In Knabb 2006: 40–1; my emphasis)

The critical shift here is the abolition of the public's role as onlookers, bit-players and 'audience'. Evoking the Brechtian concept of alienation or estrangement (*Verfremdungseffekt*), which sought to break the traditional pattern of spectatorial identification in theatre, Debord looks instead to an expanded art of self-organized urban situations which are 'lived' by those who make them. As Constant later elaborated in his vision of the experimental city 'New Babylon', the inhabitants would themselves design and construct the city in the process of living in it: 'New Babylonians play a game of their own devising, against a backdrop they have designed themselves, together with their fellow townspeople. That is their life, therein lies their artistry' (1998: 135).

The proximity of this vision to Lefebvre's concept of the city as *oeuvre* based on appropriation by its inhabitants is evident. However, the uneven history and limited success of such participatory urbanism situates the ongoing challenges to any such 'artistry'. Leaving 'space' for public participation is inevitably difficult and often risky. A rhetoric of participation in planning can all too easily become an alibi, either for 'business as usual' where models of consultation are constrained in advance (Copeland 2008), or, worse,

where DIY community initiatives become a rationale for the abandonment of state responsibility (Blackmar in Low and Smith 2006;
Finn 2014). The legacy of old urban spaces, and of old ways of
thinking and acting, means it is hard to simply invent the new artistry of urban life by an act of will. New behaviour demands new
structures (sites, institutions) and new ways of thinking, but these
also emerge partly from new practices. This circular logic suggests
that 'transitional' stages, spaces and concepts are needed, although
the SI gave little attention to theorizing this need.[8] Moreover,
refusing to specify the shape and detail of the new city can limit
its capacity to gain traction in the public imaginary. Sadler (1998)
concludes his study of the SI by observing that the group remained
marginalized in part by its own 'most radical gesture': its refusal
to generate images of utopia, preferring to take a role of general
inspiration and leaving the detail to potential users. Finally, we
might note that simply removing existing regulation around urban
planning without developing alternative settings carries the risk
of enabling *market* rather than public appropriation.[9] This history
situates a key question that remains active in the present: how is
it possible to move away from overly prescriptive design towards
an urbanism of incomplete or unfinished space, leaving room for
public appropriation without simply throwing everything back
onto a public that is often unprepared to accept the responsibility
that 'participation' carries?

Art as open work and social encounter

By the mid-1960s, the SI had expelled all its artist members, in the
process rejecting art as a viable mode of politico-urban intervention. Yet the idea does not disappear and, if anything, has become
more prominent in the present. This visibility stems from two key
trajectories. The first is the move, beginning in the early 1960s,
towards understanding works of art as open-ended, processual and
'reprogrammable', according to Umberto Eco's (1989) concept of
the 'open work'. The second is the understanding of contemporary

art in terms of its production of situated social encounters proposed by Nicholas Bourriaud (2002) in his influential concept of 'relational aesthetics' towards the end of the 1990s.

Eco's *The Open Work* was first published in Italian in 1962. It can be read as an early statement of two themes that subsequently became more prominent in his work, and in cultural theory more generally: an insistence on plurality or polysemy in cultural production; and a growing emphasis on the active role of the audience as cultural producer. Eco does not argue that the 'openness' of the modern artwork is something entirely new. He recognizes that every creative work possesses a degree of openness, which is manifest in variations in interpretation. What *is* new is the context in which the modern artwork exists. Eco proposes that the distinct intellectual context provided by modern scientific understandings of the world had led to the emergence of a new interpretative paradigm. In so far as science inaugurates a radical mode of questioning that challenges established authority by acknowledging the co-existence of different truths – or, better, different *probabilities* awaiting evidentiary proof – Eco argues that the openness of modern art belongs to a different order. The more restricted openness of traditional art gives way to a more unstable interpretative infinity:

> The work remains inexhaustible insofar as it is 'open', because in it an ordered world based on universally acknowledged laws is being replaced by a world based on ambiguity, both in the negative sense that directional centres are missing and in a positive sense, because values and dogma are constantly being placed in question. (1989: 9)

If Eco's argument involves a certain idealization of science, he takes his concept further by recognizing that certain artworks *embrace* this new sense of openness. Drawing on key modernist works including Alexander Calder's mobiles, musical compositions by Karlheinz Stockhausen, and texts by writers such as James Joyce and Bertolt Brecht, Eco argues that all these 'works-in-motion' are characterized by the artist's decision to leave the arrangement of some of their constituent elements either to the public or to chance. This decision inserts a lack of finality in terms of the work's order and 'content', and has the effect of allowing – or *demanding* – a greater degree of 'participation' from the public in the production of the work. In the process, the limited polysemy of the traditional artwork, based on a more restricted interpretative play, gives way to a more radical incompleteness. Every 'work-in-motion' remains *definitively unfinished*, to borrow Duchamp's happy description of his *Large Glass* (1915–23). As Eco puts it: 'Every performance *explains* the composition but does not *exhaust* it. Every performance makes the work an actuality, but is itself only complementary to all possible other performances of the work' (1989: 15). As I will argue below, Eco's concept offers a relevant frame for understanding contemporary media art involving multiple iterations and feedback loops linking artist and audience through a technological system.

While Eco's concept was originally proposed in relation to examples drawn from the 1920s and 1930s, it seems no accident that the concept of the 'open work' was developed at a time when art crossed the threshold that Lucy Lippard (1973) later termed the 'dematerialization of the art object'. A variety of movements beginning in the late 1950s – from Alan Kaprow's 'Happenings' to performance and conceptual art, groups such as Fluxus and the Neo-Concretists, and the beginnings of video art in the mid-1960s – collectively contributed to this major shift in art practice. When the work of art no longer consists primarily of finished objects or images, and is not necessarily wholly produced by professional artists, our understanding of art shifts. Eco's 'open work' registers this transition to a more open-ended process that often involves participation, collaboration, and even forms of co-creation, with the 'audience'.

By the 1990s such participation was no longer the exception but had become a new norm. Writing in 1998, Nicholas Bourriaud proposed a further significant shift in understanding art. Observing that participation 'has become a constant feature of artistic practice' (2002: 25), he described a series of works by contemporary artists including Rirkrit Tiravanija, Vanessa Beecroft, Maurizio Cattelan and Pierre Huyghe. Bourriaud then asked:

'How are these apparently elusive works to be decoded, be they process-related or behavioural by ceasing to take shelter behind the sixties art history?' (2002: 7). Bourriaud's proposition was that the difference between earlier modernist and contemporary projects lay in the extent to which art had begun to focus on the *process of social encounter itself*: 'The possibility of a *relational* art (an art taking as a theoretical horizon the realm of human interactions and its social content, rather than the assertion of an independent and *private* symbolic space), points to a radical upheaval of the aesthetic, cultural and political goals introduced by modern art' (2002: 14).

There are several elements in Bourriaud's framework that are germane to thinking about the capacity for contemporary digital media art to support interventions into the public realm. First, he situates the emergence of 'relational art' firmly in the conjuncture of global urban culture linked by pervasive real-time communication networks. It is the 'intensive encounters' sustained by the city that 'has ended up producing [. . .] an art form where the substrate is formed by intersubjectivity, and which takes "being-together" as a central theme' (2002: 14). Second, in so far as global society is conditioned by omnipresent digital media and the widespread privatization of public assets and public space, Bourriaud argues that art nevertheless remains an *interstice*: an area of activity that (at least in part) eludes capitalist domination. In contrast to the 'ideal subject of the society of extras' (a deliberate extrapolation from Debord's concept of spectacle) who is 'reduced to the condition of a consumer of time and space', Bourriaud (2002: 9) argues that art still has some capacity to problematize this relation. Observing that 'artistic practice appears these days to be a rich loam for social experiments, like a space partly protected from the uniformity of behavioural patterns', he suggests that relational art 'creates free areas, and time spans whose rhythm contrasts with those structuring everyday life, and it encourages an inter-human commerce that differs from the "communication zones" that are imposed on us' (2002: 9, 16). Third, Bourriaud insists that intersubjectivity forms the 'raw material' for relational art, arguing that it is 'to today's art what mass production was to Pop Art and Minimal

Art' (2002: 42). The relational artist sets out not with the ambition
of producing a work centred around a finished set of images and
objects, but with the aim of instigating new models of sociability. From this perspective, relational art is not a 'representation'
of social encounters, but the space for staging such encounters.
Bourriaud argues:

> the role of artworks is no longer to form imaginary and utopian reali-
> ties, but to actually be ways of living and models of action within the
> existing real, whatever the scale chosen by the artist. [. . .] Meetings,
> encounters, events, various types of collaboration between people,
> games, festivals, and places of conviviality, in a word all manner of
> encounter and relational invention thus represent, today, aesthetic
> objects likely to be looked at as such. (2002: 13, 28)

Bourriaud's assertions, particularly concerning the partial protection of art from hegemonic values, cannot be read as general and
generalizable principles, but need to be tested in the context of
specific interventions. It is also notable that he places relational
aesthetics in explicit lineage to Situationist practice, arguing that:
'The work that forms a "relational world", and a social interstice,
updates Situationism and reconciles it, as far as it is possible, with
the art world' (2002: 85). This 'as far as it is possible' inevitably remains contentious and contested, since it was precisely the
seeming impossibility of such a reconciliation that informed the
hardening of Debord's stance in the early 1960s. Nevertheless,
the shift that Bourriaud identifies, in which contemporary art has
become increasingly concerned with the construction of particular
social situations – 'models of action' that explore the social dynamics of 'being-with-others' – informs what is at stake in some of
the most striking examples of contemporary digital art in public
space. While these are often 'open works' in Eco's sense of enabling multiple and iterative outcomes, they are also characterized
by their concern for generating new experiences and practices of
social encounter. To what extent might such an 'art' function as a
transitional practice towards the production of a new sort of public
space?

Relational art as sociotechnical encounter

On 4 June 2010, an artificial sun was switched on in Melbourne's Federation Square as part of the annual 'Light in Winter' festival hosted at the site. *Solar Equation* was designed as a scale model of the sun, constructed on a 1:100,000,000 ratio. It comprised a large spherical aerostat (a static balloon) some 14 metres in diameter, filled with a mixture of helium and cold air, and tethered some 18 metres above ground. The aerostat was then animated by projecting video simulations of the sun's surface. This striking work was the latest in the line of 'relational architecture' projects that have been produced by artist Rafael Lozano-Hemmer since the late 1990s.[10] *Solar Equation* embodied a number of elements characteristic of the 'relational architecture' series. First, the works are all temporary installations and usually situated in public spaces rather than the physical and institutional confines of an art gallery. Second, they are designed as 'open works' in the sense Eco gave the term, although this concept is stretched and extended in particular ways by the affordances of digital technologies. Third, they deploy assemblages of digital media (video images, sensors, projection, tracking technology, robotics, computerized control, etc.) to construct situated, experimental interfaces which are accessed by the public in a variety of ways. Fourth, they focus on the social relations established and enacted in their milieu.

With *Solar Equation*, the 'openness' of the work played out across at least two dimensions. One involved the dynamic mode of producing visual 'content'. The imagery projected onto the surface of the artificial sun was derived by combining images captured from space observatories with three layers of complex mathematical equations. The result was then projected 'live' onto the spherical surface using five coordinated projectors. As Lozano-Hemmer (2010) noted:

> It's not a video that just sort of loops around, it's actually imagery taken by SOHO and SDO overlaid with equations, which faithfully simulate those behaviours on the surface. It is mathematics playing back

complex systems that will never be repeated. [. . .] I've often said, and this piece is really a good example, that these pieces are closer to water fountains than to shows. There's no beginning, there's no end, it is just a constant stream of imagery.[11]

By deploying software and algorithms, the work forms a complex system in which its 'outputs' are singularities that are unrepeatable. Lozano-Hemmer notes that adopting this kind of creative process inevitably implies a certain loss of 'authorial' control:

> By means of non-linear mathematics, like cellular automata, probabilistic ramifications, recursive algorithms or chaos strategies, it's possible to write programs whose results will surprise the author. That's to say the machine can have certain autonomy and expression because you simply capture initial 'algorithmic conditions' but do not pre-program the outcome. This is for me a gratifying post-humanist message; a message that invites humility, but one that also marks a crisis in authorship and opens a wide problematic area, and I say 'welcome' to that! (2005: 5)

Rather than being defined by the production of a finished object or set of images, this kind of open work might best be conceptualized as a *field of possibilities*, borrowing from the language of experimental physics to describe a milieu in which the complex interplay of different forces generates a range of possible events, not all of which will eventuate.

If this first level of the work's 'openness' relates to its distinctive *generative* system, a second level relates to the way it deployed a mechanism for the audience to interact with the work in some way. Lozano-Hemmer (2010) explained:

> We're developing a piece of software which allows people using an iPod or an iPhone or an iPad, to actually preview the equations, so that they get an understanding of all of the different equations we're using, and then take remote control of the sun by changing some of the variables of the equation. For instance, there's one moment where you can actually use the multi-touch surface of the device to pass your fingers

over it, and you literally see all of the turbulence of the surface of the sun react to that touch. So it's a little moment of intimacy, where, you know, you get the sense of agency in relationship to it. But I'm not underlining it too much because, unlike other interactive pieces of mine where it's all about people self-representing, this is more just like an extension of the project.

Lozano-Hemmer's statement is worth dwelling on for a moment. In *Solar Equation* what is being offered is not so much 'control' over the system as a different mode of encounter with it. User agency is kept deliberately modest: participants contribute to a set of conditions that can be perceived by others, but which disappear as the work evolves according to the process scripted by its software. If the user has a degree of agency, so does the system; it follows a logic that a user can influence but not overturn. Perhaps much the same could be said of many, if not all, human–computer interactions. What is significant is that, here, there is no final outcome or individual result to be achieved. *Solar Equation* is not about the 'usability' criteria that dominate consumer technology. Nor is it about a cyborg blending of eye and hand coordination with technical system in the name of efficient capture or kill skills that defines 'gameplay' in most video game scenarios. Rather, the experience is driven by a combination of aesthetics and algorithms, and the outcome is the shared experience of standing under an artificial sun in a public space on a winter night.

Solar Equation exemplifies the growing entanglement of experiences of public space with complex technological assemblages that are marked by aesthetic and emotional intensities as much as instrumental forms of control. Lozano-Hemmer (2000: 53) himself cites one of the most notorious examples of using electric light to create *public affect* as a precursor to his installation *Vectorial Elevation* (1999–2000): Albert Speer's 'light dome' produced for a Nazi Party rally in Nuremberg in 1935. This temporary public lighting installation was designed with the ambition of exerting maximum impact on the 'masses'. It effectively reduced 'the people' to props within an integrated spectacle. Such ambitions have often percolated into contemporary culture. Reflecting on his role as lighting designer in the context of stadium rock concerts for bands such as U2, Bruce Ramus (2011) underlines the capacity for lighting to be used as a technique for emotional control:

> in a large stadium show, you know, the audience is very controlled. They aren't necessarily aware of that, but it's there [. . .] There's a level of control that you have when you're all gathered in one space and you're all looking at one specific thing, you're all looking in one direction. [. . .] As the one who pushes the buttons with the lights and the video, we have a level of influence on where everyone looks, how they will feel at any given time.

The issue of 'who pushes the button' remains critical to understanding the differential implications of geomedia for urban space. In their 'Proposals for Rationally Improving the City of Paris' (published in the Lettrist International journal *Potlatch* in 1955), Debord and his colleagues long ago argued: 'Street lamps should all be equipped with switches so that people can adjust the lighting as they wish' (in Knabb 2006: 12). The proposal is less a practical aim than a provocation to reflect on the extent to which urban infrastructure such as public lighting is either state controlled, or managed as a large-scale commercial spectacle. This context situates the *political* import of alternative public lighting interventions such as *Vectorial Elevation*, which enabled members of the public to design urban light patterns through a web interface that controlled a battery of powerful robotic searchlights. Instead of a spectacle controlled from above, *Vectorial Elevation* used the distributed capacity of digital networks to offer the public the ability to intervene, if temporarily, in the appearance and ambiance of a large-scale and highly symbolic public space. As Erkki Huhtamo observed: 'Giving any net user the opportunity to create a display for a real-life public space was a gesture that radically disrupted the logic of traditional public light shows' (Lozano-Hemmer 2000: 108–11). When *Vectorial Elevation* was reprised for the Winter Olympics in Vancouver in 2010, nearly 22,000 designs were completed over approximately three weeks.

Lozano-Hemmer has since adapted the basic idea through a series of works such as *Pulse Front* (Toronto, 2006), *Pulse Park* (New York, 2008) and *Articulated Intersect* (Hobart, 2014), all of which enabled public manipulation of powerful searchlights located in central city sites.[12] These works enact a stronger model of participant agency than *Solar Equation*. Reflecting on the role of the public in 'co-producing' these works, Lozano-Hemmer (2009) notes: 'If no one participates the pieces simply do not exist.'

Taking part in such events can be transformative for how those inhabiting a city relate to its public domain and to each other. While it is all too easy to overstate such claims, it is equally foolish to dismiss the way in which experiences of intervening on a large scale in a public space can foster a collective reimagining of the role of complex technological infrastructure in supporting urban inhabitation.[13] Instead of the ready-made subjectivity of the 'audience' – those who receive the finished product of the urban spectacle – a new possibility is mooted of recreating urban ambiance in the company of others. What is done in the context of a special event may later play out in other contexts, including smaller and more localized forms. Once attuned to look for them, opportunities and openings can emerge in many situations.

Having argued that the issue of 'who pushes the button' remains important, I now want to switch tack slightly. I think we miss the full import of digital artworks if we judge them simply according to the degree of control they offer – or withhold. According to such an optic, artworks are always likely to fall short because they don't offer 'real' control over the urban environment. They will inevitably remain *pseudo-political* moments, as Debord eventually concluded. What is most interesting for me about Lozano-Hemmer's work is the way that, even as it supports new modes of individual and collective agency, it also asks us to reflect on the simultaneous imbrication of agency with *inscription*: with the implication of users in a network of relations that are not entirely subject to their mastery. 'Freedom' and 'control' are not opposed as neatly separable positions regulated by conscious choice but as entangled relations of human and non-human forces. Some works (like *Solar Equation*) foreground the user's relation to a technical system, while others put more weight on the mobilization of the body as a micro-public site for the work's production. But all tend to explore this balance, or imbalance, between embodied and mediated/networked experiences of social encounter in urban space. Developing an understanding of this dynamic offers a model for exploring the complexities of participation in contemporary public space, where social encounter is always already a *sociotechnical* event.

For instance, Lozano-Hemmer's *Underscan* (2005) involved thousands of 'video portraits' projected onto the ground in central city thoroughfares and public spaces. Rendered invisible by intense white light projected from above, the portraits 'appeared' only in the shadows created by the ambulant viewers. *Underscan* used surveillance technology to track pedestrian movement so that portraits could be 'placed' in a viewer's predicted path. However, instead of the conventional panoptic logic on which tracking systems are predicated (establishing patterns and profiles), here the technology is directed to framing a novel social encounter. This encounter is only partly about *watching* the portrait images, since it depends equally upon the co-presence of others at the same site. In my observation, individual participants would often respond with surprise or delight to the images that opened up in their shadow spaces. When some audience members took the opportunity to perform mock violent acts, such as stamping on or kicking the prostrate figures they encountered, this led to discussions with other members of the public concerning the ethics of these actions. The public location of the work is important in shaping its reception. When *Underscan* was staged in London in 2008, Lozano-Hemmer (2009) found the location improved this aspect of unexpected improvisation: 'The project in Trafalgar Square benefited greatly from the fact that there is already a lot of foot traffic at night. This meant people would just "encounter" the work as they went home after work, for instance, rather than having to go to a specific site to see it.'

Like a number of Lozano-Hemmer's other works, *Underscan* also actively sought to demonstrate the systems it deploys. The work 'resets' itself every seven minutes, revealing the calibration grids used by the computerized surveillance system, and making the tracking technology publicly visible. Similar explorations of the intersection between system and social encounter have guided a number of Lozano-Hemmer's gallery-based works. In *Subtitled Public* (2005), individual members of the audience were tracked by a projected word, which pinned itself to them like an illuminated brand until they discovered how to pass it on. It was only by touching someone else – a form of public intimacy, or contagion – that a word could be transferred. A work like *Sustained Coincidence* (2007) evokes the uncomfortable experience of *forced* adjacency in public encounters, using a tracking system to detect the presence and position of members of the public, and then controlling the sequencing of the light sources in such a way that different shadows are always projected onto the centre of the gallery's wall. When more than one person enters the space, this means that their shadows inevitably overlap. In this manner, strangers, even when standing at opposite ends of the room, will find themselves brought together in a form of algorithmic intimacy. The limits of 'free will' are illuminated by the protocol of a system in which your shadow is constantly redirected towards the place of the other; the more you seek to escape its effects, the more apparent the constraints become.

The capacity for digital art to combine novel forms of participation and inscription as sociotechnical encounter is perhaps best exemplified by *Pulse Room*, a work Lozano-Hemmer exhibited at the 2007 Venice Biennale. *Pulse Room* consists of a grid of 100 incandescent light bulbs suspended in a space. Activated by a sensor, in the form of a metal sculpture, which is able to register the systolic and diastolic pulses of those who grasp it, the lights flicker in response to those present, mirroring the rhythm and intensity of each person's heartbeat. Each bulb displays an individual pulse. As new users contribute their own 'data', the display moves one place along the grid. Eventually, the space is filled with the intricate percussion of 100 different heartbeats, producing complex patterns of light.

As an interface, *Pulse Room* demonstrates a triangulation of individual agency, technological inscription and collective expression.

In doing so, I suggest, it constructs a 'situation' that is emblematic of key tensions constituting contemporary public space. What kind of public encounter, as an encounter with (human and non-human) *others*, does *Pulse Room* offer? At one level, individual participation is freely chosen. You enter the space and grasp the interface, and in this gesture you contribute to the work's ongoing elaboration in the company of those around you. Upon grasping the interface, people tend to look up expectantly, perhaps in the hope of seeing signs of their own unique 'self' revealed. On witnessing her pulse translated into light, one participant when the work was displayed at Pueblo in Mexico was moved to proclaim: 'I'm all heart.'

Yet 'participation' in *Pulse Room* depends entirely on the fact that all participants evince *involuntary* signs. Clutching the sensor, one cannot 'choose' how to respond: each response is *composed* by the relation between the individual's body and the protocols of the technical system. Even more than the name or the photograph, the heartbeat is the body's signature. If this was once understood as a sign of 'inner being', it is precisely the seemingly irrefutable connection between biology and identity which underpins the shift in contemporary surveillance techniques towards biometrics, as older identity markers such as photographs give way to newer data techniques of DNA samples, cornea scans, and the like. At the same time, new possibilities for evaluating the body – its deportment, movement, breathing, temperature, gesture, facial expression, etc. – are now being deployed widely, both in the context of contemporary art but also as part of the logic of the smart city.

What redeems *Pulse Room* from this surveillant logic is what it does with this composition of body and technical protocol. Even as it animates each body's 'secret name' into a visible sign, *Pulse Room* uses the biometric signature as the means by which distinct individuals are woven into a collective electronic tapestry. This is not about averaging responses into an overall unity, nor about establishing separate individual profiles. As much as the work is – literally – about *self*-expression, *Pulse Room* builds its individual offerings into a shifting, collective expression. In this temporary collective, the 'common' is not established at the expense of the uniqueness of each member. Instead, the temporary collective resembles what

Hardt and Negri (2004) evoke as *multitude*: a collectivity that draws on uniqueness and difference as the integral basis of any relation to others. Becoming 'part' of the work is central to the experience of the audience, which finds its own affirmation as a collective in the process.

Traces of urban encounter

In the 2006 project *Rider Spoke*, media arts collective Blast Theory invited audiences to explore the city on a bike, guided by an on-board media system developed by the artists.[14] Encouraged by a series of questions and prompts – requests to describe yourself, to find a particular type of place, to observe and comment on others, or to recount past experiences – the work provided a platform for recording experiences, and also 'eavesdropping' on recordings made by others. Part of what is distinctive about *Rider Spoke* is the fact that its ambulatory orientation allowed participants to access these recordings only in the places they were made and 'deposited'. The work forms what might be called a *participatory archive* – one made and retrieved by those inhabiting the public spaces of a particular city.

The capacity to provide information 'attached' to specific locales is one of the formative conditions of geomedia. The early 2000s saw an upsurge of geotagging practices, as artists led the exploration of locative media (Wilken 2012). In one of the more thoughtful accounts of this history, Malcolm McCullough (2013) contrasts what he calls digital 'urban mark-up' with a range of older place-based communication practices from stone carving and friezes to painted and electric signs. The difference, McCullough suggests, is largely a matter of their different temporalities. Earlier forms of mark-up were slower; they not only took more time to make, but, since they were 'hardwired' into specific configurations, they constituted more durable elements in the urban landscape. Digital urban mark-up changes this in a number of ways: while it depends on an underlying platform, individual inscriptions are quick, low-cost and reconfigurable. Moreover, since the results don't need to occupy the scarce bandwidth of a sign, billboard or building, digital mark-up favours multiplicity. Digital annotation of the city has the potential to offer a practical means for addressing the contested nature of urban space, enabling new processes of 'authoring', and providing different layers of 'content' that can be accessed at specific sites. McCullough notes: 'A new kind of information commons, different from those in electronic cyberspace, may be taking form at street level' (2013: 112).

There are now numerous examples of such initiatives. In the pioneering *Urban Tapestries* (2003–4) project conducted by the UK research collective Proboscis, mobile and Internet technologies were combined with geographic information systems to enable collective 'community authorship' of the local environment. The platform enabled the annotation of different sites with data layers consisting of stories, information, pictures, sounds and videos.[15] In the organizers' words, the ambition was 'to enable people as their own authors and agents, not merely as consumers of content provided to them by telecoms and media corporations. The project centres on a fundamental human desire to "map" and "mark" territory as part of belonging and of feeling a sense of ownership of our environment.' Another mapping project originating from this time was Christian Nold's *Biomapping* (2004) which used a customized wearable device to measure participants' 'emotional arousal' in conjunction with their geographical location.[16] Drawing inspiration from the Mass Observation Movement which began in late 1930s Britain, Nold argued: 'The result is that the wearer's journey becomes viewable as a visual track on a map, whose height indicates the level of physiological arousal at that particular moment' (2009: 4). Personal user-generated data could be aggregated to produce a 'communal emotion map' of a region. These kinds of initiatives foreshadowed the enormous popularity (especially in the UK) of the Open Street Map initiative.

Geolocated data can reconfigure public space in other ways. Billibellary's Walk (2013) is an assisted-walk 'app' for smart phones that attempts an imaginative recovery of the site occupied by the University of Melbourne (where I work) from the point of view of its traditional owners, the Wurundjeri people.[17] Drawing on the example set by art walks and cultural tourism to provide alternative spatial histories, Billibellary's Walk was designed primarily as a pedagogic tool. It re-narrates familiar university landmarks such as trees and buildings, while raising questions about the impact and legacy of European 'settlement': 'Lying within the University of Melbourne's built environment are the whispers and songs of the Wurundjeri people. As one of the clans of the Kulin Nation, the Wurundjeri people of the Woiwurrung language group have walked the grounds upon which the University now stands for more than 40,000 years.'

Stop four on the tour is the Baldwin Spencer building, named after the university's foundation Professor of Biology in 1887. Noting that Sir Walter Baldwin Spencer 'was highly esteemed for his anthropological and ethnographic work, in particular that which related to Aboriginal communities', Billibellary's Walk reminds walkers – staff, students and visitors – of the political force lines embedded in traditions of academic research. 'The Aboriginal community regards Sir Walter Baldwin Spencer's work as a misappropriation of Aboriginal culture and knowledge. Today, Aboriginal communities demand control of and participation in research related to their communities and ownership of their knowledge.'

The same lines of force that have shaped research traditions also inhabit the politics of place-naming as part of the struggle over what counts as 'history' and who gets to narrate it. These kinds of conflicts are all too common in settler societies such as Australia, which has long struggled to recognize the continuing occupation and inhabitation of the land by its diverse indigenous peoples. I'm not suggesting that Billibellary's Walk is a panacea to these entrenched problems. However, in a context where the City of Melbourne is yet to establish any permanent public monuments to the history of indigenous resistance to the process of European occupation, digital annotation offers a practical means of beginning to insert these stories into the public domain.[18] The flexibility of digital annotation, and its capacity to provide public access to relevant information in specific urban sites and situations, underpins

McCullough's observation that 'the design and cultural opportunities may rival those of any past era of technological change, such as
electrification a century ago' (2013: 112).

However, McCullough immediately adds a note of caution: 'The
cultural costs could well surpass those of other ages as well, even
those of the automobile to cities' (2013: 112). While McCullough
is referring mainly to the risk of information overload, we might
recall, in this light, Nold's account of his inundation with proposals
from marketers interested in his 'emotional cartography' research.
While Nold envisaged new mapping practices enabling locally
authored and attuned representations of urban space, in which the
'data' remained at the service of those who generated it, others
viewed the technology with a more avaricious eye.

> People who actually wore the device and tried it out while going
> for a walk and then saw their own personal emotion map visual-
> ised afterwards, were baffled and amazed. But their positive reactions
> hardly compared to the huge global newspaper and TV network atten-
> tion that followed the launch of the project. People approached me
> with a bewildering array of commercial applications: estate agents
> in California wanting an insight into the geographical distribution
> of desire, car companies wanting to look at drivers' stress, doctors
> trying to re-design their medical offices, as well as advertising agencies
> wanting to emotionally re-brand whole cities. (2009: 4)

Concerns raised by Frith (2012) over differential access, and what
I have described in chapter 2 as the growing *operationality* of the
digital archive, signal the unresolved tensions that threaten to over-
shadow 'digital urban mark-up' as a means of enhancing public
space. This underlines the importance of continuing to open up
spaces in which new practices of communication and experiences
of urban inhabitation might emerge. To better understand how art
might contribute to modelling an urban archive capable of constructing a different experience of public space, I want to return
to Blast Theory's *Rider Spoke*. While the bike riders were encouraged to undertake their journey alone and the prompts invited
personal reflection, the work doesn't simply seek to construct a

private world for each participant. Rather than using technology to erect a shield between each user and those around them, *Rider Spoke* deliberately sought to engage participants in encounters with strangers. However, in so far as these were *public* encounters, they were orchestrated in a distinctive way.

The work encouraged participants to explore their emotional and psychic terrain in the context of the physical terrain they occupied. The juxtaposition proved highly evocative for many, who recounted intimate and personal experiences. How do you respond to someone you (over)hear recounting an intimate experience, or to their making the admission that they feel lonely or vulnerable? Do you offer your own story or make your own personal confession? Do you just make something up? Like a number of artworks produced by Blast Theory, *Rider Spoke* could be said to be broadly concerned with the operation of trust and intimacy in the digital milieu. However, it does not depend on the sort of public strip-mining of intimacy that is the currency of so-called 'reality TV'. Instead, it is situated in a harder to define space, somewhere between personal reverie and the more impersonal domain of public civility. If this is akin to what Jacobs evoked as the 'web of public respect and trust' (1961: 56) that supports street life, the difference here is that none of the participants meet face to face.

If each story forms a donation of experience, it is a gift offered not to a particular listener, but to an anonymous future listener or community of listeners. The fact that you can hear a story only while standing in the same place in which the teller related it makes a difference. Because the story was contributed by a particular stranger who inhabits the city around you, it produces an experience of what might be called ambient intimacy. Corresponding neither to the face-to-face encounter of traditional public assembly, nor to the abstract identification of the national 'imagined community' orchestrated by modern mass media, here the public encounter is conjugated as a particular sociotechnical modality of 'being-with' defined by deferral and delay. Sociality is marked by the archival traces of those who have gone before and those who will follow after.

There is something both very new and very old about such a meshing of stories with places. The city has always been a manifold of times. Unlocking the utopian aspirations and revolutionary energies of this heterogeneous temporality was the key ambition of Benjamin's Arcades project. Could digital urban annotation play a similar role to what Benjamin evocatively described as film's 'dynamite of the 1/10th of a second'? Could it become a technique for unlocking the experience of what Peter Osborne (1994) calls 'social time'?[19] Urban annotation projects such as *Rider Spoke* are suggestive of the potential for participatory urban archives to reconfigure public space in terms more appropriate to the diversity of inhabitants, histories and temporalities that characterize contemporary city life. This potential runs counter to the dominant trajectory of the digital which Stiegler (2011) associates with the *synchronization* of contemporary society. Developing this more complex sense of urban life situates a key fault line in the future relation between geomedia and public space.

Art and the politics of sociotechnical encounter

I often ride to work through a large park in inner-city Melbourne. It's a slightly less direct route but more peaceful, as it gets me off the overcrowded roads. At one point, there is a narrow dirt trail about 50 metres long that I use to traverse between two paved paths. It's a small example of what architects call 'desire lines' – user-created pathways where formal ones don't exist, or don't fit preferred patterns of use. Desire lines exist in all cities, particularly in the kind of abandoned or undefined sites that Papastergiadis and Rogers (1996) have called 'parafunctional' spaces. What interests me about this particular path in this context is that it is a collectively made artefact shaping a public space. It is not finished or static but has evolved over time. As a eucalypt tree near one end has grown to obstruct the original path, riders gradually began to veer wider. For a time – over several months – there were two distinct paths. Now the original path has become a faint trace.

Both the formation of the path and the process of its realignment are worth considering in the context of what I'm calling 'participatory public space'. They offer a model of loose, self-organized, collective action undertaken by a dispersed group of actors who don't know each other personally and, in fact, have never met together in person. The path has come into being because different riders have decided to take the same shortcut. Over time the marks produced by the wheels of their bikes have 'communicated' the possibility of taking a different route to others, who in turn reinforce this orientation by riding it themselves. This process of *collective attunement* enabled the smooth adaptation of the path's trajectory in response to environmental change, namely the growth of the tree. No one was formally charged with making a decision about changing the path's alignment. Rather, different users acted over time, spurred by a desire to keep the route's amenity while respecting the growth of the tree.

It's the kind of simple action that occurs commonly, yet it shouldn't be passed over too quickly. Imagine the likely situation if this was a paved – and therefore fixed – path that needed modification. Once the problem of an obstruction was identified, someone would probably have been tasked with removing the offending branch. It's quite possible they would simply cut the whole tree down. Either way, it would likely have taken thousands of dollars to formulate, plan and complete the job. Instead, a better result has been achieved for free by a loosely coordinated, distributed form of collective public action.

What can such an example teach us about the relation between geomedia and the possibility of reconstructing public space as a more participatory domain? In so far as digital networks offer the potential for low-cost, distributed communication we might anticipate they would assist the ambition of constructing urban spaces that are amenable to enhanced forms of user modification and adaptation. Yet such potentials remain underdeveloped, submerged by agendas for urban optimization, commercialization and securitization. A change in settings is sorely needed.

Stevens (2007) concludes his book on 'ludic space' by arguing that urban planners need to reconsider their overly instrumental approaches to designing public spaces, and instead take the risk of building spaces whose purposes and intended uses remain loose and ambiguous. Lack of prescription is what allows for unanticipated future uses and possibilities to emerge. However, translating such design aspirations into planning practice faces a number of challenges. Colin Ward points to the general paradox of designing 'unfinished space', in which the ideal of leaving space open for elaboration by users comes into conflict with official demands for planning detail:

> As Don Ritson of Milton Keynes development corporation explained to me in 1978: 'We can't get planning permission, even in outline, without a clear statement of what is going to happen on the site, but if we specify what is to happen we are limiting in advance the aspirations of the people who we expect to settle there. And the whole idea is to give *them* freedom of choice.' (1999: 49)

The problem resembles a chicken and egg situation. Without the 'loose' public spaces that might facilitate rich social encounters, new modes of public behaviour may not emerge, or may be stillborn and stifled, channelled in all too predictable directions. And yet designing such spaces as a way of 'leading' changes in public culture is also risky. 'Participation' may remain what Siegfried Kracauer (1995) memorably defined as a *mass ornament*: a collective image that does not emerge *from* a community but remains 'hovering above' it, unable to be understood and thereby lived.

Might digital art in public space form a transitional zone for the emergence of new practices of public participation? What is most significant about the digital artworks I have described in this chapter is that they are not purely 'bottom-up' in the sense of emerging organically from a community, but nor are they simply 'top-down' initiatives with predefined forms and outcomes. While there can be a temptation to romanticize 'bottom-up' actions, history suggests that simply asking people to participate – to appropriate, to play, to re-design, to collectively plan – rarely works, or rarely works well enough. Faced with new 'freedom', many respond by reproducing what they already know, including the same hierarchies and models of social interaction. The artworks I have described seek to provide temporary spaces for the public elaboration of new modes of social experience, fostering encounters involving experimental relations to others and to complex technical systems.

What difference do such artistic interventions make? Bourriaud notes: 'Artistic activity, for its part, strives to achieve modest connections, open up (one or two) obstructed passages, and connect levels of reality kept apart from one another' (2002: 8). Small-scale interventions are often criticized precisely because they are small, and therefore 'change nothing'. This is particularly pointed in comparison to the logic of commercial digital technology, which is all about how to 'scale-up' to factors of millions and billions. However, modest interventions have their own logic. As Jeffrey Hou notes:

> each of these acts may seem small and insignificant. But, precisely because these acts do not require overburdening investment or infrastructure, they enable individuals and often small groups to effect changes in the otherwise hegemonic urban landscapes. Although the actions may be informal and erratic, they have helped destabilize the structure and relationships in the official public space, and release possibilities for new interactions, functions and meanings. (2010: 14–15)

By establishing temporary public situations, these open, relational digital artworks offer a means of building what Sennett termed the *social skills* needed for dwelling in contemporary cities. These skills don't simply rest with the artist – the 'expert' who 'delivers' them – or with the community (the audience) who 'consumes' them, but emerge through the process of public encounter in which experimental digital interfaces are deployed to stimulate curiosity towards, and preparedness to engage with, others. By constructing open-ended, participant-driven models of public behaviour, art can help enlarge our current stock of thinking about public space and public culture. The experience of acting together with others to alter the ambience of networked public space enables a different sense of possibility in relation to the city.

Umberto Eco (1989) long ago argued that art is not simply the less 'efficient' form of communication to which instrumental rationality has so often reduced it. Inverting the cybernetic postulate that construes information with the lowest noise-signal ratio as holding the highest level of meaning, Eco suggested that art should be regarded as a 'higher' form of communication precisely because of its capacity to engage with different, often incommensurable values, scales and systems. As Papastergiadis puts it:

> Art does not proceed as an investigative exposé followed by a judicious declaration of truth. It does not possess a fixed knowledge of things but rather develops a critical attitude towards the possibilities in and between things. Art begins in curiosity, the sensuous attraction towards difference and connection, and proceeds through a relational mode of thinking that serves simultaneously as an instrument for suspending the existing order of things and as a platform for imagining alternatives. Thus affects, thinking and practice are transformed through the action of carriage and connection. (2012: 13)

Art in public space favours what Rios (in Hou 2010) calls 'negotiative' appropriation. It can foster a more polyvalent understanding of public space, based on a mode of inhabitation that is capable of recognizing plural and competing claims without needing to pre-emptively adjudicate between them by allocating exclusive possession to one or the other. Digital public art points to some of the ways that geomedia might support negotiative modes of public encounter; ones that might be practised – that is to say, *lived* – by urban inhabitants.

4

Urban Screens and Urban Media Events

A new civic media?

In Ridley Scott's film *Blade Runner* (1982), the struggle for existence in the bombed-out cityscape of the future takes place under low-cruising airships skinned with giant video screens advertising the virtues of off-world life. Scott's film proved an influential trope for understanding the large video screen as it migrated from sci-fi to real life, casting it as invasive and propagandistic. To argue for the need to move beyond this characterization is not to dispute the commercial logic that drove, and still dominates, this field. Rather, it is to suggest that change will only occur when we explore the ways in which this communication infrastructure might be repurposed towards other headings. In this chapter, I argue that large screens situated in public space should be conceptualized as a particular facet of geomedia: as media platforms embedded in specific urban locales with distinctive potential to bridge different historical conceptions of the public sphere. Focusing on the emergence of what I call 'second-generation' screens, I want to consider the capacity for this communication infrastructure to contribute to the emergence of a new kind of public space.

Drawing on fieldwork carried out in the course of several collaborative research projects,[1] I will sketch out some possible pathways for constructing 'urban media events' that utilize large screens precisely in order to experiment with new ways of 'becoming public'. If my first aim is to question the naturalization of commercial screens as a default setting, I also want to shift the debate towards thinking about what is at stake in these alternatives. As I argued in chapter 1, a richer public culture – a culture of *public civility* capable of facilitating interactions between erstwhile strangers in a context of heightened cultural heterogeneity and global mobility – depends on imagining and exploring new experiences of being together with others in public. Alternative uses of urban screens help to recalibrate our sense of what it is possible to do with screen technology and with others, as participants in micropublics with shared matters of concern. However, to maximize this potential, change is needed on several fronts, linking innovation in site design and screen operation to institutional arrangements and public cultures of use.

Relocating the screen

The cultural and political force lines demarcating the spatial settlements characteristic of the broadcast era (described in chapter 1) meant that the appearance of electronic screens in the street in the mid-1970s was not only novel but anomalous: what was 'television' doing out on the street? A landmark was the erection of the Spectacolor Board on the old New York Times building at One Times Square in 1976. Spectacolor was, in fact, not a television screen but a programmable electronic sign using an array of incandescent bulbs to produce what now seem to be fairly rudimentary monocolor graphics (Brill 2002). Its key innovation was its capacity to display variable content and to produce dynamic graphic forms. As George Stonbely, the driving force behind Spectacolor, put it: 'We had the idea of creating a broadcast medium on a sign' (quoted in Gray 2000).

The success of the new medium in attracting keen interest from advertisers meant large electronic screens were first introduced into urban spaces with a history of innovative advertising displays, such as Times Square in Manhattan and Hachikō Crossing in Tokyo's Shinjuku. While advertising remains the major driver for the development of screens situated in public space, the use of the Spectacolor screen to display Jenny Holzer's iconic 'Truisms' series in 1982 underlines the fact that artists have been interested in repurposing this communication infrastructure even from its inception.

Large-screen technologies with improved visual capabilities were developed in the mid-1980s with the release of Sony's JumboTron and Mitsubishi's Diamond Vision, each based on a matrix of smaller Cathode Ray Tube (CRT) screens. An outdoor JumboTron measuring 82 x 131 feet was famously exhibited at the 'science city' of Tsukuba near Tokyo for *Expo 85* in 1985. CRT screens of this scale had significant limitations. They consumed power voraciously, were susceptible to malfunction and produced relatively limited visual capabilities, especially in daylight. They were also hugely expensive to purchase. Nevertheless, especially once they began to display video, they found a home in premium sporting venues, particularly in the United States where there was already an established market in electronic scoreboards.

Within a few years, these stadium screens began to be deployed for a new purpose: to enhance stadium-based live rock concerts. The shift to stadium venues, which had marked the maturation of rock music as a bankable industry in the 1970s, levied new demands on both performer and audience. How could you sustain an emotional connection with a mass audience when most were located a long distance from the stage? Tours such as the Rolling Stones' *Steel Wheels* (1989) and especially U2's *ZOO-TV* (1992–3), both designed by Mark Fisher, were critical in exploring new possibilities for using large video screens in conjunction with live rock concerts (see Seigal 2002: 78–89). As Bruce Ramus (long-term lighting designer for U2) later recalled:

Prior to that, video had been a peripheral part of large-scale rock concerts. It largely sat on the outskirts of the stage. *ZOO-TV* is when we took the screens and the imagery and moved it all to the centre of the stage. We made five large video walls and had about 200 televisions dotted around the set in groups of twos and threes, making one large, albeit fractured, canvas. The whole idea was a media barrage. (Ramus 2011)

Stadium screens were mainly designed to provide image magnification so that far-flung audiences were able to experience an otherwise unattainable level of 'intimacy' with the performers. By switching between close-up images of the performers on-stage and wide shots of the audience around it, screens enabled the stadium experience to develop into a new mode of mediated collective participation.[2] The intersection between large screens and the music industry in the 1990s remains significant in this context for two reasons. First, it helped to drive technical innovations in screen technology. While the screens used for early tours such as *ZOO-TV* were all CRT-based, by 1996 LED began to be viable as a platform for large-scale video display.[3] Second, stadium concerts incubated new ways of integrating screen technologies into live experience, establishing new parameters for the 'media event'.

The switch to LED-based screens fundamentally changed the utilization of large-scale screens in the city. Because they employ solid-state technology, LED screens have significant advantages in terms of energy efficiency, longevity and reliability over earlier screen technologies. Once LEDs developed sufficient brightness for effective daylight display they became even more attractive to advertisers (Vazquez 2002). Decreases in cost, combined with improvements in image quality and operating robustness, led to urban screens proliferating in cities around the world. High-profile street installations such as Fox and Fowles' 1999 Nasdaq building in Times Square (built using a Saco-made LED screen as a curved facade) alerted designers to the more flexible possibilities of 'media facades', and promoted a new wave of experimentation mixing architecture, lighting and screen design. As Bill Mitchell points out: 'the traditional distinctions between architectural lighting design and computer graphics are beginning to disappear. Anything that lights up can be treated as an addressable, programmable pixel' (2005: 88–9). Successor to the modernist glass curtain wall, contemporary media facades enable entire buildings to become screens. This has propelled architecture towards the design of what Paul Virilio (1998: 181) aptly terms 'media buildings': structures with the primary function of providing information rather than inhabitation.

Second-generation urban screens

While large screens situated in public space had been sporadically used for a range of non-commercial purposes such as displaying video art,[4] it wasn't until the early 2000s that screens intended *primarily* for purposes other than advertising or branding began to be deployed in urban spaces on a long-term basis. These 'second-generation' urban screens were distinguished from their predecessors in several respects:

1. They were deliberately situated in traditional pedestrian areas, such as squares in city centres, rather than in high traffic thoroughfares.
2. The screens were set lower to the ground and addressed spaces in which people could assemble.
3. The screen operators sought to deliver a broader range of programming including live events and cultural content.

Three models for supporting non-commercial urban screens emerged in the early 2000s.

Public space broadcasting

This model was exemplified by the 'Big Screen' network established in the UK. Inspired by the successful use of temporary

screens for the Queen's Golden Jubilee in 2002–3, the BBC initiated a pilot programme for the rollout of up to ten permanent
screens beginning with Manchester in 2003. The site, next to the
old Corn Exchange building in Exchange Square, had been rede-
veloped following the 1996 bomb blast, and provided a ready-made
amphitheatre capable of accommodating up to 10,000 people. The
project was distinctive in being driven by a publicly funded broad-
caster. This meant that, while the screen hardware was sponsored,
advertising was not permitted. However, while the screens were
intended to display a significant amount of BBC content, the
project was not completely controlled by the BBC. Rather, each
screen depended upon establishing partnerships between the BBC,
the relevant city council and a mix of various other partners such
as art galleries and universities. In Manchester a founding partner
was the publicly funded Cornerhouse art gallery, which saw the
screen as a potential outreach site for displaying contemporary art
to audiences who would not normally enter an art gallery. As Bill
Morris (then Director of BBC Live Events) put it:

> thirty years ago we could have run the screens entirely on our own.
> We would have paid for the whole thing ourselves via the licence
> fee and we would have said exactly what was going on them at any
> time of day or night and that would have been it, wouldn't it? That
> would have been the way the BBC would have done it. Now, you
> can argue that not only would that now be wrong, it just wouldn't
> be possible. You couldn't contemplate it now. [. . .] Thirty years ago
> it would have come through the BBC's marketing arm and it would
> have been run just with BBC content and we'd have run trailers all
> over the place and adverts with BBC on it. You certainly wouldn't
> have wanted to work with community projects, arts projects, run
> local events and things of that sort. So the approach that we've taken
> is, I think, just one small bit of evidence that the BBC has to work in
> that more porous way now and that it's a two-way street. (Gibbons
> and Morris 2005)

Following the success of the pilot project, responsibility for the nine
existing 'Big Screens' was transferred to the London Organizing

Committee for the Olympic Games (LOCOG) in 2008. While the BBC remained a key partner, LOCOG was seen as a more suitable vehicle for securing the capital funds needed for the next stage of the project. Plans were made to build up to fifty screens in different cities across the UK to support the ambitious 'live site' programme planned for the London Olympics in 2012. The screens were a key part of LOCOG's pitch to the IOC but would also form part of the urban 'legacy' of games-related expenditure.[5] This initial ambition was eventually scaled back as a result of funding constraints imposed after the financial crisis of 2009. The lead-up to the Olympics saw a number of changes in the design and programming of the screens, as LOCOG sought ways to contain costs by standardizing installation and making content management less resource intensive.[6] As a result, all the screens were formally integrated into a network, with operational control centralized in Birmingham. The BBC remained the core content provider, with key programming windows allocated to LOCOG. Local 'opt out' for specific programming slots was possible, but the default setting was a more broadcast-style model of programming.[7]

By the time of the Olympics in mid-2012, twenty-four permanent screens had been installed (plus a number of temporary portables). While the 'live sites' proved to be a popular and distinctive feature of the London Games, the network soon entered a third phase in its brief history. Faced with budget cuts, the BBC handed control of the screens to their various host cities in 2013. As I write, their long-term future remains uncertain. While this shift may move the UK screens closer to the 'civic partnership' model I discuss next, it is also likely to lead to growing commercialization – if not closure or sell-off – of the screens.

Civic partnership

The civic partnership model is exemplified by the 'Big Screen' at Melbourne's Federation Square, a popular public space in central Melbourne. Instead of being anchored by a national media organization, the screen is controlled and operated as part of the site, which is managed on behalf of the Victorian State Government by Fed Square Pty Ltd under a Civic and Cultural Charter.[8] This model presents different challenges and opportunities. While lacking access to the ready content that a national media anchor such as the BBC could provide, the fact that Fed Square has been forced to find screen content has arguably produced benefits in the longer term. It has not only led to the development of new partnerships with content producers, but has also acted as a catalyst for institutional change, as the organization has had to re-evaluate its understanding of the role of the screen over time.

Even more than most 'second-generation' screens, Federation Square is distinguished by close integration of screen and site. While it is situated near a busy central city intersection, the screen does not face the road, but faces back onto a gently sloping terrace. This paved, open space is ringed by a mix of cafés and public institutions, providing formal and informal modes of seating in what amounts to an amphitheatre capable of accommodating 10–15,000 people. This high degree of integration with the site as a whole was facilitated by the fact that the screen was not introduced into an already existing space, nor added at the last minute, but was part of the site design from an early stage.[9] It creates a distinctive ambiance that indexes the challenges facing a contemporary public space. As Bill Mitchell, doyen of MIT's Media Lab, noted: 'The focal point [of Fed Square] isn't a monument, a stage, or a podium to address the masses. It's a giant LED video screen – showing, when I was last there – tennis live from the Australian Open' (2005: 44).[10]

Mitchell argued that the relationship between screen and site offered a way of confronting 'boldly and mostly successfully – the problem of public space for a postcolonial, multicultural, electronically networked society' (2005: 44). However, such a conclusion was perhaps over-optimistic and premature. When the site first opened in 2002, the screen was treated primarily as a revenue-raising asset. This meant that, while it displayed occasional live events (such as the Australian Open witnessed by Mitchell), it largely showed a mix of commercial television programming and advertising. Despite the opportunities created by integrating an urban screen in the site, it risked suffering the fate of many commercial screens – becoming mere background noise in an overcrowded cityscape.

However, following a change of management in 2005, the approach to the screen was fundamentally rethought. Incoming CEO Kate Brennan recalled: 'It seemed to me in 2005 that although Fed Square was "wired within an inch of its life", that we weren't really doing anything with that capability' (2009: 127). In order to promote change, Brennan shifted the emphasis from revenue-raising to using the screen to engage diverse communities as part of the Civic and Cultural Charter. Brennan notes:

> we were really pushed into a situation in which we had to think about what was the most efficacious engagement with the broadest possible community: how we could make the screen work better for events, how could we use it creatively, and for information. It was important to me that this wasn't cluttered up by having advertisements on the screen for X or Y. (2009: 128)

She adds: 'it seemed to me that the most obvious thing that we could do with it was to tell more stories of the community that we were part of' (2009: 127).

The success of this change in policy led to a third phase of screen operation when Fed Square Pty Ltd brought all its media operations 'in-house' in 2010. This move reflects a growing recognition of the importance of media assets – particularly the big screen – to the identity and ambiance of the site. In contrast to the perception of electronic screens as symptomatic of the incipient *placelessness* of cities in a global era, Federation Square demonstrates the potential for a public screen to become a core element of a site that is popularly acclaimed as the 'heart' of Melbourne (Coslovich 2003). I will discuss the underpinnings of such a shift in more detail below. Here I simply want to note that this model, where the screen is controlled by a publicly funded body that also has a role in managing the public space in which it is situated, has proved so successful that a number of similar screens have been opened or planned in Australia and elsewhere.[11]

Art screen

A third model for supporting a second-generation urban screen is the 'art screen' model developed by the Contemporary Art Screen (CASZ) project in the Netherlands. CASZ was located in Zuidas, a new urban precinct bridging Schiphol airport and the centre of Amsterdam. It had the distinctive mandate to display contemporary video art for at least 80 per cent of its programme time. As its inaugural curator Jan Schuijren (2008) noted when it began operation after several years of planning:

> I will [. . .] never go as far as, for example, the FACT initiative in Liverpool or what is being done [. . .] at Federation Square, where programming is partly catered to the community. CASZ is not meant to be, and will never be, a community screen – it has been conceived as an arts stage. And that's a clear difference in our intention.

CASZ emerged from collaboration between the Virtueel Museum Zuidas, the Foundation for Art and Public Space, and the Zuidas district. Because the CASZ model was rooted in the art world, rather than the community or public media sectors, its content was primarily original commissions and programmes sourced from video and film festivals. Unlike Federation Square or the Public Space Broadcasting project in the UK, CASZ did not use the screen to support live events on-site, nor did it offer familiar public screen staples such as live sport. Instead, it treated the screen primarily as an opportunity to address audiences who would not normally enter an art gallery or view contemporary video art. Beyond their potential for broader access, urban screens produce a different set of display conditions to an art gallery. As Schuijren (2008) noted, the fact that the CASZ 'audience' was mostly office workers in surrounding buildings who encountered the screen on a daily basis offered both opportunities and constraints:

> The fact that we have this 'regular' audience, so to speak, means that we have to work for them. [. . .] If eighty percent of your possible audience is returning more than four days a week, you have to be

really careful what you ask from them. And, of course, you also have to carefully decide what you offer to them, and how you offer it to them. [. . .] That's also why this repetition is important and why it's so beautiful in itself to have the opportunity to have a regular audience. This audience that comes every week, every day of the week, time and time again, allows us to actually build something over time.

Schuijren's comments highlight the way that publicly situated screens create specific viewing situations that are deeply implicated in urban rhythms and routines. This is something I will return to below. But first, it is important to note CASZ's fate. The screen faced a number of challenges from the start. Initially conceived in the context of the Zuidas station (destined to become the main inter-city and international rail hub for Amsterdam), it was shifted from its planned location at the last minute. While the new site was not far away, it lacked the volume and diversified pedestrian flow of the original location. Moreover, although CASZ faced onto a plaza between two office buildings, the space offered little invitation for people to sit or assemble. This undermined the screen's capacity to become a focal point for public gathering, and meant that, while CASZ was unique in its commitment to displaying cutting-edge contemporary art, it often lacked an audience. Following a round of funding cuts that affected a number of digital and public space art initiatives in Amsterdam, the screen ceased operation in 2011 (Cnossen, Franssen and de Wilde 2015: 4). While this fate does not necessarily invalidate the art screen model, it does indicate its vulnerability in the absence of any formal alignment with an established arts institution.

The three models I have outlined above are not meant to be exhaustive, but they are indicative of the key challenges involved in establishing and operating urban screens as public communication infrastructure. It is notable that, even where screens are intended for public communication, they have frequently been built without adequate consideration of site. It has been even more common for public screens to be planned and built with little or no budget for content. This last issue seems particularly anomalous, since in many respects public screens are directly comparable to other public cultural facilities such as libraries and art galleries, which also combine demands for infrastructure spending with the need for operating funding. Yet, it has proven difficult to accommodate public screens within existing institutional and budgetary structures. One of the ambitions of the BBC pilot project was precisely to establish the case for treating public screens as *civic* infrastructure. As Bill Morris put it:

> We would like to think that this project is creating something that is a new bit of civic architecture a bit like a decent size city expects to have its art gallery, its culture, its swimming pool, its library – that we're in that kind of territory, rather than just creating another means of contacting target consumer groups. (Gibbons and Morris 2005)

This ambition remains a work in progress. Without significant 'champions', it seems that second-generation urban screens either don't get built in the first place, or struggle to be sustained as *public* screens in the long term.[12] I would also add that successful deployment of an urban screen demands sustained rethinking of both screen and public space. As I will argue in the next section, the full benefits of public screen infrastructure will not flow simply from relocating existing visual content so it can be viewed in a different place, but arise from strategies for facilitating new forms of public encounter.

Urban screens and the media event

Second-generation urban screens create a novel amalgam of media viewing space and social situation. Large screens can be distinguished from other common forms of media use in urban spaces (such as personal mobile devices) precisely by their *fixity* and their *collective* orientation. As fixed urban infrastructure, large screens are often encountered repetitively, which means they become place-markers. Unlike advertising billboards and dynamic signage, where the aim is to capture individual attention for just a few seconds, the fact that second-generation urban screens are deliberately situated in public spaces in which people can gather, assemble, pause and sit means they are able to deploy a wider range of content, including longer form programming. How, then, should we think about these combined affordances of public assembly and public display?

In some respects, this collective viewing experience might be compared to cinema, where a group of strangers also gather publicly to watch a particular programme. But there are signal differences. Unlike the cinema, viewers are not seated in a darkened auditorium in which attention is focused almost exclusively on the screen. Instead of the cinematic norm of sedentary and silent watchers, there are a wider range of mobilities, attractions and attentive behaviours, stretching from those who simply glance at the screen as they move through a space following their own agenda, to those who allow themselves to be arrested for a moment, to those who choose to sit and watch the screen for a time. This more diverse, ambulatory and distracted mode of viewing shares similarities with how audiences encounter contemporary video art in the context of the art gallery (McQuire and Radywyl 2010).

Collective reception was one of the key factors in Benjamin's (1999) appraisal of film's radical potential in comparison to traditional visual media such as painting. A similar argument can be mounted in relation to the distinctive capacity for second-generation urban screens to support new kinds of *urban media events* based on collective experiences of public witnessing. In contrast to the 'broadcast media event' defined by Dayan and Katz (1992) that I discussed in chapter 1, in which the form of consumption is the cellular model of home-based television viewing by individuals or small groups, the urban media event is defined by new forms of collective social encounter. This also situates its primary difference from the use of digital media to carve out personalized private spaces in the public domain (Habuchi 2005). Instead, public communication infrastructure is implicated in the emergence of new kinds of public routines and social practices, which are most visible in new forms of public celebration, commemoration and mourning.

In 2005, Mike Gibbons (then Chief Project Director of BBC Live Events) recalled the telecast of an England vs. Argentina football 'friendly' as a signal moment in his understanding of the social potential of public screens. Despite bleak weather, large crowds turned out to watch the match: 'there was this real feeling of why is there 8,000 people in Victoria Square in Birmingham and 10,000 people in Manchester and 10,000 in Leeds all standing there in the pouring rain?' (Gibbons and Morris 2005). By 2006, large screens had been integrated into the FIFA World Cup programme in Germany, supporting the 'Fan Fest' tourism initiative encouraging supporters who were unable to get tickets to the matches to 'participate' by watching them on a large screen. Crowds estimated at one million per day took up the offer. Perhaps more surprising were the large crowds that turned out in the pre-dawn winter on the other side of the world, as an estimated 16,000 people gathered in Melbourne's Federation Square to watch Australia play Croatia in the same tournament.

Use of large public screens to enable new forms of collective witnessing has become an established part of many large-scale sporting events, with formal 'public viewing areas' (PVAs) now planned and advertised in advance. During the London 2012 Olympics, the network of public screens was explicitly conceived as a focal point for public engagement around the UK. These 'live sites' shape the wider event in a number of ways. By encouraging more people to experience the event in public, they amplify its 'buzz', while the 'live sites' themselves become focal points for broader media coverage, with regular photographs and live crosses appearing in the media.[13] Perhaps most importantly, live sites also offer distinctive opportunities for people to engage in collective performances of national identity. Drawing on ethnographic fieldwork carried out during the 2010 FIFA World Cup and the London 2012 Olympics, Becker and Widholm argue that the PVAs supported a range of new social practices, 'expanding the possibilities for performative and increasingly mass-participatory consumption practices' (2014: 154).[14] Paying close attention to the relation between screen content and the design, control and decoration of different sites, they observed that the PVAs were utilized by different 'actors', including local residents displaying 'home' colours, tourists displaying the symbols of their own nation, and migrants who frequently displayed hybrid identities representing both place of birth and of residence. Perhaps most strikingly, Becker and Widholm note: 'People gave many reasons for coming to these PVAs (to gather with friends, meet new people, watch the games, soak up the atmosphere, cheer on the national team or simply "have fun"), but very few people explained their attendance as a second choice or a substitute for not being at a live venue' (2014: 154).

This sense that watching an event on a public screen is no longer a 'secondary' experience is significant, and forms one of the key thresholds separating the urban media event from the broadcast media event that Dayan and Katz (1992) analysed nearly a quarter of a century ago. There are several elements to this shift. One, as Philip Auslander noted in his study of live broadcasting, is a change in how we construct 'liveness' as an audio-visual rhetoric: 'The rhetoric of mediatization embedded in such devices as the instant replay, the "simulcast", and the close-up, at one time understood to be secondary elaborations of what was originally a live event, are now constitutive of the live event itself' (1999: 25).

This change in rhetoric is now grafted onto the elaboration of new social practices, as 'live broadcasting' can be distributed not just to the home but throughout public space. If, as Becker and Widholm (2014: 165) argue, the evaluation of the 'live site' as another modality of live experience indicates the naturalization of consumption of sport through the screen, it also demonstrates the extent to which the spread of situated, real-time communication practices that is the condition of geomedia is pushing us towards a new understanding of 'presence'.[15]

While live sport is the most common manifestation of the new urban media event, equally striking are gatherings that have taken place on occasions of mourning and commemoration. Reflecting on the first two years of the BBC pilot project, Bill Morris observed:

With the London bombings [in 2005] people – not just in London but in the other cities around the country – were gathering around the screens to watch what was going on. Now, in a few cases those will be people who will simply not have access to the news in any other way, they walk into the city and just want to find out what's going on. But in other cases you actually feel that you want to be with other people. When there was the three-minute silence that happened after the London bombings, maybe a week later, people gathered in quite large numbers at each of the screen sites to observe the silence. (Gibbons and Morris 2005)

When the public screen has itself become a focal point for public ritual, the collective witnessing it enables needs to be understood less as a substitute for an event that takes place elsewhere than as a node in the enactment of a *distributed event*. Morris further recalled:

In Liverpool there was a guy called Ken Bigley, a guy from the city who was out in Iraq who was murdered in a particularly gruesome way. They really took it to heart and they held a one-minute silence and there was a service and there were more people gathered in front of the screen in Liverpool than there were at the Cathedral. And to our astonishment, people were putting flowers at the bottom of the screen. Now this wasn't planned or our assumption at all. We've been constantly surprised and challenged by what people are doing. (Gibbons and Morris 2005)

Similarly, in Melbourne, when a service was held to commemorate the victims of the 2009 bushfires that ravaged the State of Victoria (resulting in 173 deaths), Kate Brennan (then CEO of Federation Square) noted:

Even though the Service was up the road at Rod Laver Arena and our site was full of the Sustainable Living Festival, we showed it up on the screen because a lot of people wanted us to. A relatively small number of people came to Fed Square expressly to watch that up on the screen. But when asked, the person being interviewed said: 'I wanted to be where everybody else was.' I think that drive is really strong in human beings. (Brennan 2009)

Communication and media technologies have long been implicated in the orchestration – and transformation – of different kinds of social rituals (Liebes and Curran 1998; Couldry 2012). When public screens can become important sites for the collective enactment of rituals of commemoration and mourning, both the nature of the public event and the processes of social encounter have changed. If 'being with others' is one of the founding attributes of public space, the incorporation of large-screen infrastructure into central city public spaces alters the dynamic of public gatherings. A threshold example occurred in Australia in February 2008 on the occasion of the 'National Apology to the Stolen Generations' delivered by then prime minister Kevin Rudd.[16] This historical event saw Parliament House in Canberra packed with invited visitors, overflowing into indoor and outdoor viewing areas. National public service broadcasters as well as commercial radio and television stations around the country carried the speeches live from Parliament. This meant that almost anyone who wanted to could watch or listen from their home. Nevertheless, many people wanted to watch in public. In Melbourne, an estimated 10,000 people gathered to watch the telecast at Federation Square.

It is worth underlining the extent to which this turnout was unexpected at the time. Brennan (2009) recalls:

> In the lead up to the National Apology, we clearly intended to take that content. But we had no sense, really genuine sense, that the community at large would come down here in the numbers that they did to watch it on the screen. That time was an extraordinary human experience. But from the point of view of what role does Fed Square play in that life of the community, it was a great learning experience for us, and it was said to me that people do have a huge expectation of how the public realm works for them, and that we better get really good at finding ways to be responsive to that.

The fact that people could experience the National Apology while gathered together at Federation Square proved transformative in a number of ways. The Apology was an intensely moving occasion and many tears were shed. Even Aboriginal activists and others who remained sceptical as to the depth of the government's commitment acknowledged the genuine outpouring of emotion that the occasion generated.[17] The presence of a large screen capable of showing the event live in a central city public space not only allowed people to collectively experience the occasion, but provided them with an effective mechanism to participate in its construction. When the then leader of the Federal Opposition, Dr Brendan Nelson, made his reply to the prime minister's speech, offering a partial justification for past policies, many people in Federation Square turned their back on his image in order to express their disapproval. This performative gesture provided a dramatic image that suited the agenda of television news, and shots of the crowd turning away from the screen were soon incorporated into various news bulletins. By enabling such a visible and public response to Nelson's speech, the presence of the large screen in Federation Square effectively shifted the parameters of the event: it provided a feedback mechanism through which the 'audience' watching the event could become 'performers' participating in its elaboration. The 'Apology' offered a striking example of the potential for publicly situated urban screens to facilitate the appropriation of urban time and space by a city's inhabitants, enabling the viewing of remote events, but also supporting new forms of public expression as part of this experience of collective witnessing.

Large screens and transnational public communication

By 2008, it was increasingly clear that public screens no longer needed to be limited to a display-only format, but could be opened to new forms of content. Federation Square had developed a system for on-screen display of text messages, while in the UK experiments with cameras and motion sensors suggested new opportunities for public participation in shaping screen content.[18] Paralleling this heightened interest in enabling public participation to influence screen content, growth in broadband capacity meant that there was a new potential to link screens located in different sites without having to build dedicated links. These two trajectories framed the key questions of the research some colleagues and I initiated at that time: How could members of the public collectively shape the content displayed on a large screen? What would happen if the field of interaction was expanded by linking screens in different cities or even different countries?[19]

The project employed a mode of action research to explore the contours of 'transnational public space'. In other words, rather than waiting for relevant events to occur so that we could study them, we sought to initiate them (see Benford and Giannachi 2011: 8–20). To this end, the project involved commissioning artists to produce specific interactive content for simultaneous display on large screens in Melbourne and Seoul. The choice of a Korean partner reflected the new spatio-temporal contours of the digital planet: Seoul is 'closer' to Melbourne, in terms of time difference, than are some parts of Australia. By conceptualizing the urban screen as a communication platform that is *both* locally situated *and* transnationally connected, we sought to establish a frame for the creative exploration of new experiences of public communication defined by the intertwining of mediation and immediacy.

The first 'urban media event' took place in August 2009, on the occasion of the opening of 'Tomorrow City', part of a new urban precinct in Songdo, Incheon.[20] *Come Join Us Mr Orwell* involved a combination of live camera links between the two cities, screenings of artists' videos, and live performance. It also included two interactive works commissioned as part of the research project. Both used text messaging (popularly known as SMS in Australia at that time) as the interface to the large screens. *SMS_Origins* was created by Australian artists Leon Cmielewski and Josephine Starrs, in collaboration with programmer Adam Hinshaw. Participants were invited to text the details of their birthplace and that of their parents to a phone number displayed on the screen. This information was then translated by the software into vectors connecting the different cities on a world map shown on the screen. Inputs from multiple participants could be queued, while each new input was shown in close-up as it was mapped. The screen then reverts to a wide shot showing the world map with all inputs received so far. The graphic quality is deliberately simple: emphasis is on the process of active audience input rather than allowing users a rich palette for creative forms of personal expression. When the work operated, it enabled people located in the different cities to see the dynamic evolution of a single map reflecting the collective input of those gathered at each site.

The second work, *Value@Tomorrow City*, created by Korean artist Seung Joon Choi, used the screen in the manner of a public bulletin board. Audiences were asked to respond to the question: 'As a member of the future city, what do you think is the most important value?' When texts were sent, the 'values' appeared on the screen as key words in both Korean and English. If the words sent by one person were identical or similar to those used by others, the size and position of the display changed. By using the 'folksonomy' of user-tagging as the basis for the visual display, the content was responsive to user-input but also subject to a degree of self-organization.

Many lessons were learnt from this 'proof of concept' event. Getting it to happen at all involved significant challenges and compromises. Because the occasion had to run according to a strict schedule, the mode of interaction with the screen had to be more tightly defined than we might otherwise have chosen. The fact that linking screens for interactive art had not been previously attempted meant that numerous technical constraints had to be resolved, even on the night.[21] Fitting a socially oriented art project into the confines of Songdo's smart-city agenda carried its own problems. However, in this context, I want to focus on the implications of the event for thinking about the potential of large screens as public communication infrastructure. The first point to underline is the fundamental role played by choice of interface in shaping participant experience. As Drucker (2011: 12) notes, an interface is not a 'thing' but a nexus of relations that shape embodied spatial practices. A key reason for choosing the mobile phone as the primary interface to the screen was its wide availability in both Australia and Korea in 2009. Using the phone also imposed a low threshold for public involvement: texting is an everyday activity that does not involve any action that might single an individual out from the crowd in a potentially embarrassing way. The choice proved successful in maximizing public participation in shaping screen content.[22] But it also involved trade-offs. Foremost was the relatively limited options offered to participants, resulting in 'content' that is best described as user-influenced rather than user-generated. Another concern was the fact that, because texting is so inconspicuous, there was little capacity for the audience to 'snowball' by learning through observation of the behaviour of others (Brignull and Rogers 2003; Memarovic et al. 2012). In fact, this problem was not evident at the initial *Come Join Us Mr Orwell* event, which was facilitated by MCs in both cities. However, when we ran *SMS_Origins* in a more 'ambient' mode in Melbourne over the next few months, we found that providing on-screen instructions about how to participate was often insufficient. Once the project was explained to them, people would take part, often enthusiastically. However, left to their own devices, the platform would often remain unused. This lack of engagement was instructive, suggesting that beneath the surface of 'participatory culture' lies a deeper stratum in which public communication infrastructure remains out of reach, defined by a default setting of *display only*. On reflection, this is not surprising: it mirrors the dominant history of communication in public spaces of the modern city. Because most people had little or no experience of using this kind of public communication infrastructure, they were not 'primed' to explore its opportunities.

The second point I want to emphasize here is the way that the design of both artworks deliberately sought to engender collective expression without completely submerging the specificity of individual inputs. In *SMS_Origins*, this was achieved by queuing texts and highlighting the location that was 'currently mapping'. In *Value*, each user contribution was tagged with the last digits of the sender's mobile phone number. While this may seem a small point, observation confirmed how important it was for participants to recognize their own contribution to the evolving work. People inevitably waited to see their own contribution come on screen, and when they recognized it, they marked its appearance by pointing, clapping and even photographing themselves in front of it. This kind of response highlights the potential for second-generation urban screens to meet what is currently a largely unmet desire: to enable members of the public to *make their own mark* in the city centre. Too often, the scale and impermeability of the contemporary city communicates a simple overarching message to its inhabitants: you are small and insignificant, this terrain belongs to the state or the corporation and is beyond your reach. Being able to make a personal mark in a central city public space, even temporarily, constitutes an important index of contemporary social and political visibility.

As important as enabling individual expression, of equal significance is the fact that the works were designed so that individual marks were not simply left as isolated forms of self-expression. Instead, in common with some of the participatory artworks discussed in the previous chapter, these works used the iterative capacities of digital media to generate dynamic and evolving forms, or, more precisely, *networks of responses*, generated by those gathered in each city. If this orientation resembles what Kester (2004) has called a 'dialogic' model of art, in which the aim is to balance self-expression with collective and social expression, it also underlines the extent to which contemporary art practice – if not our broader sociality – is now caught up with so-called 'technical' issues: questions of interface and software design, of networks, devices and proprietary systems. 'Algorithmic' politics increasingly extends to the orchestration of social encounters in public space.

The third point I want to underline here stems from the relatively novel experience of using publicly situated large screens to 'connect' with multiple others. Comments made by many of those interviewed revealed how people in both cities were reaching to find words to describe a new kind of experience of 'being together' while also *not* being together.[23] While this paradoxical state of being has a longer history, stretching at least back to the first electronic communications in the late nineteenth century, it is worth reiterating the extent to which this urban media event decentred a range of more familiar experiences. Unlike the experience of watching an event 'live' on television while at home, the participants were part of a crowd assembled in central city public spaces, able to communicate with each other using embodied mannerisms (voice, gesture, movement, proximity, touch), while also communicating via the screen with others gathered in another city. This transnational dimension utilized a screen-based application that was not only responsive to multiple user-inputs, but was deliberately configured to display the collective responses from the micro-publics gathered in each territory. In other words, as a *public* occasion, the urban media event was designed to invite reflection on the nature of 'meeting' with others at a moment marked by global dispersion and the deployment of technologies supporting new forms of social connection.

One last point is worth making here. The nature of such works – designed, as Rafael Lozano-Hemmer puts it, as 'platforms for participation' – is that their outcomes are dependent on the specific audiences present. As 'open works', there is a high degree of contingency to each manifestation of the work. When we ran *SMS_Origins* in Melbourne shortly prior to the Australian rules football Grand Final in 2009 – arguably Melbourne's premier annual sporting event, watched 'live' by thousands on the big screen at Federation Square – we found the crowd not only indifferent but almost hostile. Clearly, the work did not fit the occasion. However, when the same work was presented at exactly the same site several weeks later, in the context of a university graduation ceremony held in a nearby venue, it was enthusiastically embraced. The graduation was attended by a large number of international students and their parents, and the capacity to publicly display family 'origins' at such a moment constituted a source of significant pleasure and immense pride to many, who photographed themselves in front of the screen as their own details were 'mapped' onto the display.

This last example situates a critical point that those concerned with programming large screens have noted: as much as they can be effectively used to relay remote content, successful screens need to respond to local context. The graduation example also underlines the *political* nature of any intervention into public space. In 2009, the political climate in Australia was marked by highly acrimonious debates over refugees and border security, resulting in a partial retreat from previously bipartisan political support for an official policy of multiculturalism. Creating the capacity for public visualization of data about place of origin constituted a very public reminder of the diversity of Melbourne's population, where more than half of the residents were either born overseas, or have at least one parent born overseas.

Following *Come Join Us Mr Orwell*, we began planning a second 'urban media event'. Moving away from language-based communication in order to better foreground the embodied dimension of public space interaction, a deliberate choice was made to use dance as the primary form of communication. While we recognized that this would significantly raise the threshold that people had to cross in order to take part, we wanted to explore the potential for embodied interaction to provide rich modes of cross-cultural exchange. Leading Australian choreographer Rebecca Hilton was commissioned to propose a concept, which was subsequently developed in collaboration with Korean choreographer Park Soon-Ho. The basic idea underpinning what became the *Hello* event in 2010 was a dance game, in which participants would teach each other simple movement sequences using screens situated in Federation Square, Melbourne, and outside Arko Art Theatre in Seoul. Realizing this concept entailed addressing a series of practical issues: How would the dances be created? How would screen connectivity be supported? How would the public spaces in which dancing and teaching took place be configured? In the process of addressing these and other questions, the parameters of the initial concept were refined as it evolved through a number of stages.

One of our starting points was the desire to engage 'contingent publics', meaning whoever happened to be near the screen at the time. Since the aim was to instigate and support open processes of communication between strangers, any 'dance' had to be easy to learn. At the same time, it was important that the dances had meaning for the participants and could form the basis for a process of communicating across cultures. In order to develop the dance sequences, the choreographers began by working with groups of young people in each city.[24] Workshops were run in which participants were invited to 'donate' their own dance moves to the project. Movements were improvised in response to a series of questions, such as: 'How would you describe Australia/Korea in one movement?' 'What's your favourite dance move?' 'How are you feeling right now?' 'What is a movement for happiness?' and 'How would you say "Hello" to someone who does not speak your language?' The two choreographers then distilled movements drawn from this collective pool into simple two-minute repertoires.

In terms of screen connectivity, a decision was made to utilize Skype rather than employ a managed service.[25] There were a number of reasons for this, but the main one was our desire to design an event that was 'light' and repeatable. This was related to our interest in using *Hello* in a more 'ambient' mode, where the connected screens might simply be left open to be used by whoever turned up. Cheap connectivity could have helped realize this ambition, but as it turned out other set-up costs limited the event to a one-off. As discussion about the event proceeded further, our Korean partners expressed their concern that 'Koreans won't dance in public'. In fact, this fear proved unfounded, but it did lead to the formative decision to build 'tents', forming designated 'interaction zones' (Fatah gen Schieck et al. 2013) in which the dancing would take place.[26]

These decisions all combined to lend *Hello* a particular feel. Participants in each city entered the tent and found themselves face-to-face with a life-size projected image of their collaborator(s). They would greet each other, usually by waving or bowing, and then one participant would demonstrate the dance while the other followed. They would then perform the movements a second time together. Following this, the 'teacher' would leave. When another participant entered in their place, the roles switched, and the learner became the teacher, teaching the dance to the next person. While the tents provided a semi-private space for teaching the dance, the whole process was broadcast on the large screens in both cities.

This combination of semi-private and public performance gave *Hello* a distinctive quality in which the different roles of teacher/learner and spectator/performer achieved a high level of fluidity. Participants reported experiencing intense one-on-one engagement with their particular dance partners, but also reflected on the experience of watching themselves (and others) in public on the large screen. Beyond the mere fact of getting people to 'join in', we were interested in how members of the public in both cities might use the networked screens to engage in spontaneous non-verbal forms of communication. 'Success' was not to be defined by accurate reproduction through transmission of the same gestures, but by the process of mutual exchange. We anticipated an itera-tive process in which the dance was transformed and mutated, in the manner of a game of 'Chinese whispers', although this was not mandated. In fact, many participants did pride themselves on the accuracy of their rendition, or worried that it lacked verisimilitude, while others acknowledged deliberately improvising.

Performing in public is a complex phenomenon that has been profoundly transformed by the growth of modern media cultures. As opportunities for appearing on screen have grown, there has been a dramatic evolution in how people compose themselves in these circumstances. Long gone is the once common reticence, and even embarrassment, at being 'caught' on camera at public events. Crowds, particularly at sporting events, are now accustomed to becoming part of the show, and many spectators have developed a repertoire – a means of producing a suitable public face – to perform when they are selected to appear on camera. In the same manner that sports professionals now rehearse their celebrations for victory or after scoring a goal, contemporary audiences are all too aware of the possibility of being filmed, and prepare themselves accordingly. An off-shoot of this situation is that, for a number of years in Federation Square, daily sessions have been run in which the large screen displays a live feed from an on-site camera. While many people pass by unaware that they are 'on screen', others not only notice but self-consciously perform *for* the screen. This behaviour frequently includes taking photographs of themselves in front of their image on screen. Some (mostly children and teenag-ers) actively seek out the camera, and work out how to position themselves so that a close-up of their face dominates the entire screen. If these responses reflect the particular novelty of seeing yourself on a large-scale screen in the city centre, they also owe much to the strong association of screen visibility with celebrity and power. As Frohne (2008) notes, screen visibility should not be regarded as a superficial rite of passage but constitutes an important mark of contemporary subjectivity in the present.

Placing *Hello* in this broader historical context is instructive. Anticipating that the presence of cameras would likely alter behaviour, we deliberately designed *Hello* so that it would be harder for participants to deploy familiar repertoires of performance. For one thing, the design of the event did not conform to the more established roles and expectations that frame participation in televised sport or in live music. We also deliberately undertook only minimal pre-event advertising, precisely so we could engage people who had few expectations about what was happening. The uncertainty as to what was expected was evident in a number of audience responses, from people worried if they were doing it 'right' to those who expressed concern as to how they would be seen by others. Comments included 'Difficult, hard to copy, didn't know what gestures to do' and 'worried about the judgement of others'. However, more evident than such concern was the palpable sense of enjoyment that most participants experienced. Laughter and smiles were the most common expressions, and far more people commented on the novel sense of 'connection' generated between participants in different cities: 'It's really amazing that those Australians were watching me and dancing and were learning from me'; 'Really nice . . . like there was a connection'; 'We used a body language. That's why we felt a sense of closeness even though we don't speak the same language'; 'We communicate with each other through the screen without actually talking to each other'; 'Without verbal communication, we communicate through bodily movements'; 'Enjoyed teaching the dance more'; 'After today's experience, I now feel like I can do anything!'

What might we make of such comments? While the encounters they describe are small in scale, they are rich in suggestiveness about how public screens might incubate new protocols of cultural exchange that include elements of intimacy and playfulness, without being based on personal knowledge of the other. Instead, 'communication' emerges from the improvised responses between strangers who are engaged in the spontaneous elaboration of a collaborative dance.

Before drawing out the deeper significance of affective communication in the public sphere, the final urban media event I want to describe here is the *Australia-Korea Dance Battle* held towards the end of 2012. The aim was to develop an event focusing on young people, given that they are frequently marginal and marginalized actors in public space. Starting out with a minimalist concept that involved simply illuminating a segment of public space to provide a 'stage' that random members of the public might occupy, the event eventually grew into a more formalized hip-hop 'battle'. This evolution was shaped by the confluence of several factors. Feedback from Korean participants after *Hello* revealed that many of them would have liked a higher quality image so they could see the face and hands of their dance partner more clearly. To achieve this higher resolution meant replacing the cheaper connectivity of Skype with a managed service.[27] Second, a new screen had opened at Northbridge in Perth, giving us the opportunity to experiment with linking three cities. However, this demanded using better vision-switching capabilities. As the event grew to include sound systems, DJs and MCs, resource constraints pushed us back towards a 'one-off' event mode. The final design involved a series of demonstration performances by dance crews in each of the cities, as well as public dance classes and open stage freestyle dance sessions.

Featuring invited performances from selected dancers (even 'amateurs') inevitably imposed a higher threshold for broad public engagement. Since for most people it is far harder to stand up and dance in public than to participate by sending a text message to a screen, this event consequently placed greater emphasis on spectating. An added factor was that the *Dance Battle* coincided with the global popularity of Psy's Gangnam Style which meant that the event received considerable media publicity. As a result, it was attended by much larger audiences than for previous events: in Melbourne, the crowds were in the thousands, while there were hundreds in each of Seoul and Perth. For all these reasons, the event ended up being far more structured in terms of public participation than either of the previous two.

In this context, I'll make two observations. First, precisely because it took place in central city public spaces, the *Dance Battle* attracted a diverse audience. This was not just about the mix of cultural and ethnic backgrounds (which is common, particularly in Melbourne), but about the capacity of the locations to solicit spontaneous onlookers. Many people who would never deliberately choose to listen to hip-hop, or go and watch hip-hop dance crews in action, encountered the event by accident. Quite a few stayed on to watch, and even to join in. The second point relates to the timeframe of the event. Because it ran for over three hours, the *Dance Battle* assumed the loose ambiance of a street festival or carnival. Not only the performers on stage and screen, but the publics surrounding them became part of the show. Even with the need to coordinate crosses between multiple screens and stages, there was still the capacity for people to move fairly freely between the roles of audience and performer. In fact, it was often younger people – children and teenagers – who had the confidence to do this.

While the *Dance Battle* was not unique in facilitating this kind of appropriation of public space, it was distinctive in using networked large screens to orchestrate a social encounter based on dancing in public with both immediate and mediated others. This situates an important liminal quality of the contemporary 'urban media event'. In the networked public spaces enabled by second-generation urban screens, the 'rules of engagement' are not yet settled. Events of this type invite public experience of – and reflection on – how new forms of social encounter and interaction might be practised and negotiated. Instead of the default assumption that public space communication is to be bought and sold, they alert us to the possibilities of participatory cultural experiences linking erstwhile strangers occupying public spaces in different cities around the world. Along such uncertain paths, a new public culture born of different choreographies and exchanges with others (human and non-human) might begin to be elaborated.

Large screens as platforms for public communication

In concluding this chapter, I want to focus on some of the deeper implications of large screens as public communication infrastructure. Writing in 1957, Guy Debord noted the potential for alternative uses of telecommunications to construct new types of urban situation: 'One can envisage, for example, televised images of certain aspects of one situation being communicated live to people taking part in another situation somewhere else, thereby producing modifications and interferences between the two' (in Knabb 2006: 41).

The recent emergence of second-generation urban screens prompts us not only to ask why the communication infrastructure of contemporary cities remains so dominated by commercial forms, but to consider possible alternatives. Exploratory uses of large screens to produce urban media events suggest new pathways along which temporary micro-publics can be formed. They signal new possibilities for appropriating public space through distinctive forms of celebration, commemoration, protest and play. They indicate a strategic capacity for public communication infrastructure to assist in 'opening up' public space to crowd-influenced ambiances, facilitating forms of loose, unfinished or incomplete urbanism. They also suggest ways that public exchange might reach beyond national borders without necessarily assuming abstract forms or subsuming local differences. The examples I have discussed above, including the modest initiatives of our research project, demonstrate a broad public appetite for the 'interferences' produced by such new experiences of 'being with others'.

This is not to suggest that large screens offer some kind of universal panacea for enhancing public participation and urban engagement. Large screens remain challenging as platforms for public communication. It proved difficult to realize our research project's initial aim of producing low-key, ambient events: while technically and aesthetically possible, such events did not easily fit the institutional imperatives of our partners, who wanted more certainty about audience involvement and outcomes. One of the operative factors here is the fact that large screens in central city locations remain relatively high-cost infrastructure. The very centrality that makes these screens symbolically powerful militates against lighter, more supple uses. Moreover, while they enable collective public reception, large screens are subject to obvious capacity constraints. Not everyone gets to program the screen, or to display their own content. The history of screens in public space demonstrates that public visibility does not necessarily mean that screens are available to be used *by* a broad public. Nevertheless, it is evident that publicly situated screens can be used in more open ways than they often have been in the past.

Siting a screen is important. Where a screen is placed, and how it is integrated with the surrounding space and structures, make a huge difference to how it 'speaks' to the public, or provides a platform for people to communicate with each other. The all too common approach of placing screens high up on skyscrapers maximizes the visibility needed for branding, but cannot support the more complex, embodied modes of communication I have been discussing. As Brian Holmes (2012) observed:

> In Shanghai and other large Chinese cities, entire buildings turn into screens at night. It's mainly advertising, sometimes state propaganda. Self-consciousness is dwarfed as the sensorium is overcome by the power to program the visual experience of the city. An impressive and sobering experience of the screen.

Nor is the 'integration' of screen with site simply a technical issue that can be confined to creating an effective media facade at the scale of a building (Schoch 2006; Hausler 2009). Rather, it demands thinking about how a specific site might work as a whole in the context of geomedia. There is still much to be learnt here, and this task signals the need for new coalitions of architects and urban planners, media producers, artists, technology specialists and interaction designers, as well as – most importantly – different publics.

What would a public space be like if it housed a 'plug and play' urban screen where anyone could simply turn up and show their own content? Like the forms of open access provided in their different ways by a speaker's corner or an Internet forum, such an ambition immediately raises many practical challenges. How should sexually explicit or politically contentious content be moderated? Who would choose the sequence in which content appeared? The point of my speculative question is not to imply the immediate practicality of providing free access to public screens, but to argue that any such development will only become possible through the maturation of a public 'culture of use' that provides a mix of formal and informal protocols for peer-based content generation, curation and reception.[28] The cultural growth needed to consolidate such models of collaboratively produced public space will not drop from the sky, but will only emerge from practice and experimentation. However, this emergence will remain still-born as long as public communication remains in thrall to the current, read-only model of commercial communication, where the market decides which messages are seen and heard on the streets of a city.

The full historical significance of second-generation urban screens can be appreciated if we locate them precisely at the crossroads of two conceptions of the public sphere that have dominated our understanding. On the one hand, the classical public sphere was conceived as rooted in physical spaces such as the agora, the plaza, the square and the street, up to and including Habermas' (1989: 33–4) coffee houses as a key site for the emergence of the 'bourgeois' political public sphere in the eighteenth century. On the other hand, this classical public sphere was precisely what was progressively displaced by the rise of 'media', including the industrialization of the press but particularly the institutionalization of broadcast television, which, for Habermas, becomes the primary institution of the public sphere in the second half of the twentieth century.

By bringing the real-time remote witnessing enabled by electronic media back into public space as a collective and embodied experience, second-generation urban screens contribute to the emergence of a new kind of public sphere in which key elements of both earlier modes are redeployed in distinctive ways. In contrast to the abstract 'global public sphere' instituted by global satellite television, second-generation urban screens conjoin the older logic of public assembly with the newer logic of the 'media event', crystallizing in the new *composition* I have called the 'public media event'. In such urban media events, the 'openness' of place described by Massey (1994) is foregrounded, as embodied and situated social interactions combine with and shape media practices that can assume global extension. In this respect, second-generation urban screens form a key site for what Sassen (2011c) calls the *urbanization* of digital technology, in which the process of 'mediation' is shaped by situated social practice, while the logic of social encounter is reconfigured by experimental deployments of 'real-time' connectivity.

The embodied-connected micro-publics initiated by urban media events also offer an as yet largely unrealized potential for incubating new kinds of *cosmopolitan* experiences, supporting spontaneous interactions between strangers in different cities and countries. One of the key lessons from our experiments in constructing a 'transnational public space' using networked urban screens is that such platforms are not exclusively – or even primarily – suited to the kind of rational-critical debate that Habermas placed as the cornerstone of his concept of the political public sphere. As Butler (2011) emphasizes, being in public is always an embodied relation of being-with-others. Urban media events such as *Hello*, with their distinctive combination of embodied interaction, remote witnessing and distributed public display, highlight the importance of *affective* relations to the contours of the contemporary public sphere. Affect here defines a mode of embodied experience, in which an improvised and spontaneous encounter with an other can become the basis for producing an emotional ambiance but also for learning a new type of social skill: the cooperative dynamic that Sennett describes as public civility. Such civility is not a function of 'intimacy' but belongs to a sharing of experience. It is enacted through the negotiation of protocols that are fully controlled by no one, but emerge in their mutual elaboration (for instance, as a game, a dance, a story, a relation to a place or a system). Developing forms of civility across transnational spaces involves establishing ongoing processes of *cultural translation*

(Barikin et al. 2014). Cultural translation is something that is constantly taking place in contemporary global society, with more or less generosity, sensitivity and success. In order to 'work', cultural translation depends on a willingness to recognize the other in their difference, while acknowledging the incompleteness of all such recognition. But it equally depends on a willingness to explore the common – what we share in and through our differences – while acknowledging the fictive and unstable nature of all such assertions of commonality.

If public civility has never been a stable body of rules and etiquette, its instability has clearly been accentuated by the global milieu of networked capitalism. Amidst widespread concerns about the future of public culture and the 'disappearance' of public space, the role of 'the media' in reconfiguring earlier forms of public interaction has too often been reduced to a simple logic of substitution or replacement. In contrast, I am suggesting that it is precisely in the new public spaces, such as those formed by second-generation urban screens, that some of the possibilities and tensions accruing around social encounters in the context of global society can begin to be addressed.

What are the limits of 'here' when I am continually linked to the 'now' of other places? How are personal and collective identities, and the complex process Stiegler terms 'individuation', transformed by new experiences of public connectivity and remote witnessing? If public space in the twenty-first century is likely to routinely include a transnational dimension constituted precisely through the intersection of earlier modes of spatializing the public sphere, critical analysis of this nexus will be a key site for exploring how the right to the city can be exercised in the future. Such experiences may yet prove critical to seeding the kinds of post-national solidarities that Stiegler has argued are necessary for moving beyond the current global impasse of 'decadence'.

5

Recomposing Public Space

In one of the most famous statements concerning the limits to the size of the classical city-state, Aristotle argues that over-extension of urban boundaries would render governance problematic: 'For who can be the general of such a vast multitude, or who the herald, unless he have the voice of a Stentor?' (1984: 2105). Such a statement should be read here less as an accurate summation of classical politics than of the gulf separating its founding assumptions from the present. This is not only a matter of exponential growth in urban scale, but also of the new capacities for projecting and archiving 'the voice'. Today, almost anyone might assume the role of Aristotle's Stentor, given the right circumstances. This is not to argue that all can speak or be heard equally, but to recognize that the redefinition of 'politics' by 'media' has been both profound and complex.

Aristotle provides a second rationale for limiting the size of the city-state, arguing that: 'in an over-populous state foreigners and metics will readily acquire the rights of citizens, for who will find them out?' He continues: 'Clearly then, the best limit for the population of a state is the largest number which suffices for the purposes of life, and can be taken in at a single view' (1984: 2105). For Aristotle, political authority is tethered to the assumption that the city-state should be a predominantly homogeneous cultural space ideally overseen by the sovereign gaze of a 'single view'. If this ideal was always somewhat mythical, it now stands as the measure of a gulf in social fact, as two centuries of mass migration have created the conditions for far more highly differentiated and volatile patterns of urban inhabitation.

And yet, despite all these alterations of polity and politics, Aristotle's mediation on governance sets out certain problematics that remain recognizable in the present. The desire of the state to regulate citizenship remains active, while longing for the urban overview seems to be intensifying even as cities assume unprecedented size and complexity. However, in the era of the megacity, the 'single view' is no longer the province of an ideal human eye, but of new forms of technological synthesis: for instance, the 'dashboards' employing diverse data-gathering mechanisms (surveillance cameras, sensor networks, drones, 'smart' documentation, etc.) that display the real-time information flows of 'smart cities'. Politics by urban design (recalling Corbusier's famous 'architecture or revolution' coda added to his *Towards a New Architecture* in 1923 (1946: 256)) is being recalibrated in favour of digital governance. Equally as significant is the fact that the operation of these technologies and analytical techniques is no longer the prerogative of the state, but is more frequently the province of private corporations (often in partnership with different arms of the state from the military to health services to local government). This is the context pushing any discussion of the future of urban public space towards contemporary debates about geomedia, smart cities, and the design and governance of protocols around data.

In this book, I have been concerned to explore the new conditions facing urban public space, at a moment when, I argue, it holds increasing importance as a contact zone: as a site for the experimental invention and reinvention of protocols for relating to others. I have focused on the nexus between geomedia and public space not because the digital is some kind of simple origin or sole cause, but because the digital threshold is increasingly bound up with transformations in urban inhabitation, social relations and the exercise of power. In closing this discussion, I want to relate these dimensions to the changed *structural* position that technology occupies in contemporary social life. Placing the emergence of geomedia in this historical context situates the stakes of current developments. It allows us to recognize the extent to which what I earlier termed the ambivalence of the digital constitutes a massive wager – a gamble with our collective future.

Capitalism has long been distinguished by its particular relation to technology. This is not simply a matter of the dependence of production on new machines that eventually coalesced into the system of industrial production, but involves the progressive integration of older processes of technological invention into an organized system of innovation. The growing dominance of what Marcuse (1998), writing in 1941, called 'technological rationality' is predicated on this new temporality, in which innovation no longer arises from invention, but increasingly seeks to *program* it in advance. As Stiegler argues:

> The reduction of transfer delays [. . .] as characteristic of contemporary technics literally leads to a confusion between technical invention and scientific discovery. Research orientations are then massively controlled by industrial finalities. Anticipation, at the most global level, is essentially commanded by investment calculation – collective decision-making, temporalization – in short, destiny is submitted to the techno-economic imperatives regarding this calculation. (1998: 42)

The emergence of this technological rationality or *technoscience* does not result in technological development becoming 'autonomous', as popular media accounts of new products often suggest. However, technology does begin to assume a 'leadership' role that creates growing instabilities within the various other systems – sociocultural, economic, biological – with which it is articulated. Stiegler draws on Simondon's argument that the creation of a system of 'industrial technical objects' begins to progressively modify the interior milieu of human desires, as 'wants are formed around the industrial technical object, which thereby takes on the power of modelling a civilization' (1998: 73).[1] For Stiegler it follows that: 'The ecological problems characteristic of our age can only acquire meaning from this point of view: a new milieu emerges, a technophysical and technocultural milieu, whose laws of equilibrium are no longer known' (1998: 60). It is in this historical context that 'the increasingly crucial question' is precisely that of the relation of the technical system to other systems: 'at stake is the organization of the future, of time' (1998: 41).

While the digital does not *initiate* this new technical milieu, the elaboration of digital platforms and networks is critical to its vastly extended reach, intensity and instability, notably by promoting the integration of technical objects and systems into more and more areas of everyday life. As digital networks merging media, communication, informational and computational techniques become integral to everyday rhythms and practices, previously untapped areas of social life are converted into 'resources', becoming the informational equivalent of what Heidegger (1977) conceptualized as the 'standing reserve' of natural resources. When all elements of 'life' threaten to become standing reserve, social relations and forms of power begin to mutate. At one level, social relations come to be centred less in processes grounded by an older sense of geography and spatial propinquity, and are instead conditioned by what Scott Lash terms the logic of 'at-a-distance'. Social encounters of all sorts become dependent on the need for combinations of extensive movement and constant mediation, promoting the disembedding of practices from spatial contexts and the acceleration of forms of exchange. Lash argues that, as a result, social relations are no longer based on spatially embedded forms of life but have become 'communicational':

> That this social bond has been in decline has been the subject of very large numbers of commentators on both left and right. More specifically, the social bond of the hegemonic order of the national manufacturing society is in decline. In the global information society, the social relation is reduced to the communication. Niklas Luhmann has most profoundly understood this. The social relation is the longer term, embedded and in proximity. The communication presumes the short term; it is disembedded (even when face-to-face) and is normally in some sense at-a-distance. (2010: 143)

As part of the same process, power begins to operate differently. One dimension of this transformation is the growing accretion of power in complex technological assemblages such as smart-city systems, digital archives, search engines and social media platforms. The challenge in understanding the terrain of what Galloway (2004) calls protocollary power, what those such as Lessig (2006) and Berry (2011) refer to as the operation of 'code', or what Beer (2009) (following Lash) terms 'algorithmic power' is partly the fact that the operations of computing and software are generally hidden. Even when not based on proprietary code, they tend to form what Thrift (2004) calls the 'technological unconscious'. This carries the risk that Crang and Graham describe as 'delegating whole sets of decisions, and along with that, the ethics and politics of those decisions, to invisible and sentient systems' (2007: 811). Developing understanding and traction in this area is limited by its dependence on specialist knowledge. This is exacerbated by the shift that Berry (2011) describes from 'hand-made' code to 'industrially-processed' code, referring to the emergence of code that is scripted through the application of other software packages. As Berry points out:

> Understanding computer code and software is difficult enough but when they are built into complicated assemblages that can be geographically dispersed and operating in highly complex inter-dependent ways, it is no surprise that we are still struggling to comprehend these systems and technologies running as code. (2011: 99)

For all these reasons, it has become critically important to pay attention to both the materiality and 'logic' of computational-informational systems, including the way they reconfigure other systems and settings. However, it is equally important not to isolate such analyses. In order to avoid reinstating 'code' as yet another in a long line of techno-determinisms, analysis of algorithmic power needs to be set alongside consideration of the institutional settings, legal and regulatory environments, business models and cultures of use that instantiate it. This is what I have sought to do in my discussion of the scenarios indexed by developments such as Google

Street View, digital public art and urban screens reconceived as public communication platforms.

Understanding the contemporary transformation of power demands more than recognizing new forms of technological 'agency'. Lash argues that we are now entering a 'post-hegemonic' order, in which 'power-over' (*potestas*) gives way to forms of power operating through 'invention'. Instead of residing in an external relation of domination, power becomes increasingly immanent:

> In the post-hegemonic order, *potestas* or domination also begins to come from below. *Pouvoir* and *puissance* somehow begin to merge into one another – become somehow fuzzy and indistinct in relation to one another. The hegemon is above. It is outside and over. In the post-hegemonic order, power comes to act from below: it no longer stays outside that which it 'effects'. (2010: 137–8)

This 'fuzziness' in which domination and invention merge situates what I have called the ambivalence of the digital. The rise of the digital and its progressive integration into everyday life through forms of geomedia has become an important site for the invention of new practices of communication, collectivity and commonality. But, at the same time, the digital is a key terrain for the orchestration of the new forms of domination that Lash describes as 'post-hegemonic'. If the everyday 'lifeworld' is becoming increasingly mediatized and technologized (which also means commoditized and branded), the corollary is that the contemporary media system manifests tendencies towards becoming increasingly 'participatory' and self-organizing. In Lash's terms, domination, which was previously extensive, operating through the commodity and the bureaucratic state, takes an intensive turn: domination becomes non-linear and iterative, achieved through micro-processes of communication and recursive feedback.

> Now domination is through communication. The communication is not above us, even as disciplinary power is. It is instead among us. We swim in its ether. When domination is through the communica-

tion, sovereignty, indeed democracy, must be rethought. Although it takes place increasingly through the media, domination was never so immediate. So unreflective. So without a separate sphere of discursive legitimation. When there is no separate instance there is only – as Lyotard said – legitimation through performance. This is the chronic decisionism that is called for by such chronic change. [. . .] We live in an age of such chronic decisionism: one in which legality as a mode of domination is displaced by performance. (Lash 2010: 144)

'Chronic decisionism' is not just a matter of the choices of this or that commodity which characterize consumer society, but also relates to the imperative for individuals to make choices in relation to broader life trajectories. Older forms of belonging based on shared experience supported through forms of physical contiguity and social continuity – whether from life-long jobs or long-term residence in a single place – have become increasingly precarious for many. The growing pressure to reflexively construct one's identity 'on the fly' imposes greater individual responsibility for negotiating the risk of different 'life choices' at all levels, from education, employment and health to the presentation of the self as a media artefact. While enhanced individual autonomy may be experienced as a form of 'freedom', the corollary has been the diminution of many older forms and sites of common experience and collective encounter. 'Decisionism' is paired with a culture of perpetual evaluation in which more and more areas of life become subject to modes of 'performance review'.

This broader historical context helps to situate the wager bound up in the condition of geomedia, in which all aspects of the human milieu become susceptible to recalibration as techniques capable of generating economic value. Stiegler relates this tendency to the historical concretization of the digital as technical object:

The technical object submits its 'natural milieu' to reason and naturalizes itself at one and the same time. It becomes concretized by closely conforming to this milieu, but in the same move radically transforms the milieu. This ecological phenomenon may be observed in the informational dimension of present-day technics, where it allows for the development of a generalized performativity (for example, in the apparatuses of live transmission and of data processing in real time, with the fictive inversions engendered therein) – but *it is then essentially the human milieu, that is human geography and not physical geography, that is found to be incorporated into a process of concretization* that should no longer be thought on the scale of the object, but also not on the scale of the system. (1998: 80, emphasis added)

In this context, our sense of sociality has become so highly conditioned by the technocultural that social encounter is to some extent 'disembedded even when face-to-face' (Lash 2010: 143). How, then, might the digital be reoriented to produce what Stiegler describes as the 'jumpstart' needed to move away from the current crisis – the inability of capitalism to instil belief in any values outside unlimited consumption?

I would argue that these are the historical stakes of the current transformation of media into geomedia: of the growing implication of urban routines and everyday life in digital networks, in the logistics of 'big data' and the operational archive. On the one hand, in so far as this profound technical restructuring remains largely tethered to the programme of contemporary capitalism, the result will be an unprecedented extension of the logic of commodification. The restructuring of industrial invention as a system of innovation will be replayed at an individual level as a demand for personal innovation, submitting individual identity to the imperatives of competitive self-evaluation and processes of self-marketing. Stiegler argues that this trajectory leads to 'a dangerous dissatisfaction with oneself and a profound loss of belief in the future' (2011: 28), constituting a vicious cycle in which urgently needed discussions of global challenges are stalled, while feeding the growing *ressentiment* manifest in bitter inter-ethnic and religio-political struggles.

Yet, as I have argued, despite – or precisely because of – its colonization of the time-space of the urban everyday, the way through the current impasse also proceeds along the tendency of the digital. The urgent need for the development of new post-national solidarities finds an historic threshold of possibility in the emergence of globally distributed communication platforms. If one challenge is to rethink the terms of operation of these platforms, this involves, as Jean-Luc Nancy (1991) has argued, rethinking 'communication' itself. One way of thinking about this is to focus on the relation between communication and the constitution of 'community'. An ongoing task in the present is to reimagine processes of inhabitation and relation to others in ways that are no longer bound by the tradition of defining the 'barbarians' as pure *outsiders*. What I have tried to establish in this book is that the intersection between geomedia and urban public space today offers a strategic site for this *political* task of reimagining communication, being-with-others and practices of inhabitation.

I suggested earlier that there is another, still largely unthought dimension to this problematic of rethinking 'communication' in the context of geomedia. This relates to the extent to which a certain thinking of 'media' has been one of the strongest investments of Western philosophy. As Derrida (1976) has shown, metaphysics is inaugurated in the privilege granted to an ideal of 'presence', grounded in an understanding of time dominated by the privilege of the present moment.[2] This historical privilege, which marks a certain course of history and inaugurates a dominant understanding of history itself, is bound up with a number of other powerful trajectories. One that I discussed earlier is the Platonic determination of mimesis (as representation, image, writing, mnemonics or sign) as a secondary relation that is understood as a modified form of presence. In modernity, this oppositional understanding of presence and absence (and its close relation to a linear concept of time) becomes implicated in a paradoxical investment in media technology. Media tends to be either a 'mere representation' that can therefore be dismissed as *less than real*, or, on the other hand, is idealized as some kind of neutral 'transmitter' of presence. Whether figured as the 'window to the world', the 'best seat in the house' or the ubiquitous means by which you remain 'in touch' with friends and loved ones today, media is offered as what might enable the overcoming and mastery of absence.

This creates a distinctive conundrum in the present. The contradictions of positioning 'media' as 'secondariness' are becoming increasingly palpable at a lived level in a moment when so much of our 'immediate experience' (as phenomenology once grasped it) is now so closely entangled with practices of real-time 'mediation'. However, instead of using this changed situation to reconsider the terms of the oppositional structure of the presence-absence rela-tion on which our dominant ideas of media and immediacy are based, this is leading to heightened levels of techno-determinism. Secondariness, distance and absence are to be transcended by a digital plenitude that has now been stripped of many of its older, utopic attributes and is defined more and more nakedly in terms of technical performance – greater speed, more bandwidth, better resolution.

As Siegfried Kracauer once noted, it is infinitely tempting *and* infinitely risky to try to correlate philosophy with history. Nevertheless, I find it instructive to see 'media history' – in the extensive sense that Stiegler (1998) gives to the history of *media*, stretching from orthographic writing through cinema and elec-tronic broadcasting to the digital, conceived as phases in the non-linear unfolding of a 'grammatization' implicated in evolu-tionary changes in the 'human' and the 'technological' as related rather than opposed terms – as the complex site for a massive wager on 'presence'. In the waning of theology, speed has become a new catechism. Modern media – indexed by all the 'teles' up to telepresence and beyond – has been the primary instrument for the pursuit of the 'now', fostering the enigmatic modern ambition of residing in the absolute instant. This is the goal of a peculiarly modern sense of mastery, not just over nature *but over time itself.* Yet, as Heidegger observed, in this pursuit we are fated to disap-pointment. The more we insist on *occupying* the instant, the more decisively it seems to elude us.

Today, the dominant orientation of geomedia means that the project of 'living in the moment' is marked by competition and a desire for mastery – over resources, events, places and time – so that it bears little resemblance to a possible attunement to the world's multiplicity. Instead, we experience the wholesale submis-sion of social time to exchange value. The pursuit of the now, in which the technologically augmented 'human' is imagined as overcoming spatial, temporal and material limits through the perpetual connectivity of real-time geomedia, has increasingly taken on an exhausting air of *keeping up*. The kind of competition that was once imagined between nations and corporations is being extended into the terrain of the individual psyche, generating new rhythms, subjectivities and anxieties in the process.

Extricating ourselves from this situation will not be easy. At the beginning of this book, I suggested that the ways in which the question of the *right to the networked city* are answered will be critical in determining what kind of cities we will inhabit and what kind of people we will become in the future. To put this proposition in the terms I am developing here, finding an alternative is not about simply *rejecting* media in the name of immediacy, but about seeking a recomposition of its dominant forms and tendencies. In particular, we need to recognize that the long-standing opposition between the human as some kind of natural living being and the technological as its invasive other is deeply implicated in the polarized and limited understanding of 'media' that I have described. Developing a different relation to media demands a different heading.

What if, as Stiegler suggests, the 'technological' is *integral* to the constitution of the 'human', is in fact one of its constitutive potentials? 'Media' would then have to be thought as part of the social relations of 'immediacy' *from the inside*, so to speak. While this proposition may seem simple to state, I am not underestimating the complexity involved in pursuing it. Thinking 'being' on the basis of a 'presence' or plenitude closely connected to a linear conception of time has always been subject to contradictions, particularly around the relations between 'consciousness' and the archiving of experience as memory. If these relations have been challenged in some ways at least since Nietzsche and Freud, this has not yet displaced our dominant frameworks for understanding media.

What I have sought to argue through this book is that the nexus between geomedia and public space is today a vital arena in which new elaborations of the digital and the technological might be attempted. This involves seizing the growing mediation of the everyday precisely as the means for exploring the historical contradictions embedded in the metaphysics of presence. In this manner we might begin to discern and develop new practices – modes of social encounter, relations to others, ways of being together with others near and far – that do not entirely conform to the contours of older logics. It is in these spaces and practices that we might begin to better discern the complex temporalities that operate in the chronically mediated face-to-face relations of the present, to recognize what might be held in common among highly differentiated and increasingly mobile urban inhabitants engaged in diverse choreographies of urban appropriation.

Notes

Introduction

1 This historic shift has been described in a variety of ways: from Weiser's (1991) 'ubicomp' to specific urban inflections such as sentient city (Crang and Graham 2007; Shepard 2011), urban informatics (Foth et al. 2011) and Adam Greenfield's witty 'every-ware' (Greenfield 2006). Ubiquity was integral to the growing interdependence between media and architecture that I have previously described as the 'media-architecture' complex or 'media city' (McQuire 2008).

2 Geographic Information Systems (GIS) that merge cartography, statistics and database technology were first developed in Canada in the early 1960s. GPS or Global Positioning Satellite technology for data capture was originally developed by the US military and operationalized in 1973. It became progressively more available for civilian use in the 1980s, but the big shift was 1 May 2000, when US president Bill Clinton ordered 'Selective Availability' to be turned off, improving the precision of civilian GPS from 300 to 20 metres.

3 On Google, see Schepke 2010. Various industry reports since have consistently proclaimed the importance of mobile location-based

services to digital media markets. While the figures will vary depending on methodology, a report from Juniper (Sorrel 2014) is characteristic in predicting a tripling of the total market over a five-year period, from $12.2bn in 2014 to $43.3bn in 2019. Almost three-quarters of that value is attributed to growth in mobile advertising.

4 Where I depart from Virilio is in his tendency to conceptualize the shift to real-time communication in terms of an opposition between an older 'concrete presence' and 'the elsewhere of a "discreet tele-presence"' (Virilio 1997: 10–11) that is always regarded as derivative and inferior. As I will argue below, ubiquitous digital networks highlight long-standing contradictions in thinking the relation between 'immediacy' and 'mediation' on the basis of a metaphysics of presence. For a more detailed critique of Virilio's humanist metaphysics, see McQuire 2011b.

5 As Derrida argues, the 'Platonic interpretation' of mimesis has persisted in, and posed as, an entire history of Western thought: 'First there is what is, "reality", the thing itself, in flesh and blood as the phenomenologists say; then there is, imitating these, the painting, the portrait, the zographeme, the inscription or transcription of the thing itself. Discernability, at least numerical discernability between the imitator and imitated is what constitutes order. And obviously, according to "logic" itself, according to a profound synonymy what is imitated is more real, more essential, more true, etc., than what imitates' (1981: 191).

6 Manifested in the Urban Communication book series (Kleinman 2007; Jassem, Drucker and Burd 2010; Matsaganis, Gallagher and Drucker 2013), the Urban Informatics series (Foth 2009; Foth et al. 2011, 2014) and the books emerging from the Media Architecture biennales (Eckardt 2007; Eckardt, Geelhaar and Collini 2008).

7 For instance, the 'research in the wild' problematic advanced by Callon and Rabeharisoa (2003) and articulated in relation to urban media by Fatah gen Schieck, Kostakos and Penn (2010).

8 Stiegler argues: 'Deconstruction is a thinking of composition in the sense that composition is "older" than opposition (what Simondon would have called "a transductive relation"): that is, a relation that constitutes its terms, the terms not existing outside the relation' (2001: 249–50).

9 In *Counter Blast*, McLuhan argued: 'new media are not bridges between man and nature: they are nature' (1970: 14).

10 Kittler argues: 'More than any other theorists, philosophers forgot to ask which media support their very practice' (2009: 24). There are some notable exceptions to this blindness, particularly Derrida and Stiegler. I return to this question in chapter 5.

1 Transforming Media and Public Space

1 The commodification of leisure has been criticized at least since the 1940s but there are significant differences in the present. Obvious examples are digital games, where players not only contribute their time and labour in order to produce much of the game 'content', but the process of play generates data which contributes to the value accrued by the platform owner. However, this logic now exceeds older modes of leisure and play and increasingly extends to the tracking and measurement of many areas of 'life', including individual patterns of communication, movement, eating and sleeping (for instance the 'quantified self' movement).

2 Wirth was writing from an urban context where rural migration to the city had been supplemented and often exceeded by migration from other countries. By 1890, fully 20 per cent of all residents of cities in the United States had been born overseas, while the concentration was even more marked in cities such as Chicago and New York. See Martindale and Neuwirth (1958: 12).

3 Wirth relied on the assumption of a normative identity needed to counter-balance anomic tendencies in order to explain the tendency for migrants to coalesce in particular urban areas (thus setting up the recurrent dilemma of the 'ghetto' in which the newcomer is forever at risk of being seen as the cause of cultural disruption). His best-known book remains his 1928 study of the American Jewish community titled *The Ghetto*.

4 This is not to suggest that Sennett's analysis of the urban present is equally optimistic. *The Fall of Public Man* describes the failure of new forms of public civility to transcend the dominant political container of the modern nation-state and so engender transnational solidarities.

5 Giedion was Secretary-General of CIAM from 1928 to 1956.

6 Giedion's statement in one of the most influential texts of modern architectural education is exemplary in its canonical call for the structural separation of motor and pedestrian transport, and housing and production precincts: 'The first thing to do is to abolish the *rue corridor* with its rigid lines of buildings and its intermingling of traffic, pedestrians and residences. The fundamental condition of the contemporary city requires the restoration of liberty to all three – to traffic, to pedestrians, to residential and industrial quarters. This can be accomplished only by separating them' (1967: 822). The logic of functional separation informed numerous post-war urban developments, including model planned cities such as Brasilia, Chandigarh and Canberra.

7 The United Nations (2014: 12) estimates that 90 per cent of the global increase in urban population to 2050 will occur in Asia and Africa, led by China, India and Nigeria.

8 These patterns include the narrowing of the urban economy as the city centre assumes a more exclusively 'cultural' function. Such developments risk further spatial stratification of lower income groups (working class, pensioners, the unemployed and the underemployed), who are increasingly relegated to distant outer-urban corridors lacking both employment opportunities and social amenities (Mitchell and Staehl in Low and Smith 2006).

9 Anderson (2008) asserted: 'This is a world where massive amounts of data and applied mathematics replace every other tool that might be brought to bear. Out with every theory of human behavior, from linguistics to sociology. Forget taxonomy, ontology, and psychology. Who knows why people do what they do? The point is they do it, and we can track and measure it with unprecedented fidelity. With enough data, the numbers speak for themselves.'

10 Batty et al. argue: 'In our vision, participation and self-organisation are the cornerstones to building a global knowledge resource that, by design, will represent a public good, accessible to every citizen, institution or business. On the one hand, people should be fully aware of the kind of public knowledge infrastructure they are contributing to, and of the potential benefits they will be able to get from it. On the other, people should be in full control of their contributed data/profiles: how their data are being acquired, managed, analysed and used, when and

for how long. Only a public system capable of delivering high-quality information within a trusted framework has the potential for raising a high degree of participation, and only large, democratic participation can ensure the creation of reliable, timely and trustworthy information about collective phenomena' (2012: 492).

11 Kitchin notes that 'city dashboards' in cities such as London provide real-time information about 'weather, air pollution, public transport delays, public bike availability, river level, electricity demand, the stock market, twitter trends in the city, look at traffic camera feeds, and even the happiness level' (2014: 7).

12 I've derived the phrase 'affordable privacy' from Gibson's *Neuromancer*, where Molly prefaces a conversation with Case by declaring: 'This is as private as I can afford' (1995: 49).

13 In 1999, Sun Microsystems' CEO Scott McNealy infamously declared: 'You have zero privacy anyway. Get over it.' Sociologist David Lyon notes: 'The modern world may be a society of strangers, but no one was able to maintain their anonymity for long. Bodies may well have "disappeared" as it became possible to do things at a distance, without direct involvement or intervention, but they were made to re-appear courtesy of surveillance' (2003: 104–5).

14 Despite this, Goffman goes on to add: 'City streets, even in times that defame them, provide a setting where mutual trust is routinely displayed between strangers' (1971: 17).

15 First recorded for his 1970 album *Small Talk at 125th and Lenox*. The peak theoretical expression of this new stance was arguably Debord's *Society of the Spectacle*, published in 1967.

16 David (2014), who makes explicit reference to Scott-Heron's 'call for action', gives the key examples of Occupy Streams (http://occupy streams.org) and the 'Arab Spring', 'where citizen video-journalism was often the only media outlet available'.

17 For Dayan and Katz, the media event has to be 'pre-planned' by broadcasters, excluding natural disasters, as well as something like the attacks on the World Trade Center towers in 2001.

18 Prior to the emergence of new delivery systems such as cable, satellite and digital broadcasting, most national territories were dominated by a small number of broadcasters operating on urban and regional scales. This began to change in the US from the 1970s, and in Europe

from the early 1980s, while in other territories such as Australia this transformation dates more from the 1990s.

19 Hence Dayan and Katz (1992) cite a limited list, including the funerals of Kennedy and Mountbatten, the wedding of Charles and Diana, the journeys of Pope John Paul II (to Poland) and Anwar Sadat (to Israel), as well as the election debates between Kennedy and Nixon, and the Watergate hearings.

20 As Auslander (1999) notes, 'live' now includes a rhetoric of instant replay. The capacity to repeat the moment of impact over and over, in the context of rolling 24/7 post-event coverage, led some US television networks to voluntarily stop replaying the footage of the planes striking the buildings, recognizing that excessive repetition risked exacerbating trauma (see Felling 2004).

21 While the 9/11 attacks are used here as a point of reference, I would argue that particular individuals will experience this kind of 'immediation' of tele-witnessing at different moments, depending on their biography and circumstances. See also Avital Ronnel's (1994) account of 'trauma TV'.

22 Economic indicators included the worst dip in the stock market since the Great Depression.

23 Hence a key regulatory objective in the period of the IIE relates to attempts by states to limit media concentration and private monopoly.

24 Stephen Graham (2010) argues that the difficulty in waging full-scale warfare in the present has given rise to new modalities of limited urban warfare in which it is increasingly difficult to identify either 'the enemy' or the 'front line'.

25 Gitlin (2003) provides a classic analysis of this dynamic in relation to the early days of the anti-war movement in the US.

26 These included: #jan25 (Egypt), #jan30 (Sudan), #feb3 (Yemen), #feb5 (Syria), #feb12 (Algeria), #feb14 (Bahrain) and #feb17 (Libya).

27 Long-standing concern about the role of PR firms in providing media content for time-poor journalists is now exacerbated by the growing colonization of social media platforms by professional communication workers.

28 While there are high levels of public mistrust in journalists, surveys suggest a remarkable faith in the neutrality of search engines. As Goldman (2010) argues, this faith is misplaced: search engines cannot

be 'neutral' but need to discriminate by ranking information in order to function at all. This situates the emerging *political* importance of search engine 'gatekeeping', and the invisibility (on commercial grounds) of search engine protocols.

2 Googling the City

1 See http://www.google.com/press/annc/maps_where20.html (accessed 25 March 2014).

2 The first Street View services outside the United States covered sections of France and Italy in mid-2008, followed by more comprehensive rollouts in Australia and Japan in August 2008. Street View subsequently deployed in Canada, New Zealand, and across numerous European countries, followed by parts of Asia, South Africa and other countries including Brazil, India (beginning 2011) and Russia (2012). Street View has also extended its service to specialized tourist sites, including national parks, art galleries and museums.

3 Unlike Google Earth, there is no standard policy on how often particular Street View sectors will be updated. But, given that most of the cost is the initial data acquisition, it is predictable that locations offering greater return on investment will be renewed more regularly.

4 Street View's low-res orientation reflected Google's premium on designing services so web pages would load quickly. As imagery has been renewed over time, resolution has been upgraded in a number of territories.

5 It is worth recalling that, while 1850s photography allowed an image to be *registered* more or less instantaneously, processing and preservation still required significant time and effort. Most of Marville's photographs were produced on glass-plate emulsions. The transformation of photography into 'mass media' did not happen until the 1880s, while the casual immediacy of digital imagery was another century away.

6 In 2011, Flickr announced it had reached 6 billion photographs. See http://blog.flickr.net/en/2011/08/04/6000000000 (accessed 25 March 2016). In a 2013 whitepaper Facebook reported: 'More than 250 billion photos have been uploaded to Facebook, and more than 350 million photos are uploaded every day on average' (2013: 6).

Instagram (launched 2010) claims more than 30 billion photos shared, with an average of 70 million uploads per day. See https://instagram.com/press (accessed 7 May 2015).

7 Benjamin argued: 'Uniqueness and permanence are as closely entwined in the [artwork] as are transitoriness and repeatability in the [reproduction]. The stripping of the veil from the object, the destruction of the aura, is the signature of a perception whose "sense of sameness in the world" has so increased that, by means of reproduction, it extracts sameness even from what is unique. Thus is manifested in the field of perception what in the theoretical field is noticeable in the increasing significance of statistics' (1999: 255–6).

8 The Stanford City Block Project was sponsored by Google from November 2002 to June 2006, when its technology was 'folded into Google's Street View'. At launch, Street View eventually used 360-degree panoramas provided by third-party Immersive Systems rather than the multi-perspective panoramas of the Stanford Project. See http://graphics.stanford.edu/projects/cityblock (accessed 3 March 2015).

9 This echoes the shift in terminology associated with big data (see Savage and Burrows 2007, 2009). Of course, Street View is still a sample: a series of snapshots 'updated' periodically. As Kitchin (2014: 9) notes, despite all its claims to scale, 'big data' is inevitably selective, filtered by sampling rates, data platforms, data 'ontology' (classification) and regulatory environment among other factors.

10 Blaise Aguera y Arcas, quoted from a video interview online at http://www.microsoft.com/showcase/en/us/details/64f1839f-db93-49cd-8e44-0729fec50ce7 (accessed 2 September 2011).

11 See http://dziga.perrybard.net (accessed 26 March 2016). The emergence of 'open' artworks will be discussed in chapter 3 below.

12 Kevin Poulsen's (2007) *Wired* article headlined 'Want Off Street View? Google Wants Your ID and a Sworn Statement' was later updated to 'Google Cuts the Red Tape'.

13 The position was not entirely clear-cut in the US. As Kevin Bankston of the Electronic Frontier Foundation observed: 'this product illustrates a tension between our First Amendment right to document public spaces around us, and the privacy interests people have as they go about their day' (quoted in Helft 2007).

14 On face blurring, see http://google-latlong.blogspot.com/2008/06/street-view-turns-1-keeps-on-growing.html. On licence plate blurring, see http://google-latlong.blogspot.com/2008/07/tour-tour-de-france-with-street-view.html (accessed 26 March 2016).

15 Reported in http://news.bbc.co.uk/2/hi/technology/8045517.stm (accessed 26 March 2016).

16 A large number of complaints concerned the fact that the inside of houses could be seen. Others concerned the growth of secondary sites using Google's photos maliciously. See http://web.archive.org/web/20091219043337/http://www.examiner.com/x-16352-Japan-Headlines-Examiner~y2009m9d4-Google-Japan-fights-concerns-about-Street-View (accessed 12 April 2016).

17 The illicit data collection began as early as 2007 and was first acknowledged by Google on 27 April 2010. In a 14 May 2010 blog post, Google's head of engineering and research Alan Eustace wrote: 'So how did this happen? Quite simply, it was a mistake.' See http://googlepolicyeurope.blogspot.com/2010/05/wifi-data-collection-update.html (accessed 26 March 2016).

18 In Europe, divisions over whether the captured data should be held for examination or immediately deleted by Google resulted in the European Justice Commission calling for a unified setting. ECJ spokesperson Matthew Newman said: 'Some countries said Google should delete the data, while some said Google should keep the data in case of legal action. We can't have a single market if we have divergent ways of dealing with the same problem.' See http://www.zdnet.co.uk/news/regulation/2011/03/17/facebook-and-google-must-follow-eu-privacy-rules-40092179 (accessed 26 March 2016). In Australia, then Communications Minister Stephen Conroy described the data capture as 'the single greatest breach in the history of privacy' (quoted in Moses 2010). While the Australian Privacy Commission found that Google had breached the Privacy Act, Australian legislation did not allow the Commission to levy a fine. Instead Google was required to publish an apology and to assess and report on any new Street View data-collection activities in Australia that include personal information.

19 See http://jalopnik.com/5671049/google-street-view-cars-collected-emails-and-passwords (accessed 26 March 2016).

20 France was the first to fine Google, levying the maximum permitted €100,000 penalty in 2011, while Germany levied a fine of €145,000 in 2013, and Italy €1m in 2014. In the US Google eventually agreed to a fine of $7m in a settlement with thirty-eight states and the District of Columbia.

21 Google Maps VP Brian McLendon (in Miller 2014) notes that Street View was conceived as a means to improve navigation by enabling users to see the surroundings near their destination, adding: 'But we soon realized that one of the best ways to make maps is to have a photographic record of the streets of the world and refer back to those whenever there's a correction.'

22 Apple's iOS6, released in 2012, was its first mobile operating system not featuring Google Maps as a 'native' application.

23 When it launched Street View, Google initially bought the street-level visual data from a third party, the video company Immersive Media, which delivered the images for the first thirty-five cities that comprised the database in 2007 (Ma 2007). After that, Google launched its own fleet of camera vehicles.

24 Subsequently, a number of other sources published similar informa-tion, including a presentation from the 2013 Google Developers' conference 'Project Ground Truth: Accurate Maps Via Algorithms and Elbow Grease' (available at https://www.youtube.com/ watch?v=FsbLEtS0uls#t=1182 (accessed 31 March 2016)) and a 2014 article in *Wired* (Miller 2014).

25 In the 'Project Ground Truth: Accurate Maps Via Algorithms and Elbow Grease' presentation (see previous note), the same relation was given but was attributed primarily to aerial and satellite imagery.

26 Apple replaced Google Maps with its own map application using data obtained and licensed from Dutch sat-nav system maker TomTom, as well as some data from Open Street Map. However, major glitches initially led to a global wave of bad publicity. Subsequent improvements in the service arose in part from Apple deploying its own fleet of camera vehicles, albeit in a more limited way than Google.

27 Uber's dependence on Google (and concern about data and costs) led in 2015 to its interest in acquiring the Nokia-owned HERE mapping service (see Scott and Isaac 2015). When this failed it made deals with

TomTom and acquired Microsoft's Bing assets as part of its move into developing its own mapping service.

28 Of course, it is not just access to data but capacity to process it that underpins Google's current dominance in areas such as search and mapping. While many processes enabling the integration of different data streams into 'Ground Truth' are automated, it is also labour intensive (Madrigal 2012b). As Levy (2011) notes, Google has a long history of building both large-scale data assets and processing capacity (analytics, storage facilities, retrieval and analytics capabilities) beginning from search and moving on to fields such as machine translation. Few national governments have similar capabilities in the present.

29 Google uses a similar argument to justify its global dominance in online search and advertising (Levy 2011).

30 Google Maps exist for around 200 countries, of which forty-three have used the Ground Truth methodology at the time of writing. Others use combinations of third-party data (e.g. state surveys) and user contributions. In particular territories (notably India) user data contributed via MapMaker plays the major role.

31 Lowering of the threshold for collecting fees from third-party use of Google Maps in 2012 was credited by Hardy (2012) with inspiring a number of companies including Foursquare to opt for using Open Street Map instead.

32 Open Street Map was initiated in the UK in 2004. Inspired by the success of Wikipedia, as well as by the lack of freely available, non-proprietary map data in the UK, its ambition has swelled to using crowd-sourced data in order to produce a free, editable world map. Like Google Maps, Open Street Map combines a variety of data sources with collaborative user-created content. It also offers a variety of use models.

33 In the 2013 Project Ground Truth video, it was noted that in 2008 it could take from six to eighteen months for Google to update a map. Errors had to be checked with third-party data providers before Google could 'publish' the correction. Bringing the map-making process 'in-house' now enables Google to update its maps hundreds of times a day in response to changing circumstances.

34 While Foursquare still claims a substantial user base of around 50 million globally, it remains a niche service compared to popular social media digital platforms.

35 Places was originally announced 18 August 2010. See https://www.
facebook.com/notes/facebook/who-what-when-and-nowwhere/
418175202130 (accessed 31 March 2016). It ceased operation just
over a year later. See http://gizmodo.com/5833712/facebook-just-
killed-places (accessed 31 March 2016). It was eventually relaunched
as a directory or 'guided local search site' in June 2014 but is not
available as a mobile app at the time of writing. See http://search-
engineland.com/facebook-launches-new-places-directory-208105
(accessed 31 March 2016).

36 This decision impacted on a number of other apps, including Assisted
Serendipity, an application for finding the gender balance in bars.
While Assisted Serendipity had previously been praised by the CEO
of Foursquare, it was unable to function with the new settings and
ceased development (Thompson 2012).

3 Participatory Public Space

1 See McQuire 1994/5. As Adorno and Horkheimer commented: 'The
National Socialists knew that the wireless gave shape to their cause
just as the printing press did to the Reformation', adding that the
charisma of the Führer belonged to the 'gigantic fact that the speech
penetrates everywhere' (1973: 159).

2 An increasingly common use of the 'two-way' architecture is the model
of content delivery coupled to a 'backchannel' reporting on consumer
choices used by streaming services such as Netflix and Spotify.

3 For instance, Jenkins et al. (2009: 4, 9) ground their argument about
paradigm change cutting across 'educational practices, creative processes, community life, and democratic citizenship' with reference
to a 2005 Pew Foundation survey showing 57 per cent of American
teenagers have 'produced' media content. But 'production' could
here refer to anything from uploading an original video to reposting
mainstream media content into a new context.

4 In their introduction to a special issue of *Planning Practice and Research*
on public participation in planning, Brownhill and Parker note:
'Increasingly, reflections on participation are tempered by a recognition of the challenges that "meaningful" participation faces and the
limitations of much past practice' (2010: 275).

5 The close relation between Lefebvre and the SI is well known, as is their split from around 1963. In this discussion, I am not interested in who 'invented' particular ideas, but note the importance of Lefebvre's (1991b) rethinking of Marxism as a problematic of everyday life, as well as their shared interest in a concept of urban 'play' borrowed from the Surrealists. As Sadler (1998: 45) notes, both Lefebvre and the SI looked to the Paris commune as the sublime 'situation' in which ordinary citizens became self-governing.

6 In his 1961 film *Critique de la séparation*, Debord argues that without true collectivity, there is no true individuality: 'Until the environment is collectively dominated, there will be no individuals – only spectres haunting the things anarchically presented to them by others.'

7 The *dérive* was defined as 'A mode of experimental behavior linked to the conditions of urban society: a technique of rapid passage through varied ambiances' (in Knabb 2006: 52). It was closely related to the Situationist concepts of *psychogeography* (the idea that the urban environment affected emotions and behaviour, consciously and unconsciously) and *unitary urbanism* (a theoretical approach to urbanism that sought to avoid the systematic separations imposed by modern functional approaches). As an experimental technique, the 'playful-constructive behaviour' of the *dérive* was enmeshed in contradictions which remain familiar to urban exploration in the context of geomedia: the oscillations between investment in a subjective language of libidinous play and appeals to a behaviouralist language of data and effects.

8 In his 1960 essay on 'Unitary Urbanism', Constant argues that the concept needs to integrate disparate phenomena including architecture, poetry, social ties and moral principles. However, such integration cannot proceed immediately because directly applicable concepts do not yet exist. 'Which is why at this stage I would prefer to define unitary urbanism as a very complex, very changeable, constant activity, a deliberate intervention in the praxis of daily life and in the daily environment' (1998: 132).

9 As Hughes observes (in Hughes and Sadler 1999: 176), key aspects of the 'non-plan' doctrine promulgated by the architects Reyner Banham, Paul Barker, Peter Hall and Cedric Price in 1969 were later embraced by the New Right for the creation of 'enterprise zones'

such as the London Docklands under the Thatcher administration in 1980.

10 *Solar Equation* was commissioned by the Light in Winter Festival, Federation Square, Melbourne. It has since been exhibited at Durham University Science Site, Durham, United Kingdom in 2013, and Ulm Cathedral, Ulm, Germany, in 2015.

11 SOHO is the acronym for the Solar and Heliospheric Observatory, an international collaboration between ESA and NASA. See http://sohowww.nascom.nasa.gov. SDO is the acronym for the Solar Dynamics Observatory, http://sdo.gsfc.nasa.gov.

12 In *Amodal Suspension* (Yamaguchi, Japan, 2003) the protocol centred on the mobile phone and SMS; while *Pulse Front* utilized a network of sensors to align the rhythm and orientation of twenty searchlights around the Toronto harbour with the pulses of passersby. In *Articulated Intersect* different banks of lights were modified by the public using a number of lever-controllers protruding from the ground.

13 As one participant commented: 'How many of you have designed light art of this magnitude? I can tell you that it is one of the greatest things I've ever experienced.' Quoted at http://www.vectorial vancouver.net/docs/VectorialAnalytics.pdf (accessed 2 September 2012).

14 *Rider Spoke* was developed in collaboration with the Mixed Reality Lab at University of Nottingham, Sony Net Services and the Fraunhofer Institute. The project was first shown at the Barbican in London in October 2007 and has since been presented in Athens, Brighton, Budapest, Sydney and Adelaide. See https://www.blast-theory.co.uk/projects/rider-spoke (accessed 31 March 2016).

15 'We have built an experimental platform that allows people to author and access place-based content (text, audio and pictures). It is a framework for exploring and sharing experience and knowledge, for leaving and annotating ephemeral traces of people's presence in the geography of the city.' See http://research.urbantapestries.net (accessed 31 March 2016).

16 The wearable device was initially a fairly crudely improvised combination of Galvanic Skin Response (GSR) and GPS. See http://www.biomapping.net (accessed 31 March 2016).

17 See http://www.murrupbarak.unimelb.edu.au/content/pages/billi bellarys-walk (accessed 31 March 2016).

18 In August 2007, a committee was convened to commemorate Aboriginal 'freedom fighters', including Tunnerminnerwait and Maulboyheenner, who were the first people to be executed in Melbourne in 1842. The Commemoration Committee called for the erection of a public monument to publicly acknowledge this story and its contribution to the history of Melbourne. The City of Melbourne voted to adopt the proposal in 2009, and finally allocated funding for a permanent memorial on the site of the execution in 2014 (Webb 2014).

19 Osborne (1994) distinguishes three broad historical approaches to time: the *cosmological* in which time is defined largely by the rhythms of 'nature'; the *lived* or phenomenological in which individual consciousness comes to the fore; and finally the inter-subjective or *social*. Osborne associates each different conception of time with different 'stages' in historical development. So-called 'pre-historic' societies are dominated by cosmological time in which continuity and cyclical processes are at the forefront. With the emergence of 'historical societies', homogeneous time moves to the centre of consciousness. Osborne argues that, as the contradictions between homogeneity and difference become apparent, we arrive at the present 'transitional' period. The emergence of what he calls 'social time' demands the abandonment of unitary history and the invention of multiple codes.

4 Urban Screens and Urban Media Events

1 These include: 'Large screens and the transformation of public space' (ARC DP0772759 2007–9) with Nikos Papastergiadis and Sean Cubitt; 'Large screens and the transnational public sphere' (ARC LP0989302 2009–2013) with Nikos Papastergiadis, Audrey Yue, Sean Cubitt, Ross Gibson and partner investigators from Fed Square Pty Ltd, Australia Council of the Arts and Art Center Nabi (Seoul); and 'Broadband-enabled public screens: from display to interaction' (Institute for a Broadband-Enabled Society 2009–11) with Nikos Papastergiadis, Frank Vettere and Martin Gibbs. I would like to acknowledge all these colleagues, as well as other researchers,

including Meredith Martin, Amelia Barikin, Xin Gu, John Downs and Sonia Pedell, who contributed to these projects.

2 As Leni Riefenstahl had demonstrated to devastating effect in the 1930s with her film *Triumph of the Will* (1935), the screen offers a flexible mechanism for the *articulation* of the individual and the masses (McQuire 1998: 75).

3 Bruce Ramus (2011) recalls: 'In 1996, we wanted to develop a new type of video system. At the time, there existed a red LED and a light green LED, like we see on little power switches on our amps and our microwaves. So we asked Saco in Montreal if they could build blue and full spectrum green LEDs, which they did. We then took that to Innovative Designs in Belgium and they made the prototype module which became the first ever LED video screen. Then we toured it in 1996–7 on the PopMart tour, which was the largest video screen yet built. It was about 70 metres wide and about 25 metres tall.'

4 The best-known example was the '59th Minute' Creative Time project which displayed short video art programmes in Manhattan's Times Square between 2000 and 2005. The art videos occupied the last minute of every screening hour outside of rush hour.

5 In its pitch for London 2012, LOCOG made broad national engagement a distinctive part of its bid, with large public screens forming a key element of this strategy. Key BBC staff from the pilot Public Space Broadcasting project, including Bill Morris and Mike Gibbons, joined LOCOG at this time, Gibbons becoming Head of Live Sites and Morris becoming Director of Culture, Ceremonies and Education.

6 While it was more cost effective, standardization of screen installation compromised the capacity for site specificity and attracted concern from CABE (2008) regarding the impact of the new screens on the urban environment.

7 When the BBC initiated their project, large screens were generally conceived and operated as stand-alone installations. Screens produced by different manufacturers not only differed in size but had different operating systems, making installation costs unpredictable. There was also the practical issue of sequencing content, which had to be done locally at each screen.

8 See https://s3-ap-southeast-2.amazonaws.com/assets-fedsquare/up loads/2014/12/Civic-and-Cultural-Charter1.pdf (accessed 3 April 2016).

9 Personal communication from Don Bates, one of the principal architects of LAB Architects who were responsible for the design of Federation Square.

10 Referring to the tennis grand slam event held annually only a few kilometres away.

11 Screens opened or planned in Australia include Dandenong, Canberra, Sydney and Perth. Federation Square was also the model for the screen built as part of the Tomorrow City complex in New Songdo City in Korea.

12 Loss of 'champions' arguably played a key role in the BBC's withdrawal of support for the Public Space Broadcasting programme, while CASZ folded in the face of such difficulties.

13 As Gibbons (2013) noted, this attention offers sponsors a valuable opportunity.

14 I am not arguing that the establishment of PVAs is always inclusive. In their study of the 2010 FIFA World Cup held in South Africa, Kolamo and Vuolteenaho (2013) observed the potential for the co-option of 'fan fest' areas into tightly controlled commercial enclaves.

15 This will be taken up further in chapter 5.

16 The background to this occasion is complex. It relates to policies enacted by Federal and State governments in Australia from the 1910s to the 1970s, in which Aboriginal children were systematically removed from their parents. While the policies ostensibly aimed to 'protect' children, the focus on removal of so-called 'mixed blood' children fitted the (often unspoken) aim of minimizing – if not eliminating – the presence of Aboriginal peoples in Australia. The effects of the policies were devastating and long lasting, creating a legacy of intergenerational dislocation and widespread child abuse. The final report of a Royal Commission of Inquiry set up to examine the effects of such policies was tabled in parliament in 1997. One of the key recommendations of the *Bringing Them Home* report was that all governments involved should make formal apologies to surviving members of the 'Stolen

Generations'. This recommendation was eventually enacted by all State governments, as well as many of the institutions (such as churches) that had been involved in removing Aboriginal children from their families. However, the Federal Government, led by conservative prime minister John Howard who had been elected in 1996, controversially refused to make a formal apology. When the Howard government lost power at the end of 2007, delivering a formal apology became one of the first significant acts of the new government.

17 The formal apology made in 2008 has to be distinguished from *legal* recognition of responsibility or payment of reparations, which still remain unresolved issues.

18 Morris noted: 'We had a virtual golf tournament a couple of weeks ago with a team playing golf in the centre of Birmingham and a team playing golf in the centre of Manchester and there's no golf courses, no holes, it was all done through virtual games. [. . .] Now we think we've only just touched the surface there, it's really early days but that kind of thing is just really opening up' (Gibbons and Morris 2005).

19 The project 'Large screens and the transnational public sphere' was funded by the Australian Research Council from 2009–15. While the research project had broader aims, including evaluation of institutional dynamics and collaborative practices, my account here focuses on three of the 'urban media events'.

20 New Songdo City, which Sassen (2011a) described as the world's best-known example of a 'smart city', included the Tomorrow City complex, designed as a transport hub and futuristic urban display venue. When our research partner, Art Center Nabi, was given the responsibility of programming the large screen situated in the public plaza of Tomorrow City, we decided to use the research project to provide content for the launch event.

21 The technical difficulties primarily concerned the need to process data 'on the fly' to accommodate different screen sizes, which led to some lags in refreshing the image.

22 Our survey data suggested that more than three-quarters of the estimated 1,800-strong Korean audience engaged with the screen using text messages.

23 Representative comments included: 'I felt connected [to Melbourne].' 'I felt difference, but I felt a sense of connection.' 'It was very new that we could directly participate [in art performance] through mobile phones.' 'My previous experience with media art was one-dimensional, where the screen images were changed responding to my movements.' 'It was fascinating to see that [I] could directly take part in the artworks through my texts.' 'People in Melbourne and I could share each other's words [values].' 'I felt very close to them as if I couldn't feel the physical distance.' 'It's hard to say that a sense of connection has been created all of a sudden. However, I feel that we [Koreans] are a little bit connected to Australia's art and media through texting and visual screening.'

24 In Melbourne, Hilton worked with young people at the Footscray Community Arts Centre, a site for culturally diverse community engagement, while Park worked at a school in Seoul.

25 A managed service provides guaranteed bandwidth, while Skype is a 'best effort' service, meaning it is more susceptible to drop-outs.

26 The cost of setting up the tents was a large part of the eventual decision to run *Hello* only as a one-off event. While the inability to repeat the event was disappointing, the tent offered unexpected benefits. Working in public space leaves an event open to different contingencies, including the weather. On the evening we ran *Hello*, persistent rain in Melbourne made us grateful for the tent, not so much for providing a semi-private space as a dry one.

27 This would have been a significant expense but fortunately the project was supported by AARNet, who provide Internet services to the Australian academic research community.

28 Comparison might be made to the peer-regulation of street art and graffiti sites in certain cities, where work of high quality is left untouched – at least for a time.

5 Recomposing Public Space

1 The quote is from Simondon's *Du modes d'existence des objets techniques* (1958), as translated in Stiegler (1998: 73).

2 Derrida argues: 'From Parmenides to Husserl, the privilege of the present has never been put into question. It could not have been. It

is what is self-evident itself, and no thought seems possible outside its element. Non-presence is always thought in the form of presence [. . .] or as a modalization of presence. The past and the future are always determined as past presents or as future presents' (1982: 34).

References

Adorno, T. W. and Horkheimer, M. (1973) *Dialectic of Enlightenment*, trans. J. Cumming, London: Allen Lane.

Ahmed, M. (2009) 'Village mob thwarts Google Street View car', *The Times*, 3 April.

Anderson, C. (2006) *The Long Tail: Why the Future of Business is Selling Less of More*, New York: Hyperion.

Anderson, C. (2008) 'The end of theory: The data deluge makes the scientific method obsolete', *Wired Magazine*, 23 June, at http://archive.wired.com / science / discoveries / magazine / 16–07 / pb _ theory

Arendt, H. (1958) *The Human Condition*, Chicago: University of Chicago Press.

Aristotle (1984) 'Politics' in J. Barnes (ed.), *The Complete Works of Aristotle*, Vol. 2 (revised Oxford translation), Princeton: Princeton University Press.

Armitage, J. (2006) 'From discourse networks to cultural mathematics: an interview with Friedrich A. Kittler', *Theory, Culture & Society* 23 (7–8): 17–38.

Auslander, P. (1999) *Liveness: Performance in a Mediatized Culture*, London and New York: Routledge.

Barikin, A., Papastergiadis, N., Yue, A., McQuire, S., Gibson, R. and Xin, Gu (2014) 'Translating gesture in a transnational public sphere', *Journal of Intercultural Studies* 35 (4): 349–65.

Batty, M., Axhausen, K. W., Giannotti, F., Pozdnoukhov, A., Bazzani, A., Wachowicz, M., Ouzounis, G. and Portugali, Y. (2012) 'Smart cities of the future', *European Physical Journal Special Topics* 214: 481–518.

Bauman, Z. (2005) *Liquid Life*, Cambridge: Polity.

Bauwens, M. (2005) 'The political economy of peer production', at www.ctheory.net/articles.aspx?id=499

Beck, U., Giddens, A. and Lash, S. (1994) *Reflexive Modernization*, Cambridge: Polity and London: Blackwell.

Becker, K. and Widholm, A. (2014) 'Being there from afar: the media event relocated to the public viewing area', *Interactions: Studies in Communication & Culture* 5 (2): 153–68.

Beer, D. (2009) 'Power through the algorithm: participatory web cultures and the technological unconscious', *New Media & Society* 11 (6): 985–1002.

Benford, S. and Giannachi, G. (2011) *Performing Mixed Reality*, Cambridge MA: MIT Press.

Benjamin, W. (1999) *The Arcades Project*, trans. H. Eiland and K. McLaughlin, Cambridge MA: Belknap Press.

Benjamin, W. (2003) 'The work of art in the age of its technological reproducibility: second version' in *Selected Writings, Volume 4, 1938–1940*, ed. H. Eiland and M. W. Jennings, trans. E. Jephcott and others, Cambridge MA: Belknap Press.

Benkler, Y. (2006) *The Wealth of Networks: How Social Production Transforms Markets and Freedom*, New Haven: Yale University Press.

Berners-Lee, T. (1997) 'Realising the full potential of the Web', at http://www.w3.org/1998/02/Potential.html

Berry, D. (2011) *The Philosophy of Software: Code and Mediation in the Digital Age*, Basingstoke: Palgrave Macmillan.

Blackmar, E. (2006) 'Appropriating "the Commons": the tragedy of property rights discourse' in S. Low and N. Smith (eds.), *The Politics of Public Space*, New York: Routledge.

Borges, J. L. (1975) 'On exactitude in science' in *A Universal History of Infamy*, trans. Norman Thomas de Giovanni, London: Penguin.

Bourriaud, N. (2002) *Relational Aesthetics*, trans. S. Pleasance, F. Woods with M. Copeland, Dijon: Les presses du réel (first published in French in 1998).

Brennan, K. (2009) Interview with Scott McQuire and Meredith Martin, Melbourne, 10 March 2009, edited version published in 'Sustaining public space: an interview with Kate Brennan' in S. McQuire, M. Martin and S. Niederer (eds.), *Urban Screens Reader*, Amsterdam: Institute of Network Cultures.

Brignull, H. and Rogers, Y. (2003) 'Enticing people to interact with large public displays in public spaces' in *Proceedings of IFIP INTERACT03: Human-Computer Interaction 2003*, Zurich: Switzerland.

Brill, L. M. (2002) 'One Times Square', at http://www.signindustry. com/led/articles/2002–05–30-LB-TimeSquareOne.php3

Brook, P. (2011) 'Google's mapping tools spawn new breed of art projects', *Wired Magazine*, 15 August, at http://www.wired.com/2011/ 08/google-street-view

Brownhill, S. and Carpenter, J. (2007) 'Increasing participation in planning: emergent experiences of the reformed planning system in England', *Planning Practice & Research* 22 (4): 619–34.

Brownhill, S. and Parker, G. (2010) 'Why bother with good works? The relevance of public participation(s) in planning in a post-collaborative era', *Planning Practice and Research* 25 (3): 275–82.

Brownlee, J. (2012) 'This creepy app isn't just stalking women without their knowledge, it's a wake-up call about Facebook privacy', at http://www.cultofmac.com/157641/this-creepy-app-isnt-just-stalking-women-without-their-knowledge-its-a-wake-up-call-about-facebook-privacy/#xithj6GiVFhduXiZ.99

Butler, J. (2011) 'Bodies in alliance and the politics of the street', at http://www.eipcp.net/transversal/1011/butler/en

CABE (2008) 'CABE concern over giant public screens', 24 July 2008, at http://www.cabe.org.uk/news/giant-screens-2012; later archived at http://webarchive.nationalarchives.gov.uk/20110118095356/http:// www.cabe.org.uk/news/giant-screens-2012

Callon, M. and Rabeharisoa, V. (2003) 'Research "in the wild" and the shaping of new social identities', *Technology in Society* 25 (2): 193–204.

Caro, R. (1974) *The Power Broker: Robert Moses and the Fall of New York*, New York: Knopf.

Castells, M. (2000) *End of Millennium*, 2nd edition, Malden MA: Blackwell.

Chun, W. (2006) *Control and Freedom: Power and Paranoia in the Age of Fibre Optics*, Cambridge MA: MIT Press.

Cnossen, B., Franssen, T. and de Wilde, M. (2015) *Digital Amsterdam: Digital Art and Public Space in Amsterdam*, Melbourne: Research Unit in Public Cultures, at https://public-cultures.unimelb.edu.au/sites/public-cultures.unimelb.edu.au/files/AmsterdamWebv2.pdf

Constant (1998) 'Unitary urbanism', reprinted in M. Wigley (ed.), *Constant's New Babylon: The Hyper-Architecture of Desire*, Rotterdam: Witte de With, Center for Contemporary Art.

Copeland, A. (2008) 'Participation and public space', *Public Space: The Journal of Law and Social Justice* 2: 1–28.

Coslovich, G. (2003) 'Federation Square captures the heart of a city', *The Age*, 11 October, at http://www.theage.com.au/articles/2003/10/10/1065676160184.html

Couldry, N. (2012) *Media, Society, World: Social Theory and Digital Media Practice*, Cambridge: Polity.

Crang, M. and Graham, S. (2007) 'Sentient cities', *Information, Communication and Society* 10 (6): 789–817.

Crary, J. (2013) *24/7: Late Capitalism and the Ends of Sleep*, London and New York: Verso.

David, S. (2014) 'The revolution . . . will be streamed', at http://recode.net/2014/01/16/the-revolution-will-be-streamed

Davis, M. (1990) *City of Quartz: Excavating the Future in Los Angeles*, London and New York: Verso.

Dayan, D. and Katz, E. (1992) *Media Events: The Live Broadcasting of History*, Cambridge MA: Harvard University Press.

Debord, G. (2006) 'Report on the construction of situations' in K. Knabb (ed. and trans.), *Situationist International Anthology* (revised and expanded edition), Berkeley CA: Bureau of Public Secrets.

Deleuze, G. (1992) 'Postscript on the societies of control', *October* 59 (Winter): 3–7.

Derrida, J. (1976) *Of Grammatology*, trans. G. Chakravorty Spivak, Baltimore: Johns Hopkins University Press.

Derrida, J. (1981) *Dissemination*, trans. B. Johnson, Chicago: University of Chicago Press.

Derrida, J. (1982) *Margins of Philosophy*, trans. A. Bass, Brighton: Harvester Press.

Dourish, P. and Mazmanian, M. (2011) 'Media as material: information representations as material foundations for organizational practice', Third International Symposium on Process Organization Studies, Corfu, Greece, at http://www.dourish.com/publications/2011/materiality-process.pdf

Drucker, J. (2011) 'Humanities approaches to interface theory', *Culture Machine* 12: 1–20, at http://www.culturemachine.net/index.php/cm/article/view/434/462

Dubai School of Government (2011) *Arab Social Media Report no. 2. Civil Movements: The Impact of Facebook and Twitter*, at http://journalistsresource.org/wp-content/uploads/2011/08/DSG_Arab_Social_Media_Report_No_2.pdf

Dyson, E., Gilder, G., Keyworth, J. and Toffler, A. (1994) 'A Magna Carta for the knowledge age', *New Perspectives Quarterly* 11 (Fall): 26–37.

Eckardt, F. (ed.) (2007) *Media and Urban Space: Understanding, Investigating and Approaching Mediacity*, Berlin: Frank & Timme.

Eckardt, F., Geelhaar, J. and Colini, L. (eds.) (2008) *Mediacity: Situations, Practices and Encounters*, Berlin: Frank & Timme.

Eco, U. (1984) 'A guide to the neo-television of the '80s', trans. B. Lumley, *Framework* 25: 19–27.

Eco, U. (1989) *The Open Work*, trans. A. Cancogni, Cambridge MA: Harvard University Press.

Ellul, J. (1964) *The Technological Society*, New York: Vintage.

Ernst, W. (2004) 'The archive as metaphor', *Open* 7, at http://www.onlineopen.org/the-archive-as-metaphor

Facebook (2013) *A Focus on Efficiency*, at http://internet.org/efficiency-paper

Fanck, K. and Stevens, Q. (eds.) (2007) *Loose Space: Possibility and Diversity in Urban Life*, London and New York: Routledge.

Farman, J. (2012) *Mobile Interface Theory: Embodied Space and Locative Media*, London and New York: Routledge.

Farman, J. (ed.) (2013) *The Mobile Story: Narrative Practices with Locative Technologies*, New York: Taylor and Francis.

Fatah gen Schieck, A., Al-Sayed, K., Kostopoulou, E., Behrens, M. and Motta, W. (2013) 'Networked architectural interfaces: exploring the effect of spatial configuration on urban screen placement', *Proceedings of the Ninth International Space Syntax Symposium*, at http://www.sss9.or.kr/paperpdf/adp/sss9_2013_ref004_p.pdf

Fatah gen Schieck, A., Kostakos, V. and Penn, A. (2010) 'Exploring the digital encounters in the public arena' in K. S. Willis, G. Roussos and K. Chorianopoulos (eds.), *Shared Encounters*, London: Springer-Verlag.

Felling, J. (2004) 'Terrorists' visual warfare uses the media as weapon', *Christian Science Monitor*, 4 August, at http://www.csmonitor.com/2004/0804/p09s02-coop.html

Finn, D. (2014) 'DIY urbanism: implications for cities', *Journal of Urbanism: International Research on Placemaking and Urban Sustainability* 7 (4): 381–98.

Foth, M. (ed.) (2009) *Handbook of Research on Urban Informatics: The Practice and Promise of the Real-time City*, Hershey PA: Information Science Reference.

Foth, M., Forlano, L., Satchell, C. and Gibbs, M. (eds.) (2011) *From Social Butterfly to Engaged Citizen: Urban Informatics, Social Media, Ubiquitous Computing, and Mobile Technology to Support Citizen Engagement*, Cambridge MA: MIT Press.

Foth, M., Rittenbruch, M., Robinson, R. and Viller, S. (eds.) (2014) *Street Computing: Urban Informatics and City Interfaces*, Abingdon: Routledge.

Franklin, A. (2010) *City Life*, London: Sage.

Frith, J. (2012) 'Splintered space: hybrid spaces and differential mobility', *Mobilities* 7 (1): 131–49.

Frohne, U. (2008) 'Dissolution of the frame: immersion and participation in video installations' in T. Leighton (ed.), *Art and the Moving Image*, London: Tate.

Galloway, A. (2004) *Protocol: How Control Exists After Decentralization*, Cambridge MA: MIT Press.

Georgiou, M. (2013) *Media and the City: Cosmopolitanism and Difference*, Cambridge: Polity.

Gibbons, M. (2008) Interview with Mike Gibbons (Head of Live Sites and UK Coordination for LOCOG, and previously Project Director, BBC Live Events) conducted by Scott McQuire, Melbourne, 4 October, partial transcription in 'Public space broadcasting: an interview with Mike Gibbons' in S. McQuire, M. Martin and S.

Niederer (eds.), *Urban Screens Reader*, Amsterdam: Institute of Network Cultures.

Gibbons, M. (2013) Interview with Scott McQuire, Melbourne, 2 December.

Gibbons, M. and Morris, B. (2005) Interview with Mike Gibbons (Chief Project Director, BBC Live Events) and Bill Morris (Director, BBC Live Events) conducted by Nikos Papastergiadis in London, 14 November.

Gibson, W. (1995) *Neuromancer*, London: Harper Collins.

Giedion, S. (1967) *Space, Time and Architecture: The Growth of a New Tradition*, Cambridge MA: Harvard University Press.

Gillespie, T. (2007) *Wired Shut: Copyright and the Shape of Digital Culture*, Cambridge MA: MIT Press.

Gitlin, T. (2003) *The Whole World is Watching: Mass Media in the Making and Unmaking of the New Left*, Berkeley: University of California Press.

Goffman, E. (1971) *Relations in Public: Microstudies of the Public Order*, New York: Basic Books.

Goldman, E. (2010) 'Search engine bias and the demise of search engine utopianism' in B. Szoka and A. Marcus (eds.), *The Next Digital Decade: Essays on the Future of the Internet*, Washington DC: TechFreedom.

Gordon, E. and de Souza e Silva, A. (2011) *Net Locality: Why Location Matters in a Networked World*, Chichester UK and Malden MA: Wiley-Blackwell.

Graham, S. (2009) 'The "urban battlespace"', *Theory, Culture & Society* 26 (7–8): 278–88.

Graham, S. (2010) *Cities Under Siege: The New Military Urbanism*, London and New York: Verso.

Gray, G. (2000) 'Streetscapes/George Stonbely: a Times Square sign-maker who loves spectacle', *New York Times*, 30 January.

Greenfield, A. (2006) *Everyware: The Dawning Age of Ubiquitous Computing*, Berkeley CA: New Riders.

Greenfield, A. (2013) *Against the Smart City*, New York: Do projects.

Habermas, J. (1989) *The Structural Transformation of the Public Sphere: An Inquiry into a Category of Bourgeois Society*, trans. T. Burger with the assistance of F. Lawrence, Cambridge MA: MIT Press.

Habuchi, I. (2005) 'Accelerating reflexivity' in M. Ito, D. Okabe and M. Matsuda (eds.), *Personal, Portable, Pedestrian: Mobile Phones in Japanese Life*, Cambridge MA: MIT Press.

Hacking, I. (1990) *The Taming of Chance*, Cambridge: Cambridge University Press.

Hardt, M. and Negri, A. (2004) *Multitude: War and Democracy in the Age of Empire*, New York: Penguin.

Hardt, M. and Negri, A. (2009) *Commonwealth*, Cambridge MA: Belknap Press.

Hardy, Q. (2012) 'Facing fees, some sites are bypassing Google Maps', *New York Times*, 19 March, at http://www.nytimes.com/2012/03/20/technology/many-sites-chart-a-new-course-as-google-expands-fees.html?_r=0

Harvey, D. (2008) 'The Right to the City', *New Left Review* 53: 23–40.

Harvey, D. (2012) *Rebel Cities: From the Right to the City to the Urban Revolution*, London and New York: Verso.

Hausler, H. (2009) *Media Facades: History, Technology, Content*, Ludwigsburg: Avedition.

Heidegger, M. (1971) 'The thing' in *Poetry, Language, Thought*, trans. A. Hofstadter, New York: Harper and Row.

Heidegger, M. (1977) *The Question Concerning Technology and Other Essays*, trans. W. Lovitt, New York: Harper and Row.

Helft, M. (2007) 'Google zooms in too close for some', *New York Times*, 1 June.

Hellerstein, J. (2008) 'The commoditization of massive data analysis', at http://radar.oreilly.com/2008/11/the-commoditization-of-massive.html

Hirschkind, C. (2011) 'From the blogosphere to the street: the role of social media in the Egyptian uprising', Jadaliyya.com, 9 February, at www.tacticalmediafiles.net/article.jsp?objectnumber=50916

Holmes, B. (2007) 'The revenge of the concept: artistic exchanges, networked resistance' in W. Bradley and C. Esche (eds.), *Art and Social Change*, London: Tate Gallery/Afterall.

Holmes, B. (2012) Post to discussion of screen technology on the *Empyre* list, 6 July, archived at https://www.mail-archive.com/empyre@lists.cofa.unsw.edu.au/msg04397.html

Hou, J. (ed.) (2010) *Insurgent Public Space: Guerrilla Urbanism and the Remaking of Contemporary Cities*, Abingdon: Routledge.

Hughes, J. and Sadler, S. (eds.) (1999) *Non-plan: Essays on Freedom and Change in Modern Architecture*, Oxford: Architectural.

Hutchinson, T. (1946) *Here is Television: Your Window to the World*, New York: Hastings House.

Ihde, D. (1979) *Technics and Praxis*, Boston Studies in the Philosophy of Science, Vol. 24, Dordrecht: Reidel.

Jacobs, J. (1961) *The Death and Life of Great American Cities*, New York: Random House.

Jameson, F. (1984) 'Postmodernism, or, the cultural logic of late capitalism', *New Left Review* 146 (July–August): 59–92.

Jassem, H., Drucker, S. and Burd, G. (eds.) (2010) *Urban Communication Reader: Volume 2*, New York: Hampton Press.

Jenkins, H. (2006) *Convergence Culture: Where Old and New Media Collide*, New York: New York University Press.

Jenkins, H., Purushotma, R., Weigel, M., Clinton, C. and Robison, A. (2009) *Confronting the Challenges of Participatory Culture: Media Education for the 21st Century*, Cambridge MA: MIT Press.

Joseph, S. (2012) 'Social media, political change and human rights', *Boston College International and Comparative Law Review* 35 (1), at http://law-digitalcommons.bc.edu/iclr/vol35/iss1/3

Kang, J. (1998) 'Information privacy in cyberspace transactions', *Stanford Law Review* 50: 1193–294.

Kasinitz, P. (ed.) (1994) *Metropolis: Center and Symbol of our Times*, London: Macmillan.

Keith, M., Lash, S., Arnoldi, J. and Rooker, T. (2014) *China Constructing Capitalism: Economic Life and Urban Change*, London and New York: Routledge.

Kester, G. (2004) *Conversation Pieces: Community and Communication in Modern Art*, Berkeley: University of California Press.

Khondker, H. H. (2011) 'Role of the new media in the Arab Spring', *Globalizations* 8 (5): 675–9.

Kitchin, R. (2014) 'The real-time city? Big data and smart urbanism', *GeoJournal* 79: 1–14.

Kittler, F. (2009) 'Towards an ontology of media', *Theory, Culture & Society* 26 (2–3): 23–31.

Kleinman, S. (ed.) (2007) *Displacing Place: Mobile Communication in the 21st Century*, New York: Peter Lang.

Kluge, A. and Negt, O. (1988) 'The public sphere and experience', trans. P. Labanyi, *October* 46 (Fall): 60–82.

Kluitenberg, E. (2006) *Hybrid Space: How Wireless Media Mobilize Public Space*, Rotterdam: NAi Publishers.

Kluitenberg, E. (2011) *Legacies of Tactical Media: The Tactics of Occupation from Tompkins Square to Tahrir*, Amsterdam: Institute of Network Cultures.

Knabb, K. (ed.) (2006) *Situationist International Anthology* (revised and expanded edition), Berkeley CA: Bureau of Public Secrets.

Kolamo, S. and Vuolteenaho, J. (2013) 'The interplay of mediascapes and cityscapes in a sports mega-event: the power dynamics of place branding in the 2010 FIFA World Cup in South Africa', *International Communication Gazette* 75 (5–6): 502–20.

Koolhaas, R. (2004) *AMOMA*, Köln: Taschen.

Koolhaas, R. (2014) 'My thoughts on the smart city', Talk given at the High Level Group meeting on Smart Cities, Brussels, 24 September 2014, transcript at https://ec.europa.eu/commission_2010–2014/kroes/en/content/my-thoughts-smart-city-rem-koolhaas

Kracauer, S. (1995) *The Mass Ornament*, ed. and trans. T. Y. Levin, Cambridge MA: Harvard University Press.

Lash, S. (2007) 'Power after hegemony: cultural studies in mutation', *Theory, Culture & Society* 24 (3): 55–78.

Lash, S. (2010) *Intensive Culture: Social Theory, Religion and Contemporary Capitalism*, London: Sage.

Latour, B. (2005) 'From realpolitik to dingpolitik or how to make things public' in B. Latour and P. Weibel (eds.), *Making Things Public: Atmospheres of Democracy*, Cambridge MA and Karlsruhe: MIT Press and ZKM Centre for Art and Media, pp. 14–41.

Le Corbusier (1946) *Towards a New Architecture*, trans. F. Etchells, London: Architectural Press (first published 1923).

Le Corbusier (1971) *The City of Tomorrow*, trans. F. Etchells, London: Architectural Press (first published as *Urbanisme* 1924).

Lefebvre, H. (1991a) *The Production of Space*, trans. D. Nicholson-Smith, Oxford: Blackwell.

Lefebvre, H. (1991b) *Critique of Everyday Life*, trans. J. Moore, London and New York: Verso (first published as *Critique de la vie quotidienne* 1946).

Lefebvre, H. (1996) 'The right to the city' in *Writings on Cities*, ed. E. Kofman and E. Lebas, Oxford: Blackwell (first published as *Le Droit à la ville* 1968).

Lessig, L. (2004) *Free Culture: How Big Media Uses Technology and the Law to Lock Down Culture and Control Creativity*, New York: Penguin.

Lessig, L. (2006) *Code: Version 2.0*, New York: Basic Books.

Levy, S. (2011) *In the Plex: How Google Thinks, Works, and Shapes Our Lives*, New York: Simon and Schuster.

Liebes, T. and Curran, J. (eds.) (1998) *Media, Ritual and Identity*, London and New York: Routledge.

Lim, W. (2012) *Incomplete Urbanism: A Critical Urban Strategy for Emerging Economies*, Singapore and Hackensack NJ: World Scientific Publishing.

Lippard, L. (ed) (1973) *Six Years: The Dematerialization of the Art Object from 1966 to 1972*, London: Studio Vista.

Lovink, G. (2008) *Zero Comments: Blogging and Critical Internet Culture*, London and New York: Routledge.

Low, S. and Smith, N. (eds.) (2006) *The Politics of Public Space*, New York: Routledge.

Lozano-Hemmer, R. (2000) Interview with Geert Lovink, in R. Lozano-Hemmer, *Vectorial Elevation*, Mexico City: CONACULTA: Impresiones y Ediciones San Jorge, S.A. de C.V.

Lozano-Hemmer, R. (2005) Interview with José Luis Barrios, in the *Subsculptures* catalogue by Gallery Guy Bärtschi, Switzerland (English translation by Rebecca MacSween).

Lozano-Hemmer, R. (2009) Interview with the author, part published in McQuire 2009b.

Lozano-Hemmer, R. (2010) Interview with the author, Melbourne, 30 May, part published in McQuire 2010.

Lynch, K. (1960) *The Image of the City*, Cambridge MA: MIT Press.

Lyon, D. (2003) *Surveillance After September 11*, Malden MA: Polity Press in association with Blackwell.

Lyotard, J.-F. (1984) *The Postmodern Condition: A Report on Knowledge*, trans. G. Bennington and B. Massumi, Manchester: Manchester University Press.

Ma, W. (2007) 'Riding shotgun with Google Street View's revolutionary camera', *Popular Mechanics*, 19 November, at www.popularmechanics.com/technology/gadgets/news/4232286?page=1

McCarthy, C. (2010) 'The dark side of geo: PleaseRobMe.com', *CNET. com*, 17 February, at http://www.cnet.com/uk/news/the-dark-side-of-geo-pleaserobme-com

McCullough, M. (2004) *Digital Ground*, Cambridge MA: MIT Press.

McCullough, M. (2013) *Ambient Commons*, Cambridge MA: MIT Press.

McLuhan, M. (1970) *Counter Blast*, London: Rapp and Whiting.

McQuire, S. (1994/5) '"The go-for-broke game of history": the camera, the community and the scene of politics', *Arena Journal* 4: 201–27.

McQuire, S. (1998) *Visions of Modernity: Representation, Memory, Time and Space in the Age of the Camera*, London: Sage.

McQuire, S. (2008) *The Media City: Media, Architecture and Urban Space*, London: Sage/Theory, Culture & Society.

McQuire, S. (2009a) 'Mobility, cosmopolitanism and public space in the media city' in S. McQuire, M. Martin and S. Niederer (eds.), *Urban Screens Reader*, Amsterdam: Institute of Network Cultures.

McQuire, S. (2009b) 'Making images with audiences', *Realtime* 89, at http://www.realtimearts.net/article/issue89/9337

McQuire, S. (2010) 'Sun work: mathematics as media', *Realtime* 97, at http://www.realtimearts.net/article/issue97/9863

McQuire, S. (2011a) 'The art of interactive lighting', *Realtime* 104, at http://www.realtimearts.net/article/issue104/10388

McQuire, S. (2011b) 'Virilio's media as philosophy' in J. Armitage (ed.), *Virilio Now: Current Perspectives in Virilio Studies*, Cambridge: Polity.

McQuire, S. (2014) 'Let there be light: behind the trend of illuminating cities for art', *The Conversation*, 23 May, at https://theconversation. com/let-there-be-light-behind-the-trend-of-illuminating-cities-for-art-26449

McQuire, S. and Radywyl, N. (2010) 'From object to platform: digital technology and temporality', *Time and Society* 19 (1): 1–23.

Madrigal, A. (2012a) 'How Google builds its maps – and what it means for the future of everything', *The Atlantic*, 6 September, at http://www. theatlantic.com/technology/archive/2012/09/how-google-builds-its-maps-and-what-it-means-for-the-future-of-everything/261913

Madrigal, A. (2012b) 'Why Google Maps is better than Apple Maps', *The Atlantic*, 13 December, at www.theatlantic.com/technology/archive/2012/12/why-google-maps-is-better-than-apple-maps/266218

Manovich, L. (2000) *The Language of New Media*, Cambridge MA: MIT Press.

Manovich, L. (2006) 'The poetics of augmented space', *Visual Communication* 5 (2): 219–40.

Marcuse, H. (1998) 'Some social implications of modern technology' in D. Kellner (ed.), *Technology, War and Fascism: Collected Papers of Herbert Marcuse*, Vol. 1, London: Routledge.

Martindale, D. and Neuwirth, G. (1958) 'Preparatory remarks: the theory of the city' in M. Weber, *The City*, ed. and trans. D. Martindale and G. Neuwirth, Glencoe: Free Press.

Massey, D. (1994) 'A global sense of place' in *Space, Place and Gender*, Cambridge: Polity.

Matsaganis, M., Gallagher, V. and Drucker, S. (eds.) (2013) *Communicative Cities in the 21st Century: The Urban Communication Reader III*, New York: Peter Lang.

Mattern, S. (2013) 'Methodolatry and the art of measure: the new wave of urban data science', *Places Journal* (November), at https://places-journal.org/article/methodolatry-and-the-art-of-measure

Matusitz, J. (2013) *Terrorism and Communication: A Critical Introduction*, Thousand Oaks: Sage.

Memarovic, N., Langheinrich, M., Alt, F., Elhart, I., Hosio, S. and Rubegni, E. (2012) 'Using public displays to stimulate passive engagement, active engagement, and discovery in public spaces' in MAB '12: Proceedings of the 4th Media Architecture Biennale Conference: Participation, at http://www.mediateam.oulu.fi/publications/pdf/1460.pdf

Miller, G. (2014) 'The huge unseen operation behind Google maps', *Wired Magazine*, 12 August, at http://www.wired.com/2014/12/google-maps-ground-truth

Mitchell, D. (2003) *The Right to the City: Social Justice and the Fight for Public Space*, New York: Guilford Press.

Mitchell, W. (1995) *City of Bits: Space, Place, and the Infobahn*, Cambridge MA: MIT Press.

Mitchell, W. (2005) *Placing Words: Symbols, Space, and the City*, Cambridge MA: MIT Press.

Moores, S. (2003) 'The doubling of place: electronic media, time-space arrangements and social relationships' in N. Couldry and A. McCarthy (eds.), *Media Space: Place, Scale, and Culture in a Media Age*, London and New York: Routledge.

Morley, D. (2009) 'For a materialist, non-media-centric media studies', *Television & New Media* 10 (1): 114–16.

Morozov, E. (2013) *To Save Everything, Click Here: The Folly of Technological Solutionism*, New York: Public Affairs.

Morris, M. (1988) 'Things to do with shopping centres', Issue 1 of *Working Paper*, University of Wisconsin, Milwaukee Center for Twentieth Century Studies.

Moses, A. (2008) 'Smile Australia, you're on Google's candid camera', *The Age*, 5 August, at http://www.theage.com.au/news/biztech/global-backlash-as-google-launches-street-view/2008/08/05/1217701932020.html

Moses, A. (2010) '"Petulant" Conroy accuses Google of "single greatest privacy breach"', *Sydney Morning Herald*, 25 May, at www.smh.com.au/technology/technology-news/petulant-conroy-accuses-google-of-single-greatest-privacy-breach-20100525-w937.html

Mouffe, C. (2007) 'Art and democracy: art as an agonistic intervention in public space', at www.onlineopen.org/download.php?id=226

Nancy, J.-L. (1991) *The Inoperative Community*, trans. P. O'Connor, L. Garbus, M. Holland and S. Sawhney, Minneapolis: University of Minnesota Press.

Nissenbaum, H. (2011) 'Contextual approach to privacy online', *Daedalus* 140 (94): 32–48.

Nissenbaum, H. and Varnelis, K. (2012) *Modulated Cities: Networked Spaces, Reconstituted Subjects* (Situated Technologies Pamphlets 9), New York: Architectural League of New York, at http://www.archleague.org/PDFs/ST9_webSP.pdf

Nold, C. (ed.) (2009) *Emotional Cartographies: Technologies of the Self*, at http://emotionalcartography.net/EmotionalCartography.pdf

O'Connor, J. (2006) *Creative Cities: The Role of Creative Industries in Regeneration*, Renew Intelligence Reports, North West Development Agency, Warrington, at http://eprints.qut.edu.au/43879

O'Reilly, T. (2005) 'What is Web 2.0? Design patterns and business models for the next generation of software', at www.oreilly.com/pub/a/web2/archive/what-is-web-20.html

Ortiz, A. and El Zein, R. (eds.) (2011) *Signs of the Times: The Popular Literature of Tahrir*, at https://issuu.com/arteeast/docs/shahadat_january25_final/13?e=2775683/3006

Osborne, P. (1994) 'The politics of time', *Radical Philosophy* 68: 3–9.

Papastergiadis, N. (1999) *The Turbulence of Migration*, Cambridge: Polity.

Papastergiadis, N. (2012) *Cosmopolitanism and Culture*, Cambridge: Polity.

Papastergiadis, N. and Rogers, H. (1996) 'The parafunctional' in J. Stathatos (ed.), *The Dream of Urbanity*, London: Academy Group.

Park, R. (1967) 'The city as social laboratory' in *On Social Control and Collective Behavior: Selected Papers*, ed. R. Turner, Chicago: University of Chicago Press (essay first published 1929).

Penny, S. (2011) 'Towards a performative aesthetic of interactivity', *Fibreculture* 19, at http://nineteen.fibreculturejournal.org/fcj-132-towards-a-performative-aesthetics-of-interactivity

Poulsen, K. (2007) 'Want off Street View? Google wants your ID and a sworn statement', *Wired Magazine*, 15 June, at http://www.wired.com/2007/06/want_off_street

Pratt, A. (2008) 'Creative cities: the cultural industries and the creative class', *Geografiska annaler: Series B – Human Geography* 90 (2): 107–17.

Ramus, B. (2011) Interview with the author, Melbourne, 10 June, part published in McQuire 2011a.

Ronnel, A. (1994) 'Trauma TV: twelve steps beyond the pleasure principle' in *Finitude's Score: Essays for the End of the Millennium*, Lincoln: University of Nebraska Press.

Rushe, D. (2012) 'Google's Mr Maps sets his sights on world delineation', *Guardian*, 7 December, at http://www.theguardian.com/technology/2012/dec/07/google-maps-street-view-world/print

Sadler, S. (1998) *The Situationist City*, Cambridge MA: MIT Press.

Sassen, S. (1991) *The Global City: New York, London, Tokyo*, Princeton: Princeton University Press.

Sassen, S. (2006) *Territory, Authority, Rights: From Medieval to Global Assemblages*, Princeton: Princeton University Press.

Sassen, S. (2011a) 'Talking back to your intelligent city', at http://voices.mckinseyonsociety.com/talking-back-to-your-intelligent-city

Sassen, S. (2011b) 'Open source urbanism', *New City Reader* 15, at http://www.domusweb.it/en/op-ed/2011/06/29/open-source-urbanism.html

Sassen, S. (2011c) 'The global street: making the political', *Globalizations* 8 (5): 573–9.

Savage, M. and Burrows, R. (2007) 'The coming crisis of empirical sociology', *Sociology* 41 (5): 885–99.

Savage, M. and Burrows, R. (2009) 'Some further reflections on the coming crisis of empirical sociology', *Sociology* 43 (4): 762–72.

Schaffers, H., Komninos, N., Pallot, M., Trousse, B., Nilsson, M. and Oliveira, A. (2011) 'Smart cities and the future internet: towards cooperation frameworks for open innovation' in J. Domingue et al. (eds.), *Future Internet Assembly*, Berlin and Heidelberg: Springer.

Schepke, J. (2010) 'Google Place Search: location information just became more critical', at http://searchenginewatch.com/sew/news/2066103/google-place-search-location-information-just-became-more-critical

Schoch, O. (2006) 'My building is my display: omnipresent graphical output as hybrid communicators', Swiss Federal Institute of Technology, Faculty of Architecture, archived at http://e-collection.library.ethz.ch/eserv/eth:30097/eth-30097-01.pdf

Schuijren, J. (2008) Interview with Scott McQuire, Melbourne, 5 October, edited version published as 'Putting art into urban space: an interview with Jan Schuijren' in S. McQuire, M. Martin and S. Niederer (eds.), *Urban Screens Reader*, Amsterdam: Institute of Network Cultures.

Scott, M. and Isaac, M. (2015) 'Uber joins the bidding for Here, Nokia's digital mapping service', *New York Times*, 7 May, at http://www.nytimes.com/2015/05/08/business/uber-joins-the-bidding-for-here-nokias-digital-mapping-service.html?_r=0

Seigal, J. (2002) *Mobile: The Art of Portable Architecture*, New York: Princeton Architectural Press.

Sennett, R. (1978) *The Fall of Public Man: On the Social Psychology of Capitalism*, New York: Vintage Books.

Sennett, R. (2012) *Together: The Rituals, Pleasures and Politics of Cooperation*, New Haven: Yale University Press.

Shepard, M. (ed.) (2011) *Sentient City: Ubiquitous Computing, Architecture, and the Future of Urban Space*, Cambridge MA: MIT Press.

Simmel, G. (1971) 'The stranger' in *On Individuality and Social Forms: Selected Writings*, ed. D. Levine, Chicago: University of Chicago Press (originally published in German in 1908).

Soja, E. (2000) *Postmetropolis*, Oxford: Blackwell.

Sorkin, M. (ed.) (1992) *Variations on a Theme Park: The New American City and the End of Public Space*, New York: Hill and Wang.

Sorrel, S. (2014) *Mobile Context and Location Services: Navigation, Tracking, Social and Local Search 2014–2019*, Juniper Research.

Souza e Silva, A. de (2006) 'From cyber to hybrid: mobile technologies as interfaces of hybrid spaces', *Space & Culture* 9 (3): 261–78.

Stenovec, T. (2014) 'The future of TV may look a lot like the present', *Huffington Post*, 29 April, at http://www.huffingtonpost.com/2014/04/29/future-of-tv_n_5215120.html

Stevens, Q. (2007) *The Ludic City: Exploring the Potential of Public Spaces*, London: Routledge.

Stiegler, B. (1998) *Technics and Time 1: The Fault of Epimetheus*, trans. R. Beardsworth and G. Collins, Stanford: Stanford University Press.

Stiegler, B. (2001) 'Derrida and technology: fidelity at the limits of deconstruction and the prosthesis of faith' in T. Cohen (ed.), *Jacques Derrida and the Humanities: A Critical Reader*, Cambridge: Cambridge University Press.

Stiegler, B. (2010) 'Telecracy against democracy', *Cultural Politics* 6 (2): 171–80.

Stiegler, B. (2011) *The Decadence of Industrial Democracies. Volume 1: Disbelief and Discredit*, trans. D. Ross and S. Arnold, Cambridge: Polity.

Thatcher, J. (2014) 'Living on fumes: digital footprints, data fumes, and the limitations of spatial big data', *International Journal of Communication* 8: 1765–83.

Thompson, C. (2012) 'Foursquare alters API to eliminate apps like Girls Around Me', 10 May, archived at https://web.archive.org/web/20130502072720/http://aboutfoursquare.com/foursquare-api-change-girls-around-me

Thrift, N. (2004) 'Remembering the technological unconscious by fore-grounding knowledges of position', *Environment and Planning D: Society and Space* 22 (1): 175–90.

Thrift, N. (2009) 'Different atmospheres: of Sloterdijk, China, and site', *Environment and Planning D: Society and Space* 27 (1): 119–38.

Townsend, A. (2006) 'Locative-media artists in the contested-aware city', *Leonardo* 39 (4): 345–7.

Townsend, A. (2013) *Smart Cities: Big Data, Civic Hackers, and the Quest for a New Utopia*, New York: W. W. Norton.

United Nations (2014) *2014 Revision of World Urbanization Prospects*, at http://esa.un.org/unpd/wup/Publications/Files/WUP2014-Report.pdf

Vazquez, R. (2002) 'LED as an alternative?' *Sign Industry.com*, at http://www.signindustry.com/led/articles/2002–07–13-RV-LEDalternative.php3

Vertov, D. (1984) *Kino-Eye: The Writings of Dziga Vertov*, trans. K. O'Brien, ed. A. Michelson, Berkeley: University of California Press.

Virilio, P. (1986a) 'The over-exposed city', trans. A. Hustvedt, *Zone* 1/2: 14–31.

Virilio, P. (1986b) *Speed and Politics: An Essay on Dromology*, trans. M. Polizzotti, New York: Semiotext(e).

Virilio, P. (1989) *War and Cinema: The Logistics of Perception*, trans. P. Camiller, London and New York: Verso.

Virilio, P. (1994) *The Vision Machine*, trans. J. Rose, Bloomington and London: Indiana University Press.

Virilio, P. (1997) *Open Sky*, trans. J. Rose, London and New York: Verso.

Virilio, P. (1998) 'Architecture in the age of its virtual disappearance. An interview with Paul Virilio by Andreas Ruby, 15 October 1993' in J. Beckmann (ed.), *The Virtual Dimension: Architecture, Representation, and Crash Culture*, New York: Princeton Architectural Press.

Virilio, P. (2000) *A Landscape of Events*, trans. J. Rose, Cambridge MA: MIT Press.

Ward, C. (1999) 'Anarchy and architecture: a personal record' in J. Hughes and S. Sadler (eds.), *Non-plan: Essays on Freedom and Change in Modern Architecture*, Oxford: Architectural.

Wark, M. (1994) *Virtual Geography: Living with Global Media Events*, Bloomington: Indiana University Press.

Watson, S. (2006) *City Publics: The (Dis)enchantments of Urban Encounters*, London and New York: Routledge.

Webb, C. (2014) 'City of Melbourne plans memorial to indigenous men executed in 1842', *The Age*, at http://www.theage.com.au/victoria/city-of-melbourne-plans-memorial-to-indigenous-men-executed-in-1842-20140424-zqz08.html

Weber, M. (1958) *The City*, ed. and trans. D. Martindale and G. Neuwirth, Glencoe: Free Press (first published 1921).

Weber, M. (1968) 'The city', ch. XVI in *Economy and Society: An Outline of Interpretive Sociology*, Vol. 2, ed. Guenther Roth and Claus Wittich, Berkeley: University of California Press.

Weiser, M. (1991) 'The computer in the 21st century', *Scientific American*, Special Issue on Communications, Computers and Networks (September), at http://web.media.mit.edu/~anjchang/ti01/weiser-sciam91-ubicomp.pdf

Whyte, W. (1980) *The Social Life of Small Urban Spaces*, Washington: Conservation Foundation.

Wilken, R. (2012) 'Locative media: from specialized preoccupation to mainstream fascination', *Convergence: The International Journal of Research into New Media Technologies* 18 (3): 243–7.

Wilken, R. (2014) 'Mobile media, place, and location' in G. Goggin and L. Hjorth (eds.), *The Mobile Media Companion*, New York: Routledge.

Williams, R. (1974) *Television, Technology and Cultural Form*, London: Fontana.

Winner, L. (1977) *Autonomous Technology: Technics-out-of-Control as a Theme in Political Thought*, Cambridge MA: MIT Press.

Wirth, L. (1994) 'Urbanism as a way of life' in P. Kasinitz (ed.), *Metropolis: Centre and Symbol of our Times*, London: Macmillan (first published 1938).

Wohllaib, N. (2008) 'Smart homes, smart cities', *Pictures of the Future* (Fall), Siemens Corporation, at http://www.siemens.com/content/dam/internet/siemens-com/innovation/pictures-of-the-future/pof-archive/pof-fall-2008.pdf

Wolf, M. (2011) Interview with the *British Journal of Photography*, archived at http://web.archive.org/web/20110214094713/http://www.bjp-online.com/british-journal-of-photography/news/2025845/world-press-photo-google-street-view-photojournalism

Wolman, G. (1956) 'Address by the Lettrist International Delegate to the Alba Conference of September 1956', at http://www.cddc.vt.edu/sionline/presitu/wolman.html

Zukin, S. (1982) *Loft Living: Culture and Capital in Urban Change*, Baltimore: Johns Hopkins University Press.

Index